AROUND THE DAY IN EIGHTY WORLDS

THOUGHT IN THE ACT

A series edited by Erin Manning and Brian Massumi

AROUND THE DAY IN EIGHTY WORLDS

POLITICS OF THE PLURIVERSE

Martin Savransky

DUKE UNIVERSITY PRESS · *Durham and London* · 2021

Library of Congress Cataloging-in-Publication Data
Names: Savransky, Martin, author.
Title: Around the day in eighty worlds : politics of the
pluriverse / Martin Savransky.
Other titles: Thought in the act.
Description: Durham : Duke University Press, 2021. |
Series: Thought in the act | Includes bibliographical
references and index.
Identifiers: LCCN 2020038096 (print) | LCCN 2020038097 (ebook)
ISBN 9781478011989 (hardcover)
ISBN 9781478014126 (paperback)
ISBN 9781478021438 (ebook)
Subjects: LCSH: James, William, 1842–1910. |
Pluralism—Political aspects.
Classification: LCC B945.J24 S28 2021 (print) |
LCC B945.J24 (ebook) | DDC 147/.4—dc23
LC record available at https://lccn.loc.gov/2020038096
LC ebook record available at https://lccn.loc.gov/2020038097

Cover Art: Brie Ruais, *Circling Inward and Outward, 128 lbs*,
2020. Glazed ceramic, rocks, hardware. 96 × 92 × 3 inches.
Image courtesy the artist and Night Gallery.

CONTENTS

Acknowledgments · vii

CHAPTER ONE · Ongoing and Unfinished · 1

CHAPTER TWO · Runaway Metaphysics · 25

CHAPTER THREE · Trust of a Held-Out Hand · 49

CHAPTER FOUR · Worldquakes · 70

CHAPTER FIVE · Pragmatism in the Wake · 91

CHAPTER SIX · The Insistence of the Pluriverse · 113

Notes · 133

Bibliography · 163

Index · 177

ACKNOWLEDGMENTS

Can one ever say when a book *begins*? Or when it ends? This one has, indeed, been long in the making. But, thinking back, it seems impossible now to pinpoint precisely when it begun. It certainly did not begin when I started writing it. For the fact is that, if I started writing it, it's only *because* it had already begun, in some other form, insisting in whatever else I was doing, making me hesitate, insinuating itself in the form of a generative problematic that, with the force of an imperative, turned me into its prey and compelled me to turn to it, to do what I could to develop it, to respond to its demand while intensifying the possibility that it could, in fact, be written. Which is to say that the book was already ongoing when I started writing it, and now that it is out of my hands, it remains unfinished, insisting and persisting in yours, unexpectedly morphing into whatever might come after it. The book is ongoing and unfinished, much like what is *in* the book—much like the runaway philosophical and political experimentation that turned me into its means and that, with the help of William James, I seek to activate through it, to make felt by means of it. The "and" trails along every edge, along every sentence: Ever not quite! Which is why, while this book is written in gratitude for, and in honour of, a whole host of relations (intellectual, personal, institutional, political, enduring, and ephemeral) through which it became composed, it is the ongoing and unfinished nature—of every book, perhaps, but certainly of this book—that overwhelms my capacity to name every one of those relations here.

And yet, as James himself told his editor upon submitting his thousand-page, two-volume manuscript *The Principles of Psychology*, "No subject is worth being treated of in 1000 pages!" If ongoing and unfinished (and it is clear that his was just as ongoing and unfinished as this one, albeit significantly longer), a book must have, if not necessarily an introduction and a conclusion, then at least a "before" and an "after." Above all, one must do one's best to avoid turning it into what, in his letter, James called "a loathsome, distended, tumefied, bloated, dropsical mass." The same goes, because of my own incapacity to name them all, for the relations I can and must strive to invoke by name here. Thus, I will try to exert some self-restraint, and restrict these thanks to those whose mark has been most patently felt in the weaving of this text. It goes without saying, but not without thanking, that this book would not be what it is without the warm and generous support from Erin Manning and Brian Massumi, who have been keeping the flame of speculative experimentation burning in extremely generative ways, and who enthusiastically welcomed the inclusion of this book in their brilliant Thought in the Act book series. Deep gratitude also goes to Ken Wissoker, Ryan Kendall, Annie Lubinsky, and two anonymous readers, who asked thoughtful questions, made perspicacious and invaluable suggestions, and carefully saw the book through its various stages of development and production. Their attentive, careful, and responsive editorial work is second to none, and it made the entire process a true pleasure.

Goldsmiths, and in particular the Department of Sociology, have provided the increasingly rare space of refuge within which a book like this could even be conceived, let alone developed. As it now faces—like many other institutions in the UK and around the world—new threats of intellectual devastation, this book is a modest thank you to everyone and everything that for years has made of Goldsmiths a place where thought can be cultivated pluralistically, along lines of divergence that connect it to the possibility of creating another possible university, of thinking, writing, and teaching for another possible world, even when the worlds we trust are possible are not always the same world. Inside it, even today, hindrance and experiment go all the way through.

Among colleagues and friends, this book is particularly indebted to some without whose careful questions, comments, and suggestions—or indeed, without their patient reading of too much of the text, at various stages—it would not be what it has become. In this sense, I am especially thankful to Monica Greco, Isaac Marrero-Guillamón, Rajyashree Pandey, Marsha Rosengarten, Sanjay Seth, and Isabelle Stengers, for their always generative and generous engagements, provocations, and propositions. Others who have enabled the composition of this book, through their helpful comments and suggestions on various chapters, sections, or passages or simply through their close intellectual friendship and support while the book was in the making, include, among others, Andrew Barry, Vikki Bell, Steve Brown, Felicity Callard, Nerea Calvillo, Didier Debaise, Vinciane Despret, Craig

Lundy, Cecile Malaspina, Patrice Maniglier, Mariam Motamedi-Fraser, Dan Neyland, Dimitris Papadopoulos, Melanie Sehgal, Shela Sheikh, Peter Skafish, Katrin Solhdju, Paul Stenner, John Tresch, and Alex Wilkie. I thank them for reminding me, each in their own divergent way, that the book might, just perhaps, be worth writing in spite of all.

This book was written in the thick of it, amidst all other goings-on, without the benefit of sabbaticals, fellowships, or other such contemplative pleasures. On occasion, such escapes might have been welcome. And yet, in this particular case, the fact is that the writing benefited from the messy buzz of sociality, from the multifarious stream of life. Above all, it benefited from the interstices of thoughtful, collective experimentation that the MA and PhD students that attended my Politics & Difference masters module engendered each year for the last five years. Their willingness and ability to consent to experiment with a whole array of decidedly strange philosophical propositions; with even stranger beings; their capacity to put themselves at risk and their values in question as they groped for the possibility not only of making sense of obtuse ideas but of learning to think, live, and be connected to one another otherwise, gave me vital energy to carry on snatching bits of time here and there to enable the writing to continue its course, and to continue instilling joy, inside and in spite of the institutional demands of the day. At a time when universities seem increasingly unworthy of our attempts to defend them against their own devaluation, they persuade me that it is not the idea of the university, but something that can happen inside and in spite of it, something that brings us in and brings us back, which must be defended at all costs.

And those interstices are sometimes created, too, in rare spaces of scholarly exchange, through talks and seminars and meetings. In this sense, I've had the privilege of being invited to present and discuss aspects and parts of this book in various, immensely enriching contexts, with thoughtful audiences and participants. I am particularly grateful for discussions that took place at the Centre for Philosophy and Political Economy (CPPE) and the Business School at the University of Leicester (with thanks to Maria Puig de la Bellacasa for inviting me), with the Groupe d'Études Constructivistes (GECo) at the Université Libre de Bruxelles (with thanks to Didier Debaise and Isabelle Stengers), with the Unité de recherche en métaphysique et theories de la connaissance (MéThéor) at the Université de Liège (with thanks to Vinciane Despret), at the Wellcome Centre for Cultures and Environments of Health at Exeter University (with thanks to Lara Choksey), at the Experimental Speculation/Speculative Experimentation meeting at Europa University Viadrina/Diffrakt Centre (with thanks to Melanie Seghal), at the Instituto de Altos Estudios at the Universidad de San Martín (with thanks to Lucía Ariza), and at the Pontifica Universidad Católica de Chile (with thanks to Manuel Tironi, Felipe Palma, and Martin Tironi).

It was on a certain afternoon—which might as well have been one of many hesitant beginnings—with Inês Violante, that the story of the first circumnavigation that opens this book began to insinuate itself in the midst of our conversation. It is to her, to life with her, that I am most grateful. May that remain, like a book, like the insistence of the pluriverse itself, always ongoing and unfinished.

CHAPTER ONE · Ongoing and Unfinished

———————

Damn Great Empires!—including that of the Absolute.
WILLIAM JAMES

These days, my notion of the fantastic is closer to what we call reality.
Perhaps because reality approaches the fantastic more and more.
JULIO CORTÁZAR

ONE AND MANY · Ours is a tempestuous time. In the wake of the multi-farious storms pouring over worlds for the last five hundred years, of imperial conquests and colonial projects, of capitalist supply chains and industrial progress, of rational knowledges and ecological devastation, it has long been a time of endings. Yet despite the ubiquitous resurgence of the term *apocalypse*, this is not the end to all endings, it is not for all that the end of time. Not yet, perhaps not ever. For in the end—to borrow Aimé Césaire's words—it is The End of the World that is the only thing in the world that's worth *beginning*.[1] Which is to say that it is the possibility of other worlds in this world that is beginning amidst all endings. The possibility of other stories, ongoing and unfinished, in-the-making in spite of all. Stories which offer neither the comfort of redemption, nor the foundations of a new and better civilization. But in the eye of the storm, they counter any sense of finality and trouble all fantasies of totality.[2] Pluralizing the present, these other stories, these other worlds in this world, precipitate a pragmatics of collective imagination against ongoing desolation. Which is why it is possible that perhaps, just perhaps, by attending to stories where other worlds remain ongoing and unfinished, by experimenting with the possible beginnings such worlds might open up, the impossible itself can crack open, and an adventure in divergence around the day in eighty or a thousand worlds may once again become worthy of a certain kind of trust. This, indeed, is the speculative wager of this book, its groundless gamble, its throw of the dice: the wager on the possibility of rendering ourselves capable of thinking, against all odds, for other times to come, for worlds to be otherwise composed. To think, while we still can, in the hold of an improbable but insistent *perhaps*. One that, after William James—that most singular, divergent, and adventurous of American philosophers—we might call a *pluriverse*: a pluralistic universe underway and yet to be made, one and many, ongoing and unfinished.[3]

What might a radical pluralism look like, in the hold of perhaps? What politics of the possible might the pluriverse open up? Let me begin by beginning again, hesitantly, with a series of partial stories in the form of a list threading some loosely connected worlds through which openings make themselves felt in spite of all. A list which, like all good lists, is neither definitely finite nor statically infinite, but always *indefinite*, without beginning or end, ongoing and unfinished, always beginning with "And" and ending, provisionally, with "et cetera":[4]

And there is this world where, for much of the year, the sun doesn't set, either east or west, until a green and yellow night erupts to cover all hours of the day.

There is this world in which people cultivate their existence in the sea, learning to move, and think, and live under water for tens of minutes on end.

There is this world where elves are real, living underneath rocks. Meddling in human affairs, they're called the *huldufólk* (the hidden people), and often force modern infrastructural development projects to slow their pace and change course.

There is this world where ghosts are real, requiring the same things that humans require, making demands for care and justice after a disaster, and often receiving offerings of food and drink, money, clothing, and even bicycles and motorbikes.

There is this world where immortality is real, enjoyed by strange fungal beings that, borne of deforested landscapes, do not die unless they are killed.

There is this world where shamanism is real, releasing its forces with the thawing advent of spring, which pushes forward a permanent state of transition after socialism, with or without shamans.

There is this world where soybeans, real soybeans, kill, actively taking the lives of peasants in expanding monoculture plantations.

There is this world where sorcery-lions are real, haunting their victims at night by means of direct, deadly attacks, or more slowly, by poisoning the health of their victims.

There is this world where characters are real, fictional characters borne of novels and stories who then come to inhabit the private spaces of people entering into conversations with them, making suggestions, offering advice.

There is this world where Gods and Goddesses are real, some revolutionary, some impersonal and remote, some extremely personal, engaging in intimate exchanges with those who learn how to trust them.

There is this world where yellowish moldy things, unicellular beings with no brains or nervous systems, inhabiting suburban backyards, can think and select and make logistical decisions that at times are as efficient as those made by human engineers.

There is this world where healers, developing the appropriate techniques, can extract gray, visible spirits from people's bodies, relieving them of their pain and suffering.

There is this world where oracles pronounce indubitable truths, truths that can sooth or bewilder those who consult them but which are never put into question, never doubted, for doubt is irrelevant to them.

There is this world, which are many, where Pachamama—or what, inadequately, some of us call Nature—has a real existence and even the right to integral respect for its ongoing existence despite persistent assaults by extractivist practices.

There is this world where the dead are real and present in the lives of those who go on living, often appearing in the guise of birds or cats, transforming the habits of those who love and remember them.

(Etc.)

There are more, many more little worlds in this world, many et ceteras to be added to this permanently unfinished list. But here's the thing: this is not a list of imaginary places or legendary lands. These are neither parallel universes, little freestanding units, nor utopian scenarios. When I speak of these many beings as *real*, I do not speak metaphorically. I am not simply claiming certain people *believe* them to be real, that they belong to some exotic *worldview* or to other modes of *knowing* the world, and I am not even saying they correspond to so many ontologies, or to *theories* of what is. All such formulations would leave the foundations of our modern world, of what some call "reality," ultimately unscathed. These are many little worlds insofar as their *realities* diverge radically from each other, and from the heavily policed borders and deep foundations of the modern, Western ploughing of the world. But their differences are immanent. Rather than absolute separations, they trail along the "and" that, James proposed, makes the world *both* one and many.

Indeed, divergence does not oppose, but presupposes, togetherness. Already in 1907, James argued that the problem of whether the world is one or many was the most pregnant of all philosophical problems, the one with the largest number of consequences, such that if you know whether someone is a decided monist or a decided pluralist you perhaps know more about their outlook on life than if you give them "any other name ending in *ist*."[5] But James was also aware then of what no philosophy can any longer pretend to ignore: that the problem of difference, of one and many worlds, has always been more than philosophical. For indeed, in the wake of the tangled catastrophes of capitalism, colonialism, and extractivism, the mass disqualification of differences through which the modern world was born has radically devastated the very conditions of livability of myriad human and more-than-human worlds in this world. In relay and return, to experiment with differences under the sign of a radical pluralism requires that we trouble those facile images of diversity and sameness in a unified cosmos capable of containing difference in its midst. For the pluriverse is speculatively situated in the "*and*" that connects "one" and "many" through divergence, holding the many connecting frictions in generative tension. Standing resolutely against the absolute, before the beyond, without foundations, the pluriverse trembles in the interstices between the one and the many, insinuating the possibility of other worlds in this world, of differences all the way down.

The possible it intimates is an urgent and insistent one, for it lurks there where the seams of the modern modes of worlding the world have begun to burst. As such, while its degrees of oneness and unity ultimately remain an open, empirical question, permanently up for verification and transformation, its ongoing insistence is in the form of partial stories, of loosely connected and disconnected realities, of eighty or a thousand "little hangings-together" in continuous processes of unification here, and pluralization there, without amounting to an encompassing unification yet, or perhaps ever.[6] For these realities, spread across South and North, the West and "the rest," frequently derided and condemned, often hard-won, when not reluctantly conceded and dimly disclosed, nevertheless subsist precariously. They persist in intimate friction with and in spite of the ongoing and unfinished project of what I would call the modern *monification* of the world: the disqualification and devastation of differences brought about through capitalist supply chains and corrosive forms of laughter, through rational knowledges and colonial expansions, through development programs and socio-ecological plundering.[7] These realities are many, but in some respects, in some planetary respects, we're all in the same multifarious storm, to swim or sink together—literally.[8] It is the reality of such realities—one and many, ongoing and unfinished—that the pluriverse insinuates as an insistent possibility. And it is this possible to which this book seeks to respond.

THE FEELING OF REALITY · In spite of all, worlds still abound, unbound, they stir trouble and pose problems, they insist and persist. There are now a host of efforts in fields as diverse as philosophy, geography, postcolonial studies, anthropology, theology, political theory, and the nascent environmental humanities that seek to engage with the insistence of differences and the troubles they precipitate so as to try and cultivate a radically pluralistic politics that may work to displace and counter the modern monification of the world—in other words, to reimagine the possible conditions for its livability in the plural. And it is precisely in the interstices of these various diverging paths that, in *Around the Day in Eighty Worlds*, the effort involves something altogether different from the attempt at writing another exegetical commentary or an interpretation of James's thought, which still appears to produce contemporary exegetes who conclude that his work provides us "with little discussion of social issues that appear central at present."[9] What I seek instead is to *relay* aspects of the thrust of his thought as a hand held out from a past that has never left our present. A held-out hand which perhaps another hand—one that quietly but irreverently sidesteps the fate of much of James's reception among avid commentators—may speculatively experiment with, may seek to relaunch and reactivate, to turn it once again into a generative and demanding proposition.[10]

To relay James today is not, therefore, to attempt yet another faithful exposition, another go at "building up an author's meaning out of separate texts" so as to assess their inward coherence, or lack thereof.[11] Relaying is above all an art of consequences. It is experimental or it is nothing.[12] As such, it requires not fidelity but the risky cultivation of a certain form of trust, and its efficacy consists precisely in the extent to which such an experiment may manage to grasp something of James's "centre of vision, by an act of imagination," breathing a bit of new life into propositions that might otherwise fade away.[13] Such is the task before us. Relaying James's pluralism as a proposition that is at once dramatically political, radically empirical, and fugitively metaphysical, I hold out a trusting hand as I seek to forge new and always partial connections among a multiplicity of divergent paths. For indeed, as it happens in this overspecialized academic habitat we inhabit with difficulty while we still can, these diverging projects speak to each other less than one might wish, expressing the somewhat troubled dissonance created by the "and" that turns "the one and the many" into a problem on which we cannot turn our backs any longer.

Seeking to construct the theoretical conditions for a decolonial option to a global future, the tradition of postcolonial thought, for instance, is of course acutely sensitive to the ways in which the imperialist system of knowledge and capitalist production that Walter Mignolo, for convenience (I hope), dubs the "Western code," the code by which European modernity proclaimed its own historical exception, has operated in such a way as to override and strip divergent worlds from their generative liveability.[14] Postcolonial and decolonial thinkers are sensitive, that is, to the fact that Euromodernity continues its expansion on the alleged achievement of a universal thought that may finally be called "rational," while doing so at the expense of the experiences, values, and knowledges of the those that have been on the receiving end of its imperialist operations. Their plight is poignant and urgent, and aspects of their proposals continue to inspire and inform the experiment that this book sets in motion. At the same time, however, divergences abound and proliferate. For I fear that as they seek to uncover the foundations of a post-Occidental reason, their concern with epistemology and identity, and their profusion of neo-Kantian diagnoses on the coloniality of knowledge, of power, of being, and so forth, often draw many a postcolonial thinker back into the modern quicksand of the Western code itself, not only presenting the latter as a homogenous and accomplished block but as a "coloniality at large," endowed with a reality no other decolonial "option" appears capable of resisting, or even putting at risk.

A fertile and divergent path is being traced by a growing number of contemporary anthropologists, philosophers, and political ecologists.

They have radically turned the tables on the Eurocentric game of cultural relativism by appealing to the language of multiple ontologies and comparative metaphysics.[15] In so doing, they sometimes have created quite wonderful openings for beginning the task of taking seriously the realities of these many worlds outside the modern West. Indeed, if I find myself drawn to an experiment in relaying James's pluralistic problematic today, it is no doubt thanks to what they have taught me. *Around the Day in Eighty Worlds* holds out a hand to them too, in generous affinity with their efforts. Alas, I'm not an anthropologist. Yet it is our shared interest in the "permanent decolonization of thought" that leads me to experiment, beyond an analytics of ontology, with the divergences, connections, and transformations that are made and unmade by the ongoing and unfinished adventures of many other worlds in this world.[16] For while possibly appropriate to those others who have a stake in the theorization of their own modes of experience, it is worth continuing to remind oneself, now and again, that "ontology" is not everybody's problem. Its significance belongs above all to a world which, to varying degrees, still keeps alive the flame of that questionable tradition that so comfortably has split the world into epistemologies and ontologies, appearances and realities, what things are and what they look like. Which is why it is the great merit of these adventurous anthropologies to have resisted the habit—to borrow Eduardo Viveiros de Castro's apt words—of relating to other cultures "as solutions to those problems posed by our own," attempting instead to create the means to attend to the divergent ways in which others pose problems of their own. And it is in alliance with them that what I seek to intensify throughout this book is precisely the possibility of giving to those differences and divergences the power not to solve but to induce a metamorphosis of the manner in which we might come to pose our own problems.[17]

This is to say that, in seeking to stimulate a new appetite for trusting the pluriverse, what I hope to do in the course of this book is not to solve but to learn to inhabit the problem of differences, of the one and the many, to *feel* this "and," in its viscosities and its openings, in its violences and its possibilities. If the problem of the one and the many is so crucial today, then it's because it evokes in its most dramatic stakes the need to pay attention to what James called "the feeling of *and*."[18] It is, in other words, because this "and" matters: because any clear-cut, either/or solution, while possible in the abstract, is practically unworkable. "Things are with another in many ways, but nothing," James protested, "includes everything or dominates over everything. The word 'and' trails along after every sentence. Something always escapes. 'Ever not quite' has to be said of the best attempts anywhere in the universe at attaining all inclusiveness."[19] Pluralism is not an unproblematic celebration of the many. It is an ongoing response to a generative problematic, an insistence that calls for no jubilant solution but for careful and pragmatic experimentation. This is what the anaphoric operation that composes the list above ("There is this world . . .") tries to evoke: this *and* that, one *and* many, same *and* different, ongoing *and* unfinished. For as James argued, when the problem is addressed pragmatically rather than abstractly, "the world is one just so far as its parts hang together by any definite connexion" and "it is many just so far as any definite connexion fails to obtain."[20] And it is growing more and more unified or pluralized as the many practices that compose it continue to intervene in it. The pluriverse insists and persists in the interstices between the one and the many, rejecting either as final solutions to its ongoing problematic insistence.

The kind of pluralistic variation I am after, therefore, is one concerned with the pluralization of this element over which the modern world has claimed exclusive jurisdiction—a pluralization of this thing, of this *king*, called "reality." Pluralism's trusting hand is held out to manifold *realities*, loosely connected, partially open to each other and to their own becoming, composing a precarious cosmos that is diverging with itself all the way down—one and many, ongoing and unfinished. For if an ontology is always in some sense the handmaiden to some metaphysical system, *reality*, the sense of reality—suggested James, sneakily, in the middle of his treatise on psychology—"feels like itself, that is about as much as we can say."[21] *Reality feels like itself*: a demanding formulation that needs no phenomenological subject, no human agent, and no cultural whole, to be already there (where?), doing the work of feeling. Reality *feels* and *is felt* – a formulation which, put in the general language of serious metaphysicians, might perhaps read like this: "reality" may be said of everything that feels and is felt anywhere in the universe. Or as James put it elsewhere: "Everything real must be experienceable somewhere, and every kind of thing experienced must somewhere be real."[22] Indeed, it is precisely in this sense that *Around the Day in Eighty Worlds* sets out to relay James's thought: as the anti-imperialist efforts of a runaway metaphysician. For while he may be better known as a mere psychologist or, at best, a philosopher of "experience," it is also James who, bit by bit, makes experience and reality coincide in an irrepressible and generative plurality, such that while experience is the "primal stuff or material in the world" of which "everything is composed," there is also "no general stuff of which experience at large is made. There are as many stuffs as there are 'natures' in the things experienced."[23] Reality feels like itself, in the plural.

Feeling like itself, "reality" doesn't always need to come wrapped up in proper names—like Amerindian, Cuban, Western, Melanesian, and so on—because it hasn't yet learned that it is indecent for it to go out naked. To those who are heirs to the musings of modern European philosophy, this may sound like a minor, technical distinction, but the pragmatic difference it can make is, I suggest, significant. Because the modern tradition is also the one that has turned its own metaphysics into an empire, deploying its trained realism into a weapon of mass disqualification that creates and polices the border between what may count as real and what is dismissed as illusory, fantastical, superstitious, magical, or whimsical, no matter where (or when) it is found. Which is also to say that, as I gasp for another chance to regenerate my imagination while I still can, in this book I find myself entertaining pluralism, after James, as an ongoing, anti-imperialist effort dedicated to *our own metaphysical indetermination*—a speculative pragmatism that is not *against* the work of metaphysics as such, but resolutely *other* to its imperial expansions into an all-inclusive system.[24] More than a straightforward multiplication of the many, then, pluralism animates the politics of a world that persistently resists the assaults that would turn it into a single order, risking its own unfoldings and refoldings into an irreducible and insistent pluriverse. This kind of pluralism is thus a vector for a speculative, decolonial imagination.[25] One that instead of opposing power to power, instead of confronting the empire of modern realism with the anti-realism of deconstructive critique, lays siege to empire by embarking on the adventure of cultivating a realism generous and generative enough to travel around the day in eighty or a thousand worlds. A pluralism *trusting* enough to wager on the possibility that, as Indian writer and activist Arundhati Roy once reminded the World Social Forum, "another world is not only possible, she is on her way. On a quiet day, I can hear her breathing."[26]

STORIES WITHIN STORIES, WORLDS WITHIN WORLDS · Other worlds underway, ongoing and unfinished, trust we must. Isn't this what Gilles Deleuze meant when he implored that the most urgent and most difficult task before us today is precisely to believe in the world? The urgency of this task, one that requires a "mode of existence still to be discovered," and a problematic "we" yet to be composed, signals that this is not a matter of cultivating an *amor fati* toward an impending apocalypse.[27] To trust the world, to insist on living in it, to persist in it, is urgent because it demands that we insist on *another* world in this world, and that we trust *that*. This is what Fred Moten beautifully calls the "the joyful noise of the scattered, scatted eschaton," the refusal of a modern eschatology that has gone to great lengths to bring about its miraculous discoveries and creations, and now begins to wonder whether those same lengths may well bring about the end.[28] But while possibly joyful, this possible refusal is no doubt also the most difficult. Because, as Deleuze acknowledged, "we have so many reasons not to believe" in the world, "we have lost the world, worse than a fiancée or a god."[29] More than that, we continue to lose it. Indeed, it was the impending loss of the world, the progressive erasure of differences propelled by the imperialization of America, that marked James's anti-imperialist pluralism at the turn of the twentieth century, and against which he sought to cultivate a risky, experimental trust in the insistent possibility of an irreducible pluriverse.[30]

What has happened to us? What have been the lengths that this modern eschatology has gone to such that it could have partly succeeded in creating the foundations for a narrow form of reason fundamentally pitted against trust, and turned its provincial realism into a weapon of mass disqualification? We could recall Max Weber's nostalgic lament about the modern disenchantment of the world generated by the growing rationalization of a culture finally freed from all illusions.[31] This is a fine story, but I fear it is not the one the urgency of the task demands. Because any (re) enchantment of the world has disenchantment built into it.[32] And Weber's romanticism, for its part, is the child of a modern epoch that accepts as *fait accompli* a fate that is still ongoing and unfinished. A fate many of those other worlds are either indifferent to, or keep plying against as their "outsized realities," to borrow Gabriel García Márquez's words. The realities of hidden people, of gods and ghosts and soybeans and oracles and sorceries, were never "enchanted" to begin with. [33] They just feel like themselves.

Thus, in attempting to scat the eschaton, to disclose its enclosure such that another throw of the dice may become possible, perhaps we can experiment with a different tale. One whose memento will neither lead us to simply ponder where the magic has gone, nor set the mythological foundations for the complete erasure of a memory that, however sad, is still ours, to which we are today called upon to respond. The challenge is whether we can explore the possibility of asking other generative questions that may in turn make the monumental challenge of trusting the other worlds in this world possible. With that in mind, let me propose a *failing* story of origins of the modern project of world-monification, one whose implausible plot is I think as interesting as its unraveling. This is a tale, in other words, about the turning of the world into a *globe*. It is a tale I entertained for a short while (only to be amazed at its unraveling, and humbled by my own learned ignorance) when trying to imagine that, just as the moderns were supposedly able, according to their own stories, to leave the Middle Ages behind—that is, in the middle of their path to "progress"—by realizing that the innumerable marvels and wonders that fascinated Europeans at that time were not real because the world, now enlightened, had never in fact been populated with divine presence;[34] that this might have been made possible, in turn, by the fact that they had *already* discovered that those other worlds in this world could not in any genuine sense be *real*, either. While today, out of tolerance and goodwill, one may call them cultural, metaphorical, magical, traditional, or religious, they could not possibly be real because it was the turning of our unbounded reason into technologies of circumnavigation that gave us Columbus's egg and Magellan's voyages, that gave us the modern Age of Empires and enabled us to settle, once and for all, that the world is *not* many, for contrary to medieval wisdom, the earth is not flat, but round.

One could imagine how, rightly or wrongly, the event of the first successful circumnavigations would have been key to this process. First, because of the economic and geopolitical accession to world-wide trade and processes of enslavement and colonization of non-European peoples, but also, importantly, because of the geometrical discovery of a spherical Earth, perfectly self-contained, with no cliff-edges, and no possible worlds beyond. A round world mirroring in earthly experience the theologics of the One.[35] Indeed, as the modern epic goes, Columbus held the enlightened but then unpopular conviction that the Earth might in fact turn out to be round, and had to overcome the calumnies of the assembled clerics at Salamanca to get a hearing with the Spanish monarchs to gain their support for the expedition that would open a nautical path between the Spanish Kingdom and the Far East. For this reason, when they reached what later became known as America, Columbus was convinced he had actually arrived in Asia. It was thanks to this cosmographical mistake, therefore, that Europe was placed at the center of the map as well as of history—a gesture that prompts postcolonial philosopher Enrique Dussel to make the provocative suggestion that, rather than having been born of its own accord, through the miraculous inventions of an enlightened techno-scientific culture, it was Columbus who in fact inaugurated Modernity.[36]

Columbus, however, didn't make it to Asia, and so he never quite managed to bend the medieval map. It was the Portuguese renegade Fernão de Magalhães who, as is known, is credited with having led, between 1519 and 1522 (and with Spanish funding), the first voyage around the world—not quite in eighty days like Phileas Fogg, but in well over a thousand. Unlike Columbus, who described his voyages as the discovery of "another world,"[37] Magalhães was still adventurous but a lot less speculative, simply seeking westward access to the Spice Islands promised by Columbus but never delivered, a kind of access that, if achieved, would have enabled Spain to lay sovereign claim to part of the Portuguese-dominated spice trade. Assisted by his Malaysian polyglot slave Enrique, a fleet of five ships, 230 men, copious artillery, and promises of massive future dividends, he sailed south alongside the African shore, and made the Atlantic crossing south of the Equator to reach southern Brazil. From then on, they continued sailing along what would now be the Uruguayan and Argentinian shores.

For reasons far more numerous than I can here relate, this was a dangerous trip. Suffice it to say that, on their way down the American coast, Magalhães and his fleet came across "hogs with navels on their haunches, clawless birds whose hens laid eggs on the backs of their mates, and others still, resembling tongueless pelicans, with beaks like spoons." They also encountered "a misbegotten creature with the head and ears of a mule, a camel's body, the legs of a deer, and the whinny of a horse."[38] And as they found shelter in the natural harbor of what later became known as Puerto San Julián in the Argentinian Patagonia, Antonio Pigafetta, a Florentine member of the fleet who kept written records of their journey, writes that they encountered a giant who, at the glance of a mirror, "was greatly terrified, leaping backwards" and making "three or four men fall down."[39] This was, of course, less than half of the trip. Navigating through the strait that crosses the southern tip of the continent on to the Pacific Ocean, the other half also included internal rebellions and desertions within the crew, food shortages, generalized cases of scurvy, and violent encounters with indigenous peoples from Micronesia—until at least part of the fleet made it to the Philippines and then on to the much sought-after Spice Islands in what is now the Indonesian archipelago. After spending some time stuffing themselves on cloves and cinnamon, they eventually reentered the Atlantic and made the final stretch back to Spain.

The map was bent. If, as the Martinican philosopher and poet Édouard Glissant put it, "the first Colonist, Christopher Columbus, did not voyage in the name of a country but of an idea," then presumably Ferdinand Magellan, the first circumnavigator, would have literally *brought home* the idea that, contrary to medieval wisdom, the world was not flat but round—without worlds beyond, wholly and ecumenically one.[40] As he turned the cliff-edges into a challenging but united mass of water, and established a definite connection around the many little worlds for the first time, the Dark Ages drew to a close and the colonial monification of the world was thus initiated. Indeed, in some regards, this was a critical event. Not only was the very construction of the fleet responsible for "the final demise of the forests of the Mediterranean and the beginning of an intensive exploitation of wooded parts of the Baltic, Scandinavia, Russia, and eventually, the Americas,"[41] but as historian Joyce E. Chaplin has argued, having succeeded in turning the globe into a real object, the expedition also made "plans for global empire real."[42] The Global World, the Age of Empires, and Cheap Nature Capitalism were thus born as triplets, and modernity began to lose the world as soon as it had finally managed to capture the globe.[43]

That said, a contemporary historian may understandably want to burn me at the stake for this story. Others may object that it risks creating too strong an association between modernity and the West, thus giving a free pass to the Eurocentric character of many a story of the advent of the modern age. They would remind us that "the West" is little more than an abstraction, that modernity was neither an exclusively European invention, a historical rupture with a pre-modern past, nor a fully successful achievement. They would argue that despite its furious disavowals, modernity is itself multiple and plural. They need not be wrong either. As far as I am concerned, "modernity" is the heteronymic name for a host of different stories we tell. Which is not to say that these are "just stories." Stories do things, they infect our lives and practices, they weave and tear worlds, they shape how they might come to be inhabited. We live and die by the stories we tell. Thus, no story can claim innocence.[44] No story can disentangle itself from what it omits, any more than it can distance itself from the consequences it precipitates, or the difference it might be liable to make. Each involves a risk, a wager on the worlds we might seek to weave. Which is why it matters how stories are told. With some stories we are lured into the surreptitious instabilities of the modern, looking for the persistent ambivalences of that which its most Eurocentric and self-indulgent versions would disavow. With others, we're prompted to sail in the search for alternative configurations of what being modern might involve. But perhaps other stories, like the one I'm in the midst of telling, might yet take us along different paths, not always marked on a map. By *provincializing* the modern, by rendering it a mode of ploughing and of inhabiting a world-turned-globe that has become dominant but never total, by conceiving it as a project and a force that has proven extremely effective but never finished nor entirely successful, perhaps these kinds of stories create the possibility of something else. Perhaps they enable us to affirm that while we're heirs to colonizing and imperial histories that persist in the worlds we might seek to weave—*ever not quite*, there are other worlds in this world; other ways of inhabiting worlds are possible in spite of all. Perhaps stories like this might also precipitate the possibility of telling other stories, ones which might lure us to the sense of an opening, transforming thought through a pluralistic variation of interests.

That, for better or ill, is the risk I take—the risk, that is, of experimenting with such stories in order to throw the dice and begin again. But I do so with some hesitation, for hesitation is at the heart of this story I'm trying to tell. It simultaneously subtends and upends it. After all, compared to the monistic elegance of most stories of origin, pluralism "offers but a sorry appearance. It is," James insisted, "a turbid, muddled, gothic sort of affair, without a sweeping outline and with little pictorial nobility."[45] Muddle things I must! For it is not just that while Magalhães did made history, he didn't actually make the entire journey, having died somewhere along the way at the hands of Filipino soldiers defending themselves from invasion. Nor is it just that, by the time the fleet reached the South Asian Sea, it would have probably been Enrique, the Malaysian slave, who was the first person to have completed a journey around the world. The fascinating unraveling of this story begins when we note that much of its "pictorial nobility" hinges on the bending of the medieval flat-Earth map. Enticing as it is, I found out rather quickly and with some embarrassment that this could not, in and of itself, have been the inaugural event of the modern monification of the world—at least not without unraveling the untimely thread that connects the event of circumnavigation in the early sixteenth century with another event that took place much later. Which is to say, not without considering that most things happen through the *resonance* of events, "point of view on a point of view, displacement of perspective, differentiation of difference,"[46] stories within stories, worlds within worlds.

By this I mean that, if we follow the story linearly, Magellan's circumnavigation could not have constituted the birth, or rather, the rebirth—which is to say, the *Renaissance*—of the self-contained, spherical Earth, for the simple reason that the Earth of the Dark Ages was never flat to begin with. This is where the other story in this story opens up. Contrary to the epic tale, this other story notes that the ancient insights of a spherical Earth achieved by the Greeks never quite faded, and "all major medieval scholars accepted the earth's roundness," at least in principle, "as an established fact of cosmology."[47] In fact, the natural historian Stephen Jay Gould writes of this other story that apparently only two medieval scholars espoused such flat cosmologies. One proposed an account whereby people at the antipodes "might walk with their feet above their heads in a land where crops grow down and rain falls up," while the other championed a literal interpretation of a biblical metaphor which suggested that the Earth was "a flat floor for the rectangular, vaulted arch of the heavens above."[48] But both of them were largely marginal figures in medieval scholarship, not least because they wrote in Greek and remained untranslated during a time when the *lingua franca* was Latin. To muddle things further, back in the enlightened imperial center of the world, monsters, curiosities, and other wild facts and outsized, extraordinary realities still populated fairs, coffeehouses, and publications until well into the eighteenth century. After all, it was at that time that the Académie Royale des Sciences printed Leibniz's account of a dog that could bark out about thirty words![49] As this other story goes, it was not until the last couple of decades of the nineteenth century that the epic story of the flat Earth took hold, and was introduced on a massive scale in history textbooks pretty much until today, with the sole purpose of supporting the place of Darwin's theory of evolution as the latest episode of "a tale of bright progress continually sparked by science."[50] The introduction of the flat-Earth story in history textbooks was, as Gould suggests, a chapter written by modern historians in their equally implausible story of the development of human civilization as an ongoing strife between Science and Religion.

A *failing* story of origins indeed—for neither the circumnavigation, nor the nineteenth-century campaign led by historians, will singly help us pinpoint its beginning. But something is underway nevertheless. Something is engendered in the resonance between these events; another story within these stories is woven through them, one which opens up what has effectively constituted an epochal transformation, underway throughout the last few centuries, and lacing itself around many other stories of the rise of the "new sciences" and Newtonian physics,[51] the bifurcation of nature,[52] the rise of natural law in both science and politics,[53] and the birth of the human sciences.[54] This transformation that we have come to call "modern" extracted elements of such divergent stories with a view toward the general orchestration of a dominant story of order that would bring together, into an encompassing scheme, the laws of nature and the laws of nations. And in so doing, it embraced the arrival of what in hindsight we might call a new, modern metaphysics of an ordinary, uniform, and unexceptional order of nature. Conflating it with reality as such, modernity celebrated its intellectual, political, and social implications. Stephen Toulmin had a point, then, in associating the "hidden agenda" of modernity with a *counter-renaissance* that, in conflating reason with the boundless, the general, the universal, the certain, and the timeless, poured scorn on everything specific, local, timely, and uncertain.[55] Writing a historiography of backward pasts to accompany a geography of living anachronisms, this new metaphysics spread throughout philosophy, science, and the arts in the form of a modern realism that rendered the imagination dangerous and the extraordinary vulgar, and thus transformed the way in which the event of circumnavigation came to matter. According to its own story, going around the world was no longer merely a nautical success, nor even just a political achievement. Instead, it represented the absolute victory of a finally boundless reason over a world whose unruly edges and extraordinary multifariousness could then safely be ignored, and eventually banished. A mode of inhabiting the world where one would no longer be compelled to believe in other worlds in this world, or to trust anything beyond what this domesticated orthodoxy now deemed possible. And yet, ever not quite: the story is still ongoing, the agenda is still unfinished.

WHAT IS REALITY CAPABLE OF? · In knitting together certain forms of naturalism, of rationalism, and of colonialism, what these connected stories animated, therefore, is the conjuring of an order of the possible in a now self-enclosed world.[56] This is why rather than choosing between them, I propose these stories-within-stories as a kind of *opening*, one perhaps capable of *dis*-closing the closure brought about by the progressive plot of the epic tale of the nineteenth century, one providing a possible resource to counter the process of monification and to reimagine the stakes of trusting the world and its pluralization again. Rather than simply arguing for a (re)turn to the flat Earth, then, I propose to invert the direction, which is to say the sense, of Magalhães's and Fogg's travel—*around the day in eighty worlds*. What is at stake here is neither the affirmation of many little separate worlds in isolation, nor the number eighty, but the wresting of the adventure of voyaging from the dreams of the colonial project by going around a pluralistic universe of partial stories and connections. In other words, it is a matter of attempting to rescue realities in the plural from the hands of modern realists *and* anti-realists alike. Of course, disputes over some form of "realism" or another may have been around ever since Plato expressed his distrust of art and sought to expel poets from the Republic, but these connected stories have enabled the modern flame-keepers of Platonism to truly spread across the contemporary world.[57] And today, while the list of disqualified realities rises exponentially in a world without refuge, "realist" thinkers fight over whether one should be a realist either about the past *or* about futures, a realist about natural kinds *or* about human kinds, a realist about things-in-themselves *or* about things-as-related, a realist about objects *or* about relations, a realist about substances *or* about processes, or a realist about stars but not about the occurrence of the sequence "777" in the number π.[58] Which begs the question: other than by its love for the unexceptional, how should modern realism be characterized? What is the patterning through which it ploughs the world?

Given that no "cat-on-the-mat" argument is capable of singlehandedly ploughing the world, and given that, as I have just suggested, so-called realist philosophers may disagree about whether one should affirm the reality of the cat, or the mat, and would probably frown upon any modest attempt to affirm the reality of the *on*, my suggestion is that modern realism can be characterized neither as a philosophy, a theory, nor even as an intellectual position. Consider the supposedly standard definition of realism, which states that among its basic premises are that "the world consists of some *fixed* totality of mind-independent objects" and that "there is exactly *one* true and complete description of 'the way the world is.'"[59] What is this if not a legislative decree? What is this if not the arbitrary definition of an abstract *boundary*? What difference does this definition make, if not that of inspiring distrust in other worlds by insisting dogmatically in the fixed and single nature of *this* world as *the* world? Which of the many other worlds could possibly survive it? Alas, poor ghosts, poor hidden people, poor giants and oracles, poor gods and goddesses and the dead; poor Pigafetta, poor our own imaginations, apparently so mind-dependent; poor the relationships and partial connections we're in; poor novelty; but also poor Darwin, poor James, poor Deleuze, poor our sense of curiosity, discovery, and invention; poor the possible itself.

Because it is a moving border legislating on the kinds of questions that can be asked, the meaning and function of modern realism is first to be defined negatively. Just like the notion of Enlightenment itself,[60] this order of the possible for which modern realism is a nickname is largely defined by what it excludes, which is to say, by what it opposes, such that we may as well imagine it rather as an order, both metaphysical and political, of the *impossible*. More than a philosophical doctrine with an affirmative proposition about what reality *is*, modern realism must thus be pragmatically understood, first and foremost, as a belligerent operation, as an entire mode of inhabiting and engaging the world and its forms of divergence, a mode which makes its own militant legislations percolate into every encounter, into every feeling of *and*. This modern-realist operation functions primarily as an act of policing that, aided by the rise of an unexceptional metaphysics and the global expansion of European empires, consists in marshalling a distrust for the world as it travels around it, undertaking the ongoing—but I insist, unfinished—task of legislating what is real from what is illusory or superstitious, what is possible from what is impossible. With no patience for generative questions, it behaves like the schoolmate of Julio Cortázar, the Argentinian writer in whose honor I've titled this book. This was a classmate to whom Cortázar lent a book by Jules Verne; after a few days the boy brought it back and, to Cortázar's surprise, said: "I can't read this, it's too fantastical."[61]

Were it not for the fact that European colonization turned this distrusting realism into an imperial machine of its own, we would not need be concerned with it. But its ubiquitous presence today, its capacity not only to disqualify anything it faces but to transform the very mode of judgment, cornering those who seek to think the possibility of another world in this world into the defeat of an equally distrusting anti-realism, makes its consequences felt with an urgency that one can no longer afford to ignore. Because while abstract philosophical arguments cannot singlehandedly shape the world in their own image, philosophies nevertheless are, as James said over a century ago, "intimate parts of the universe," such that "with our theories," even with our modern realist theories-of-no-theory, the universe "may trust itself or mistrust itself the more, and by doing the one or the other, deserve more the trust or the mistrust."[62] This is why, animated by James's proposition that reality feels like itself, this books sets out to invert Magellan's journey, and go around the day in eighty worlds. Because it seems to me that the first task to be undertaken in the permanently ongoing and unfinished project of our own metaphysical indetermination, one that might perhaps enable us to regenerate our trust in this world and its possibilities, is the task of refusing the modern-realist operations by snatching realism from its modern alliance with monism. Which is to say, the task of laboring against the empire of mistrust that the metaphysics of an ordinary nature has instilled in our practices and imaginations. Because what distrusts itself deserves to be mistrusted.

Édouard Glissant once wrote that decolonization "will have done its real work" when it goes beyond the limits of the oppositional logic that defines it as the negative of colonialism.[63] Seconding him, I would say that it will then have *resumed* its work on and in reality. More than a deconstructive critique of coloniality, refusing the reasons that give rise to opposition requires a *pluralistic realism* that works experimentally to cultivate an ongoing and unfinished pluriverse, diverging with itself all the way down. Not, therefore, a relativist "anything goes," but a pluralist "many things *are!*" Laboring toward metaphysical indetermination, I want to associate this kind of pluralism with the paradoxical figure of a *runaway metaphysics*, unhinged from first principles and apocalyptic endings, permanently ongoing and unfinished: an exercise that has certainly nothing to do with the modern systematic search for the ultimate structure of a boundless reality principle, to be discerned above and beyond the multifarious realities of this world. It is the modern justifications for the distrust in the world that a runaway metaphysics rejects, and it is the temptation to be absolved in yet another boundless beyond that it resists. As such, it will favor no system, condone no systematic distrust, and authorize no principle of neglect. Unhinged, its task is that of an ongoing experimentation, a permanent effort in generative feeling, an ongoing and unfinished art of noticing and learning, not from a realm of a higher denomination but from the multifarious, empirical "reality where things *happen*," without exception.[64] A runaway metaphysics must thus go wandering South and North in the search for possible alliances with other little hangings-together, with realities lost, suppressed, marginalized, and derided, with realities fantastical, incomprehensible, and implausible; always in touch with other worlds underway and yet to be made, insisting in the distrusted rubbles that modern-realist operations have disavowed. And it insists in them to make felt, always a bit more, always a little differently, that if reality needs no other justification than experience itself, there is no one substance of which all experiences are made. That there are other worlds in this world, underway and yet to be made. That reality feels like itself, in the plural.

A thoroughly realistic project, albeit of an unusual sort: pluralistic, un-principled, counter-ecumenical, pragmatic, radically empirical. Going around the day, it will perhaps resemble the kinds of realism we enter-tain during the night, when even the most skeptical of the moderns can be shaken at the glimpse of the shadow of a possible ghost. Such a pluralistic realism would no doubt be unusual because, instead of beginning with either positive or negative doctrines, with so many determinations and definitions distinguishing what is real from what is not, it must always begin again, with a generous and generative question that modern-realist operations have made almost impossible to utter: "*what is reality capable of?*," and stay to hear the responses. It is clear that this question will not, by itself, solve any of our problems. Worse, it will take away our favorite weapon for dealing with them. In so doing, it is likely to create new, prag-matic problems of learning to inhabit a pluralistic world without founda-tions. But, perhaps, just perhaps, these new problems may change the ones we've got. Perhaps they may be able to create the possibility of something unexpected to happen on a day when we have learned to expect nothing. And perhaps, just perhaps, giving this possible a chance matters. With it, perhaps the pluriverse may trust itself a little more. This, at any rate, is what I'm trusting.

························

Like a many-storied universe, *Around the Day in Eighty Worlds* unfolds and enfolds experimentally, through piecemeal approximation, stuttering its most humble questions while holding out a hand to a host of different worlds it trusts may meet its hand. Cultivating a pluralistic art of noticing other worlds in this world, the book thinks with what some of their many stories may demand of our own concepts and propositions in relay and re-turn, so as to render each other capable of response, capable of trusting reality to feel and be felt in the plural. In so doing, each chapter attempts to relay relevant aspects of James's thought by situating it in generative and generous alliances with ethnographic stories of other fellow day-travelers as well as with a host of other thinkers inhabiting the interstices of this plu-ralistic manifold in and out of Europe. Chapter 2, "Runaway Metaphysics," undertakes the initial task of articulating the stakes and demands of our own metaphysical indetermination by following the story of the fractious exchange between anthropologist Harry West and Lazaro Mmala, a schoolteacher and veteran of the Mozambican war of independence, on the question of whether the sorcery-lions that populate the Mueda Plateau can be understood as political "symbols," or whether, as Mmala forcefully insists, we must come to terms with the fact that they are indeed *real*. The attempt to take Mmala's response seriously precipitates nothing less than a pragmatic revaluation of the ways in which we have come to approach the politics of difference. Relaying aspects of James's thought in conversation with postcolonial scholars and contemporary cultural anthropologists, I suggest that rather than a matter of choosing between "epistemological" or "ontological" pluralisms, the adventure in divergence opened up by a runaway metaphysics calls for nothing less than the *decolonization of the plural* itself.

By threading together a speculative exploration of James's concept of trust with anthropologist Tanya Luhrmann's story of evangelicals who learn to trust in the reality of God standing by their side, with love, Chapter 3, "Trust of a Held-out Hand," examines and dramatizes the implications of James's generative proposition that reality feels like itself. Countering the modern histories that reduced the realities of gods and spirits to the realm of "religion," and turned "belief" into a weapon of de-realization of other worlds, I suggest that trust is the *generic* name James gave to the feeling of reality in the plural. And in this sense, it designates an immanent, living disposition that impregnates, always differently, the multifarious ways in which the inhabitants of the many worlds in this ongoing and unfinished world live, think, feel, and act. Trust, in short, characterizes a living attitude of *consent* to the world: a feeling-with one's world. As such, whenever James is concerned, trust constitutes an immanent metaphysical ultimate, capable of generating a transformation of our concept of reality and an opening to our own metaphysical indetermination. For what the practices of these evangelicals make perceptible is that it is possible to *learn* to trust another world in this world. Trust, therefore, does not simply subtend the manifold relationships people establish with their worlds in this world, but simultaneously opens these relations up and creates the possibility of extending them, to a whole array of "ifs" and "maybes." Learning to trust, I suggest, precipitates a pluralistic event: the partial, fragile, ongoing, and unfinished weaving of a tremorous form of togetherness that obtains thanks to, and not in spite of, divergence. And for that reason, the risky cultivation of trust is a requisite for the pluriverse's own verification.

Trust is therefore what a radically irreducible politics of difference *requires*, interrupting the modern habit of considering ourselves free to translate and redefine the ways in which others inhabit their world. What it makes possible is a felt approach to the turbulent insistence of the pluriverse itself. Indeed, it is this interstitial trembling, the partial connections between its different little worlds, that makes the pluriverse felt. On a quiet day, one can hear it breathing. Modern realism has always despised the tremors, going to any lengths to hold *our* world fast, deploying its weapons of de-realization to countervail the quickening of our own foundations. Approaching this tremorous togetherness can hardly be achieved, therefore, without experiencing something of our own metaphysical indetermination as another world passes into our experience. This is what, in Chapter 4, I call a "worldquake": the insinuation of another world underway, of a buzzing multiplicity of other worlds in this world, of the feeling of another world passing into one's experience. By threading Edith Turner's experience of seeing a visible spirit coming out of a woman's back in Zambia, together with James's own experience of a mild earthquake and some of his reflections on the relationships between percepts and concepts, it is the aim of this chapter to *dramatize* the experience which worldquakes precipitate.

A worldquake, I propose, puts all general principles out of their depth, making perceptible the radical contingency of any and all responses to the feeling of difference in the concrete. As such, it helps us understand that a politics of the pluriverse is neither a matter of articulating equanimous responses, singlehandedly capable of putting us and others on symmetrical footing, nor is it only about a politics of translation, of choosing between betraying either the language of origin or of destination. Rather, worldquakes require that one grants the trembling of togetherness the power to transform our stories and concepts, to let oneself be transformed by them. They prompt what, throughout this book, I call an *intranslation*: an entirely nonsymmetrical act, at once conceptual, political, and pragmatic, of *introducing* ("intraduire") and precipitating generative vectors of alteration, curves of divergence, variations of interest, the many boiling over the one, a pinch of chaos in the cosmos.[65] Worldquakes leave us without foundations. They make present that there is something tragic in every decision, in any response. The ongoingness of the pluriverse itself is at stake, and just as there are novelties, there will be losses. Which is why a runaway metaphysics cannot but keep stuttering out its most humble needs like a foolish little child in the eyes of reason. Thus, the test of its experiments cannot be any other than a thoroughly *pragmatic* one: what difference might this make? With our responses and additions, does the pluriverse *"rise or fall in value? Are the additions worthy or unworthy?"*[66] Chapter 5, "Pragmatism in the Wake," explores the generativity of James's pragmatism as an experimental and speculative response to events that make such radical contingency felt. And it does so by threading his thoughts on the pragmatic method together with a most dramatic story: that of the profusion of ghosts that emerged in the aftermath of the tsunami that hit the coast of Japan in 2011, killing 18,000 people, and of the improvisational practices that a group of Buddhist, Shinto, and Protestant priests articulated in the wake of the disaster. Eschewing the strictures of their doctrinal knowledges and languages without surrendering to the professed modernity of contemporary Japan, these priests developed a host of spiritual care work practices across divergent forms of religious faith to address not only the trauma of the survivors, but also the suffering of the dead who lost their living to the wave. In so doing, I suggest that their practices dramatize the most generative feature of pragmatism: the speculative wager on the feeling of *if*, the insistence on the possibility that caring for other stories can lead, in turn, to composing ways of living and dying well with others, of rendering each other capable of response, of enabling the pluriverse to trust itself a little more.

Building on the preceding explorations, the final chapter, "The Insistence of the Pluriverse," brings aspects of James's melioristic thought to bear on contemporary debates around what I refer to as the emergence of an interest in political cosmology. Which political dreams and fears, hopes and perils, might the Jamesian pluriverse animate? By relaying a story of James's own visit to a sort of concrete middle-class utopia, the Methodist retreat at Chautauqua, the chapter places James in conversation with a renewed engagement among postcolonial thinkers in the very idea of a "pluriverse," and dramatizes the possible alliances and divergences that are made present between them. Whereas contemporary thinkers tend to associate the notion of the "pluriverse" to a cosmology where many worlds "fit," and some even characterize it as a new *universal* project from below, I argue that the Jamesian pluriverse conjures a political cosmology that rejects all cosmopolitan dreams of transcendence. Instead, the cosmology arising from James's world-picturing activity is that of a precipitous manifold, a permanently ongoing and unfinished composition of forms of divergence, togetherness, and experiment. The pluriverse, I suggest, is the name for a *perhaps* that insists and persists. And pluralism, in relay and return, is but a pragmatics of the pluriverse—the art of relaying the dynamic of collective invention through which myriad divergent practices, in and out of Europe, cultivate their own forms of trust in the possibility of another world while consenting to the possibility that the worlds they trust are possible are not the same world.

CHAPTER TWO · Runaway Metaphysics

The word "or" names a genuine reality.

WILLIAM JAMES

Philosophy may not neglect the multifariousness of the world—
the fairies dance, and Christ is nailed to the cross.

ALFRED NORTH WHITEHEAD

A PLURALISTIC REALISM · There is an ancient Andean saying, I am told,
which teaches that in order to grasp the universe in its totality, the only
way to do it is by beginning to notice each of its components, one by one,
until we fall asleep.[1] It seems to me that there is something remarkably
perceptive about this pearl of wisdom. With a subtly cosmic humor, it confronts the impetus of many modern metaphysical projects—with their perennial constructions of philosophical castles to provide a final, general,
and anonymous account of the nature of reality—and turns them on their
head: displacing the hubris of the modern-realist operation ("this is real,
this is not . . .") with the humor of its own situated art of noticing, bit by
bit, the multifariousness of the world. And this is a situated art indeed,
not least because noticing, one by one, the many components that make
up a universe—exploring their contrasts and differences, their edges and
relations, their forms of connection, their constraints and possibilities,
their singular modes of divergence—circumvents and aerates the stuffed

habits of those who will not let themselves count in the mix. It counters the projects of those who will step away from the multifarious mess of things so as to come back from a transcendental beyond with their own, disowned, dispassionate, higher-order consideration of the "really real" nature of things. Noticing the many realities that make up the mess, like counting stars with our backs stretched against the soil that holds us, involves instead an intimate and tangled experience, a plunging in the midst of things not in order to sort out the mess but to pass on and through, to incessantly experiment with the possibility of experiencing the universe in its branching and refolding, in its generative divergence. Without guarantees.

These pluralistic arts of noticing, therefore, cannot afford the operation of "scaling up" their questions and procedures. They cannot proceed by simply noticing a few elements here or there and apply what they have learned elsewhere, to greater scales, without at the same time being forced to relearn the lessons, without being confronted with the interruptions and radical differences that other elements and their relations make felt. This is not surprising. For as anthropologist Anna Tsing has pointed out, this "ability of a project to change scales smoothly without any change in project frames," which she calls "scalability," is at the very heart of capitalist industrialization and modern imperialist expansion.[2] Indeed, it is hardly a coincidence that the birthplace of such modernizing experiments in scaling were the European colonial plantations set up in the American continent. As Tsing argues, the introduction of sugarcane from New Guinea into colonial Brazil was made possible by a series of displacements of dislocated cloned planting stock and forcedly displaced slave labor. These displacements and uprootings had the effect of making every relevant part interchangeable, and subjected parts to new processes of standardization of production brought about by technologies of central milling, such that "all operations had to run on the time frame of the mill."[3] In this way, the plantations' "contingent components—cloned planting stock, coerced labor, conquered and thus open land—showed how alienation, interchangeability, and expansion could lead to unprecedented profits."[4] Colonial plantations served thus as one of Empire's key political-economic machines of what I have called the modern metaphysics of ordinary nature, effectively ploughing the world after its own principles of domestication, interchangeability, and regularity. Precariously situated, by contrast, the arts of noticing cannot but remain non-scalable. They must always begin somewhere, must always be held by some generative soil and develop their activity piecemeal, errantly moving from element to element, from this reality to that, combing "through the mess of existing worlds-in-the-making, looking for treasures—each distinctive and unlikely to be found again, at least in that form."[5] With each new element, with each new event, the question is posed anew: *What is reality capable of?*

Situating oneself in other worlds in this world by way of a wandering exploration of its many existing realities, the many realities underway and yet to be made, until we fall asleep, seems like an apt refrain for this un-principled, empiricist, and counter-ecumenical pluralism that I have associated with the task of a *runaway metaphysics*. Indeed, through another resonance of events, another displacement of perspective, this pearl of Andean wisdom is a sort of pluralistic proposition *avant la lettre*. In *A Pluralistic Universe*, William James confessed that, save for the sheer existence of monists, he found "no good warrant for even suspecting the existence of any reality of a higher denomination than that distributed and strung-along and flowing sort of reality which we finite beings swim in."[6] For that reason, he suggested that instead of the monism of modern-realist operations, which erects metaphysical empires to legislate over the jurisdiction of this unity, this "all-form" called reality, and does so at the peril of all those little hangings-together left on the other side of its borders, pluralism wagers that any philosophic attempt to define nature or reality all at once, by way of a series of abstract principles, "so that no one's business is left out, so that no one lies outside the door saying 'Where do *I* come in?' is sure in advance to fail."[7]

Here the resonances between these Andean arts of noticing and the possibility of a runaway metaphysics go even further. The pluriverse, on-going and unfinished, underway and yet to be made, also relays their cosmic humor. Because while these worldly manifolds may, at the end of the day, add up to a *universe*, there is always an after to the end of days—any final count of its parts is always unfinished. "This world *may*, in the last resort," James allowed, "be a block-universe; but on the other hand it may be a universe only strung-along, not rounded in and closed. Reality *may* exist distributively just as it sensibly seems to, after all. On that possibility I do insist."[8] And as one, going around the day in eighty or a thousand little worlds, responds to the insistence of this possibility, the parts that are disconnected now may in some way become connected tomorrow, and one may discover along the way that in this strung-along reality "a thing may be connected by intermediary things, with a thing with which it has no immediate or essential connexion. It is thus at all times in many possible connexions which are not necessarily actualized at the moment."[9] What's more, with the many activities of monification and pluralization that constitute the pluriverse's generative insistence, what reality is not capable of today she may be capable of tomorrow—new conjunctive and disjunctive relations are engendered at every step of the way, and the many *possible* connections and disconnections that may come into existence across and among its little hangings-together demand to be noticed too. They also ask, "Where do *I* come in?" As James suggested, "the word 'or' names a genuine reality."[10] Little worlds in this world, here and there, yesterday and tomorrow, they are too many to count fully. And as the suns of the pluriverse begin to set, as they do in different ways and at different times of the day, sleep befalls upon those who travel the day passing on and through its many little worlds. Ever not quite!

Like the Andean arts of noticing, then, pluralism "lets things exist in the each-form or distributively."[11] Without recourse to the scaling powers afforded by general principles and transcendental foundations, it must travel around the day carrying out its task piecemeal, beginning with any one of the many little worlds, and see whither it's bound, with what other worlds it is connected, which other "ands" trail along its edges, which outside worlds make its intimate environment.[12] Thrown in the middle of the world's multifariousness by virtue of its generous and generative question, it is thus that a runaway metaphysics becomes an entirely unprincipled and radically empirical adventure. Unable to decide in advance what should and should not be real, it proffers the possibility of a *pluralistic* realism. For indeed, as James noted, "every smallest bit of experience is a *multum in parvo* plurally related" and "each relation is one aspect, character, or function, way of its being taken, or way of its taking something else." Refusing to disqualify what would oppose the principles it doesn't have, it can neglect nothing that is "empirically realized in every minimum of finite life,"[13] no matter how minute, implausible, fantastical, or extraordinary it may be. Its challenge, instead, is that of learning, against the empire of modern-realist operations, to trust that those extraordinary realities, those other worlds in this world, can be, in Cortázar's words, "as acceptable, possible, and real as having soup at 8 p.m."[14]

A most demanding task, no doubt. One that requires arts of noticing to be necessarily collective, comprised of a multitude of ally day-travelers, already existing and in the making, who may be willing to risk passing on and through the smallest and widest bits of reality, to trust the furthest and closest worlds in this world, so as to multiply the echoes of this curious metaphysical experiment. But this is also a task that, at the same time, requires day-travelers to refuse the reasons, to counter the habits of thinking and feeling, both colonial *and* critical, with which modern-realist operations have, since Magellan, turned world-traveling into world-monification—those that will make reality feel like something other than itself, and turn every other world in this world into a matter of symbols, of cultures, of worldviews, of so many ways of knowing or representing *one* world, of so many ways of conceptualizing what the world, *our world*, is. A task underway and yet to come, ongoing and unfinished.

"THESE LIONS, THEY ARE REAL" · Let us then heed the advice of the Andean arts of noticing and begin to dramatize some aspects of this task by noticing one of the many worlds in this world that form part of that ongoing and unfinished list included in the previous chapter. Geographically situated on the Mueda Plateau in postcolonial, post-socialist Mozambique, the humble but striking story through which it comes into our focus is related by ally anthropologist Harry West in his book *Ethnographic Sorcery* and relayed here.[15] Toward the end of his ethnographic work in the region in 1994, West was asked by the provincial office of the Arquivos do Patrimônio Cultural (ARPAC, Cultural Heritage Archives) to give a series of lectures to a mixed audience of indigenous residents and government functionaries from the provincial departments of education or culture, in order to "give something back to the institution" in return for the help he received during his fieldwork.[16] It was not that ARPAC did not have any ethnographers of its own. It did, West tells us, have "half dozen staff researchers" with "far more ethnographic fieldwork experience" than he had. The issue, as he then saw it, was rather that none of them "had much formal training in anthropological theory and methodology" and thus "they hesitated . . . to analyze or interpret what their informants told them." Seeking to allay such hesitations, West thus took up the task of providing a brief introduction to anthropological theory, and in particular, to Victor Turner's symbolic anthropology, with the aim to "inspire them to move beyond the cataloguing of data and the verbatim quotation of informants that characterized their publications."[17]

Keen to present a piece of his own ethnographic work-in-progress, he made use of aspects of Turner's thought while engaging with stories collected in the course of his own research in the plateau. He began by summarizing for the audience "what most already knew":

when a lion was seen in or around a plateau village, people often speculated that it was not an ordinary lion, not an *ntumi wa ku mwitu* (bush lion); rather, they often suggested, it was a *ntumi wa nkaja* (a settlement lion), meaning either that it was a sorcerer who had turned into a lion, in which case it might also be called an *ntumi munu* (lion-person), or that it was made by a sorcerer, in which case it might also be called an *ntumi wa kumpika* (a fabricated lion). Sorcery lions devoured the flesh of sorcerers' rivals, neighbors, and kin, sometimes through visible attacks and sometimes through invisible ones that produce chronic illness. To deal with such a lion—most of my audience, again, already knew—a specialist was summoned to discern the lion's true nature and to prepare medicinal substances that rendered the beast vulnerable to hunters. At the same time, people continued to deliberate on the identity of the person associated with the lion and on the identity of the lion's intended victim.[18]

An ideal case for a symbolic analysis, he reckoned, because such a situation brought Muedans to examine collectively the possible transgressions of egalitarian norms, the appropriation of the wealth of others without honest work. It brought them, that is, to interrogate "who among them was 'predator' and who was 'prey,'" and in so doing, "their anger and distrust were infused with, and heightened by their fear of the lion."[19] Interpreted in this way, the lions could thus be seen as a symbol that connected the ideological and sensory poles of the Muedans' experience, and both represented "social predation" and "also symbolized nobility and power." For indeed, it was the task of the historically most respected and feared elders on the plateau, the *vahumu*, to monitor "the hidden realm of *uwavi* (sorcery), bringing their power to bear on sorcerers whose acts threatened the well-being of the settlement." Following "Turner's mandate" of symbolic interpretation, West eventually concluded his talk by proposing to his audience that "the lion not only symbolized both dangerous predator and regal protector but also symbolized a deep ambivalence about the workings of power in the social world. Simultaneously, the lion, as symbol, expressed the ideas that power was necessary to produce and secure the common good and that power constituted an ever-present threat to the community's many members."[20]

His words were followed by a long silence and "several awkward interjections about minor ethnographic details, as most people in the room fidgeted nervously." Indeed, the story so far has nothing remarkable about it. Quite to the contrary, it might appear as yet another instance of a colonial anthropology coming to save non-European natives from their own fears and superstitions. West may not have explicitly uttered the adverbial weapon that is quintessential to modern-realist operations, but he didn't need to—his argument gave it away. As it became clear a bit later, the initial silences and interjections testified to the fact that his was something of a poisoned gift. While attempting to repay his debt to the institution by offering an introduction to symbolic anthropology, his overcoming of the local ethnographers' *hesitation* simultaneously involved the expulsion of sorcery-lions from the world. They were *really*—this is the adverbial weapon—but symbols through which Muedans worked through real issues of politics and inequality in a world that was indeed "social" not least because it did not include either settlement-lions, lion-persons, or fabricated lions among its real existents.[21] In so doing, West's talk dramatized once again what in *The Invention of Africa* V. Y. Mudimbe had damningly said of European colonial anthropology more generally: that it itself was "the distance separating savagery from civilization on the diachronic line of progress," such that "there is nothing to be learned from 'them' unless it is already 'ours' or comes from us."[22] World-monification incarnate.

What is most striking about West's story, however, is what happens next. For while this tale flows through the opening pages of his book, there is no celebratory tone in them, but a much more humble and curious sense of *his own hesitation*. The prolonged silence and nervous fidgeting that followed his talk was ultimately interrupted, he tells us, by the arresting moment when Lazaro Mmala—"a graduate of the elementary school at the Imbuho Catholic mission, a schoolteacher by training, a veteran of the Mozambican guerrilla war for independence, and, now, an officer of the veterans association"—cleared his throat and, addressing West by his Shimakonde name, said: "Andiliki, I think you misunderstand." Increasingly anxious about the challenge, West asked him how he meant that, and Mmala replied: "These lions that you talk about . . . they aren't symbols—they're real." With some trepidation, Mmala therefore took the risk of insisting on what modern reasons could not but distrust: reality in the each-form, the extraordinary existence of another world in this world. A world in which sorcery-lions are not symbols, but may instead be as real as symbols—as real as everything else. Mmala thus made present to everyone in the room that if anything could indeed be *learned* from the Muedans, it had to be precisely that which symbolic anthropology was not already, that which did not already come from it. After Mmala's intervention, a "collective sigh enveloped the room. A lively discussion ensued to which nearly everyone present contributed accounts of incidents that they had experienced, or stories that they had heard, about lions stalking, attacking, and devouring people, as well as about the envious neighbors and kin who were to blame for these events."[23]

Notwithstanding the colonial undertones that infuse this extraordinary encounter, let us not congratulate ourselves just yet by performing on the critical register what West dramatized in the anthropological mode—surreptitiously replacing the pluralistic generativity of difference with the reassuring recognition of those familiar stories we already know how to criticize, those of a colonial anthropology carried out by and for Europeans, of non-European peoples dominated by European powers.[24] The refusal of the modern-realist operation is more demanding than that. And if the possibility of a runaway metaphysics requires that we affirm every smallest bit of experience to learn to trust the world and its possibilities again, which is to say, to insist on the persistence of other worlds in this world, it is from them, and not from our own consensual critiques, that such learning needs to be attempted—however necessary those critiques may still be. Thus, while it cannot be denied that the events of West's story reenact a familiar pattern in the imperial history of modern world-traveling, it cannot be accepted that it simply represents yet another case of a coloniality coated in scientific knowledge. After all, the text *begins* with this story, and it is not precisely in order to authorize a book-long argument about the alleged backwardness of the Muedans. More generously, West's *Ethnographic Sorcery*—the title is telling—is an attempt to come to terms with this extraordinary and generative encounter. Like other anthropological works concerned with the postcolonial entanglement of seemingly traditional practices such as sorcery, witchcraft, and the occult together with "properly" modern phenomena like statecraft, capitalism, or democracy, West's exploration might be better characterized as belonging to what is known as the tradition of "the modernity of witchcraft."[25] What was at stake was not so much the scientific confirmation of the Muedans as living anachronisms, clinging to premodern beliefs and traditions that no longer had a place in a postcolonial, post-socialist, "developing" Mozambique. Rather, it was the recognition, as West puts it a bit later in the book, "that sorcery constituted a language through which the Muedans . . . comprehended and . . . commented upon the workings of power in their midst," such that in order to "discern how Muedans understood the social, political, and economic transformations they experienced," he had to "learn the language of sorcery."[26]

If anything, then, what seems to have prompted West's presentation and subsequent book is rather a critical postcolonial gesture, which sees in the Western focus on the exotic, extraordinary nature of non-Western practices the kernel of colonialism's political-epistemological war on non-European worlds, an Archimedean lever of disqualification in an increasingly monistic, self-enclosed world: *give me an extraordinary reality, and I will turn it into a backward people.* The exotic text is indeed one of the three genres of "speeches" that, Mudimbe suggests, have contributed since the seventeenth century "to the invention of a primitive Africa," only to be complemented by Enlightenment "hierarchies of civilizations" and nineteenth-century "explorers' sagas, anthropologists' theories, and the implementation of colonial policy."[27]

Just like other scalable operations, this was not restricted to the African continent. In his magisterial *Orientalism*, for instance, Edward Said suggests that throughout the nineteenth century the scientific discoveries of things Oriental were crucially encompassed and enveloped by a "virtual epidemic of Orientalia" that ignited in Europe a general enthusiasm for everything Asiatic as "wonderfully synonymous with the exotic, the mysterious, the profound, the seminal."[28] These modern ethnographic and historiographical cabinets of curiosities did not just gloss over with an allure of romantic exploration the imperial expansion and colonial expropriation of Asian worlds that were at their heart. They also served as scholarly tools that would progressively enable the radical difference of the non-Western world to be tamed in order for the modern monification of the world to become achievable: "the Orient needed first to be known, then invaded and possessed, then re-created by scholars, soldiers, and judges who disinterred forgotten languages, histories, races, and cultures in order to posit them—beyond the modern Oriental's ken—as the true classical Orient that could be used to judge and rule the modern Orient. The obscurity faded to be replaced by hothouse entities; the Orient was a scholar's word, signifying what modern Europe had recently made of this still peculiar East."[29]

Recalling the material connections brought about by Ferdinand de Lesseps's construction of the Suez Canal, which by joining the Mediterranean and Red Seas opened up an unimpeded path between Europe and Asia, Said argued that just "as a land barrier could be transmuted into a liquid artery, so too the Orient was transubstantiated from resistant hostility into obliging, and submissive, partnership."[30] Thus, while a fascination for strange facts and extraordinary events ignited the imagination of medieval European naturalists with an open curiosity about what Nature might be capable of, it quickly passed into its modern opposite.[31] The romantic, European exultation of the exotic became thus a scalable *exoticization* which, paradoxically but effectively, served to pacify differences— rendering others culturally incomprehensible but epistemologically accessible and politically powerless vis-à-vis the modern West. After all, a lever works both ways, and it is the very scalar working of this Archimedean lever that in turn raises the modern West to the very measure of forward-looking, culturally civilized, epistemologically sound progress.

Colonial exoticism became thus an essentialist, metonymic weapon of disqualification and imperial rule coated in romanticism, where extraordinary realities—always relative and situated—were wrapped up in proper names, stood in for entire peoples, and became tokens of rational primitiveness, economic underdevelopment, moral immaturity.[32] Which is to say that, in reducing extraordinary realities to metonymic tokens of backwardness, colonial exoticism domesticated the multifariousness of the world in the name of a progressive, "world-historical" reality. A reality whose final accomplishment—also known as Modernity—would both transcend the many strung-along, loosely connected realities that make this a many-storied universe, and would justify their devastation. It is G. W. F. Hegel, that great philosophical flame-keeper of Orientalism and the Great Empires, who with characteristically epic prose dramatized this modern eschatology in his 1830 *Lectures on the Philosophy of World History*:

> Even as we look upon history as an altar on which the happiness of nations, the wisdom of states, and the virtue of individuals are slaughtered, our thoughts inevitably impel us to ask: to whom, or to what ultimate end have these monstrous sacrifices been made? This usually leads in turn to those general considerations from which our whole enquiry began. From this beginning, we proceeded to define those same events which afford so sad a spectacle for gloomy sentiments and brooding reflection as no more than the means whereby what we have specified as the substantial destiny, the absolute and final end, or in other words, the true result of world history, is realised.[33]

In other words, once it is incumbent upon thought to fully embrace the modern realization of this providential—or eschatological—plane of reality, this "all-form" known as World History, the scalable plantations of the colonies become their own reality principle, Empire turns metaphysical, and anything goes: evil, wickedness, human miseries and slaughter, not to mention—indeed, it doesn't get mentioned—socio-ecological devastation, the expulsion of sorcery-lions, ghosts, giants, hidden people, all other worlds in this world.[34] Anything goes, *absolutely*: a very different kind of relativism indeed. A relativism that, rather than supposedly derived from the rejection of all principles, is instead authorized by *absolute* foundations, a thought thus *absolved* from noticing, and contending with, the many "ands" that trail along modern edges. James was not exaggerating, therefore, when he said of Hegel's philosophy that it "mingles mountainloads of corruption with its scanty merits."[35] For as he argued, "Tho the absolute dictates nothing, it will *sanction* anything and everything after the fact, for whatever is once there will have to be regarded as an integral member of the universe's perfection."[36] In relay and return, I incant James once again: "Damn Great Empires!—including that of the Absolute."

DECOLONIZING THE PLURAL? · One can thus see why postcolonial thinkers, in the social sciences and elsewhere, have unceasingly warned against celebrations of the exotic and its trap of prolonging the colonial politics of knowledge by other means, under different names. Plying against this kind of world-monification, they have adopted an anti-essentialist philosophical sensibility where an inappropriable and ambiguous alterity insists and persists in and out of Empire. The postcolonial refusal of such modern eschatology, therefore, consisted in articulating a counter-imperial politics by seeking to decolonize the foundations—cultural, philosophical, historiographical, epistemological—on which certain stories of modernity rest, a decolonization pursued through manifold projects which, nevertheless, can broadly—if imperfectly—be characterized as comprising two intertwined gestures. First, a textual, radically deconstructive theoretical activity that seeks to unmoor the essentialist operations that go into the making of modern representations of difference so as to reveal the hybrid, fluid, and ambivalent interstices lurking in their midst.[37] And second, a counter-epistemological attempt that contests modern operations of disqualification, and specifically its "epistemological exclusions," as Dipesh Chakrabarty has called them, by pluralizing the many forms of thinking, knowing, and representing the world in and out of Europe.[38] In so doing, it seeks to provincialize the Eurocentric reasons through which the modern politics of knowledge disqualifies other forms of rationality and knowledge-making and continues to present modern knowledge as "the point of arrival and the guiding light of all kinds of knowledges."[39]

My sense is that the effort carried out by Harry West after his encounter with Lazaro Mmala, wherein he sought to regenerate his imagination about sorcery and sorcery-lions on the Mueda Plateau, could well belong to this latter approach. It is not, in other words, that sorcery was a sign of the Muedans' primitiveness. Reflecting on his presentation at ARPAC, West became aware that Turner's logic inadvertently situated him in a position he hadn't chosen and had him asserting, "with echoes of colonial condescension," that Muedans "failed to recognize their own symbols (or metaphors)" and thus "mistook allegories for identities." In other words, despite his best intentions, he found himself affirming "that Muedans deceived themselves . . . that their understanding of the world in which they lived was a form of false consciousness."[40] Forced by Mmala's riposte to throw the dice again, to begin thinking and noticing again beyond his initial position, West's study sought to recognize, rather, that just like the moderns use the language of politics and law, sorcery was a discursive means that the Muedans deployed to "facilitate their appreciation for the complex dilemmas created by the elusiveness and capriciousness of power in their midst."[41] In other words, his developed approach led him to characterize sorcery fundamentally as an indigenous epistemological repertoire, carried out by postcolonial *agents* of knowledge, actively expressing a non-Western worldview and capable of representing and mediating the world according to their own deportment, for their own reasons, with their own criteria, and in relation to their own concerns.

This involves a profoundly de-exoticizing operation indeed. Rather than marvel at the mysterious otherness intimated in Muedans' engagement with sorcery and turn their failure to recognize their own symbols into a sign of the distance that separates them from modern reason, this counter-epistemological gesture works inward, as it were, turning the modern engagement with the language of politics and law into one among many other ways of understanding the world. By way of a decolonization of our own reasons and languages, it thus provincializes modern knowledge, and seeks to pluralize epistemology by recognizing instead that sorcery is a knowledge-practice like any other, a means through which humans historically construct their social, cultural, and political worlds. It is not, therefore, that Muedans' failed to recognize their symbols—it is we who disqualified the Muedans as we failed to recognize our own! Once enthroned by colonialism, modern rationality now finds itself "tottering on its pedestal."[42] In this way, this counter-epistemological gesture of provincializing modern knowledge has enabled a generative array of attempts that, by pluralizing the many ways of knowing and understanding the world in and out of Europe, affirm that another knowledge is possible. In their ongoing struggle to contest the global sovereignty of modern science and philosophy by reminding them that their reasons are not the only reasons, that their purposes are not the only purposes, that their means are not the only means, such gestures have often proven critical in efforts made across the world to resist the modern-realist operations of disqualification that thwart the ways in which knowledge-practices diverge.[43] If the pluralistic world is one in some respects and many in others, knowledge-making is not only itself unambiguously manifold. As it adds new relations to a multiplicity of related hangings-together, as it invents new and multiple transitions through paths that were theretofore impossible, knowledge-practices, in the plural, are generative *vectors* of plurality.[44]

That said, from the perspective of a runaway metaphysics, the centrality that this counter-epistemological gesture has acquired in critical efforts everywhere at pluralizing the world is not without dangers of its own. To be sure, it does succeed in provincializing modern knowledge and challenging the epistemological Eurocentrism that modern-realist operations espouse, when these stipulate that only those things which can unequivocally be claimed to be mind-independent can be real, *and* that only modern thought possesses the methods capable of establishing mind-independent facts. Indeed, "realism" becomes here the enemy's very name, for as Said put it, the philosophical "language, thought, and vision" of Orientalism, and of colonialism more generally, "is a form of radical realism" that "will designate, name, point to, fix"—in other words, essentialize—what it is addressing, in such a way that it "then is considered to have acquired, or more simply to be, reality."[45] Postcolonial thought, then, denounces this modern-realist operation as a form of coloniality that, Aníbal Quijano has argued, works "above all, over the modes of knowing, of producing knowledge, of producing perspectives, images and systems of images, symbols, modes of signification, over the resources, patterns, and instruments of formalized and objectivised expression, intellectual or visual."[46]

And yet, in endowing *epistemological* coloniality—and epistemological decolonization—with such primacy, this postcolonial gesture confronts this pillar of modern realism with a critical anti-realism. Indeed, against the Hegelian eschatological plane that celebrates modernity as the providential realization of the fully developed conditions for rational thought to finally coincide with reality, postcolonial critics adopt instead a historicized and pluralized Kantianism, whereby *no reality can be felt* except as it is mediated through the historical, cultural, and political conditions under which it comes to be *represented*.[47] In so doing, this kind of postcolonial critique challenges colonial essentialism but not without simultaneously surrendering realism, and reality, altogether.

That Immanuel Kant, of all philosophers, should be the silent force behind the cultivation of an anti-imperial pluralistic politics is something that ought to give us pause. After all, not only is he rightly considered one of the fathers of modern European philosophy, but his thought has pervaded with tectonic force every domain of modern culture, from science to literature.[48] And his legal-political thesis on *perpetual peace*, which has revived modern and contemporary cosmopolitan thought, is precisely a plan for a kind a peace whose "conditions of possibility"—as he liked to put it—were not only reliant upon an impoverished geography replete with all manner of racist and statist claims about the inhabitants of the Earth, but indeed required the envisioning of a regulative cosmos, given in advance, that would organize difference by right toward the progressive constitution of a "universal law of humanity."[49] Few ideas could be further from the insistent pluriverse I am trying, with James's help, to conjure.

But never mind Kant. My main objection to the negative operation performed by such anti-realism is a pragmatic one. That is, it concerns the question of what difference it might make, or fail to make, to the pluralistic task of trusting the many worlds in this world again. I fear that the price anti-realism pays for escaping the trap of a colonial exoticism and pluralizing epistemologies is precisely that of becoming unable to shout "hands off!," of rendering oneself incapable or unwilling to affirm that realism need not be essentialist, that reality cannot be surrendered, that there is more to it than the essentialism and impoverished realism of modern-realist operations would allow, that something else exceeds it, that something that *should* not be subsists, insists, and persists in it. Indeed, despite his efforts, Harry West cannot respond to Lazaro Mmala's insistence that sorcery-lions are real except by affirming that the reality of sorcery is *discursive*, in the sense that Muedans "engaged with the world of sorcery in a discursive field to which they themselves made substantial contributions. Not only did they, like me, experience sorcery's reality *through* its verbal constructs, but they conceived of sorcery and the words that spoke its reality as one and the same."[50] The difference upon which Mmala insisted is thus still transformed—not into an unacknowledged symbol that disqualifies the Muedans, but into an epistemological pluralism that makes of sorcery and anthropology two equal but different modes of experiencing *the same world* of politics and society. Indeed, in an interesting reversal that is the reason for the title of West's book, he proposes that since sorcery is fundamentally a discursive means of making and remaking the world by articulating interpretations of the world remade, and since sorcerers and counter-sorcerers make and remake their worlds as they articulate new interpretations of it, "the same must be said of anthropological visions of the world."[51]

Ultimately, the pluralistic problem of the one and the many is here solved by the introduction of a thoroughgoing chasm between what reality may be capable of and how different peoples may be capable of interpreting it. About the latter, we can indeed affirm that the "hows" are plural; about the former, we must all forever remain silent. This postcolonial gesture, then, offers an epistemological response to a metaphysical problem. But in elevating epistemology, this response poses itself a problem. For this counter-epistemological postcolonialism does trust knowledge: it trusts what it can do and what it can't; it trusts that knowledge is plural and situated, and that "objectivity" and "impartiality" are suspect propositions with a dodgy history; it trusts that other knowledges are possible and that they are already underway in practices and legacies that modernity has disavowed.[52] But this approach does not seem to trust that knowledge is cultivated out of worlds it can never hope to exhaust; it does not trust that between what things are and how they're known there may be no chasm but rich and generative exchanges; it does not trust that reality may be capable of more than what it is known as; it does not trust, in short, that there can be no politics of knowledge without a politics of reality, *that it is the plural itself that must be decolonized, pluralized all the way down.* As such, this approach seems to neglect the fact that, according to West's story, what Muedans knew is that these real sorcery-lions are liable to *attack and kill* their victims, whereas anthropological discourse, while occasionally powerful, does not have that efficacy. But more than that, it appears to neglect that this chasmic solution is itself a quintessentially modern solution, proper to those who have inherited the tradition that has split the world into epistemologies and ontologies, appearances and realities, what things are and what they are known as, and did so precisely so as to tame the insistence of many other worlds in this worlds, so as to accommodate them in such a way that one could still hang on to what John Law has succinctly called the "metaphysics of the one-world world," articulated as it is through a whole array of modern imaginaries and operations.[53] Finally, and not by chance, it is a *scalable* solution. More than scalable, this response *only* works so long as we affirm, even if just tacitly, that reality, like spoiled milk, comes already split—everywhere, for everyone.

THE WORD OR NAMES A GENUINE REALITY · Mmala's insistence stirs trouble. And it is one that a runaway metaphysics must stay with, for it dramatizes this radically empiricist proposition, that reality feels like itself. Indeed, I am ineluctably reminded of the contention put forth by Italian anthropologist Ernesto de Martino, who in 1972 opened his book *Primitive Magic* with the provocative proposition that the "first barrier to our penetrating the secrets of the world of magic is prejudice. Prejudice, particularly, against the idea of magical powers. It is usually perfunctorily and automatically supposed," he continued, "that magicians' claims are clearly false or misguided and that magical phenomena are at best illusions, and at worst, fakes." It will be clear by now that "prejudice" would not be my word of choice to characterize the reasons that a runaway metaphysics must refuse, and the problems it must contend with. But it cannot be denied that "sooner or later there must be some consideration given to the fact that this problem involves not just the quality of magic powers, but also our concept of reality."[54]

Indeed, what the above discussion hopefully makes present is that the generative problematic of the one and the many, for which the pluriverse is a nickname, opens up a veritable throw of the dice, of the kind that James, in his famous essay "The Will to Believe," would call a *genuine option.*[55] That is, it is a problematic whose force demands a living, momentous, and forced response. Living, because it belongs to our epoch, because it impregnates the questions upon which decisions are made as to what may cease and what may go on existing, as to whether, at the end of the day, we might find ourselves swimming or sinking. Momentous, because we live in a time that seems to be running short, and responding to it requires that we jump with both feet off the ground of our modern habits and take the risk of inventing new ways of trusting the many worlds in this world again. And it is *forced* because, while we must insist on participating in the redetermination of the problematic, while we must insist on developing it, on addressing it pragmatically rather than abstractly, on thinking again about what doing metaphysics might entail, the problematic cannot be dodged—the risks it poses cannot be avoided, "there is no standing place outside of the alternative." Even if one were to try, as some postcolonial critics have, to turn it into an epistemological question of whether there is one or many ways of *knowing* the world, this attempt cannot avoid the metaphysical stakes of its own response.[56] Thus, as we take stock of the lessons of those who have pluralized and politicized epistemology, we must also confront the fact that, if the discrediting of realism and metaphysics is such that it now seems impossible to trust the world and its possibilities again, a counter-epistemology is no longer enough to develop the pluralistic problematic.

At this stage, we can take the risk of heeding James's advice, that the task before us is not so much to go "*through* Kant as *round* him to the point where we now stand."[57] We may do well, in other words, to outflank the epistemological transposition and seek to reclaim a pluralistic politics of reality by learning to be situated by and into the many worlds in this world, looking for treasures while we try and cultivate a feel for the fantastic, for the extraordinary and the implausible, for the pluriverse's many existing realities, those underway and yet to be made, until we fall asleep. Thankfully this is no longer a solitary task. It is perhaps a hopeful sign of these eschatological times that in areas as diverse and divergent as anthropology, theology, animal studies, philosophy, science and technology studies, political theory, and the environmental humanities, there has recently been a nascent but marked shift away from the dominance of the counter-epistemological Kantianism of yesteryear and toward the rekindling of an appetite for a more open-ended and adventurous day-traveling of a world that may, in spite of all, still retain vital signs of resisting the persistent assaults to turn it into a single order. Those pursuing this shift are many and follow their own divergent and diverging paths, making contributions to these ongoing and unfinished pages, and to other debates that (alas) escape them, in their always singular ways. Indeed, they remain key allies, fellow travelers around the day in eighty worlds. Thus, I could not even attempt here the impossible task of somehow summarizing or painting a picture of their endeavors, which, rather appropriately, span an impressive and multifarious landscape of sites, practices, beings, and problematics: from the ontological multiplicity of the body in modern medical practices, the plurality of ways of "becoming salmon" through aquaculture practices, to the disconcerting mode of existence of numbers in Yoruba mathematical practices, to name only a few.[58] What I pursue instead is a narrower and more modest aim, namely, to notice and explore the emergence of a certain gesture, and a certain language, that has sometimes been used to craft a response to the distrust bred by anti-realist critiques of modern realism in the presence of other worlds in this world, a gesture that seems to have proven fecund across many of these projects—that is, the pluralization of "ontology." Or, rather, of *ontologies*.[59]

At stake in this gesture is nothing less than the possibility of a radical regeneration of the decolonial imagination. A pluralization of the plural, or "a permanent decolonization of thought," to borrow the apt words of Eduardo Viveiros de Castro, whose ethnographies of Amerindian perspectivism have in some way pioneered this shift.[60] *Round* Kant, some of these ontological pluralisms dramatize the proposition that epistemology cannot solve metaphysical questions, that no perplexity stirred by the feeling of difference can be solved by claiming that there is a mind, or a culture, knowing it. Instead, just as James affirmed that relations are as real as the hangings-together they relate, many of those who have been articulating a possible pluralization of ontologies insist on the possibility that differences have a force of their own. As such, what is required of an art of noticing is not learning to see things differently, but learning to see different things. What is more, *round* modern realism, this transmutation also involves an important revaluation of this feeling that colonialism has weaponized, this feeling of "or" that difference generates. For it is one thing to remember and denounce the role that colonial exoticism has played in taming and subduing difference, but it is another to conclude that no divergence can be affirmed that is not already complicit in such histories of disqualification, domination, and colonization. Indeed, Eduardo Kohn puts it very perceptively when he writes that "this would be the final act of colonization, one that would subject the possibility of something else, located in other lived worlds, human and otherwise, to a far more permanent death."[61] World-monification reincarnate! And yet—ever not quite. By decolonizing the plural, the task of traveling around the day in eighty or a thousand worlds, insisting that *there is* another world in this world, suddenly becomes possible again. What these allies make present in their various philosophical and anthropological tongues is that a radically empiricist, collective art of noticing the many realities that compose the pluriverse requires an effort not of deploying our own modern conceptual apparatus to interpret them, but of thoroughly *transforming* our concepts so as to enable these realities to feel like themselves.

"These lions, they are real": It is not a matter of asking how it is that Lazaro Mmala and the Muedans may come to *know* and *represent* the world such that they can arrive at that proposition, indeed to defiantly insist on it in the face of anthropological knowledge. That would amount to constructing an epistemology for people who do not construct it for themselves. It is a matter, rather, of hesitating about our own metaphysical foundations, of pluralizing "our own concept of reality" (to recall de Martino once again) in the face of extraordinary realities that do not conform to what our modern principles would anticipate. Indeed, it involves the risk of asking what reality may be capable of, and seeking to learn how to trust Mmala's proposition instead of explaining it (away). If those involved in the pluralization of ontologies are very close allies, then, it is not just because their travels profoundly enrich the collective arts of noticing passing on and through extraordinary realities to be noticed, but also and crucially because, at their best, their "abiding concern with *freeing thought* from all metaphysical foundationalism"[62] involves a counter-metaphysical gesture that turns world-travel into day-travel, and the politics of knowledge into a politics of reality. For indeed, "to subjunctively present alternatives to declarations about what 'is' or imperatives about what 'should be' is itself a political act—a radical one, to the degree that it breaks free of the glib relativism of merely reporting on alternative possibilities ('worldviews,' etc.), and proceeds boldly to lend the 'otherwise' full ontological weight so as to render it *viable as a real alternative*."[63] Thus, these gestures open up generous and generative possibilities of trusting the world, the many worlds in this world, once again.

But alliances are fertile when the possibility of appreciating and learning from the practices of others is cultivated not in the name of a general consensus but by the generativity of our subtle divergences. I salute and celebrate their counter-metaphysical experimentations, and appreciate how, given the legacy of anti-realist critique, the gesture that has given rise to the language of ontology can regenerate our imaginations, revitalize more adventurous forms of comparison, and allow us to explore the question of what reality might be capable of in new and productive ways. But in and of itself, such language cannot exhaust the pluralistic response to this question. It hardly needs saying, I hope, that the reason for this is *not* that there is only *one* ontology, the one that modern-realist operations have sought to plough the world with. As many of them have shown, there are of course "multiple ontologies," in the sense that there are others in and out of modernity that have actively engaged, for their own reasons, with their own means, in the problems of conceptualizing what is and what is not, or what, if anything, it might mean to be.[64] And in this respect the language of ontology undoubtedly enables a more generative mode of at-

tentive and equivocal translation, one whose effect is no longer the neu-
tralization or disqualification of others but, as Eduardo Viveiros de Castro
provocatively put it, the "conceptual" and "ontological self-determination
of people. Or peoples to be more exact."[65] One can't fail to note the very deliberate playfulness involved in a proposition that by pluralizing ontologies
leaves entirely open the question of what "ontology," "self-determination,"
and "peoples" might *be*. In the same breath, one cannot fail to insist on
the fact that, while many hangings-together in all corners of the Earth
have suffered the consequences of modern-realist operations turning
them into a series of "nothing buts"—nothing but belief, superstition,
culture, epistemology—at stake are not only "concepts," "ontologies," and
the "self-determination of peoples," but the feeling of reality itself. Which
is why, once it becomes detached from its transgressive gesture, from its
disruptive force in simultaneously subtending and upending the labor of
counter-metaphysical translation, once it becomes an established analytics, a "turn" approaching every practice with the question "What ontology
do you espouse?," one is in danger of seeing the tools of decolonial experimentation surreptitiously *turn* against themselves, constructing ontologies for practices that have no need for them. What's more, one might also
risk *turning* the pluriverse, both one *and* many, modern *and* other-than-
modern, ongoing *and* unfinished, into so many universes, each with their
own distinct ontology, many so long as there are countless ones. Of course,
some of the proponents of the "turn" are aware of the risks and advise us to
read references to "ontology" in a purely methodological sense, as a heuris-
tic device relevant only to the internal relational economy of anthropological inquiry.[66] As far as argumentative consistency is concerned, this may
be an elegant move, with the only problem being that it defuses much of
the political potential of such counter-metaphysical experiments, casting
them as little more than analytical exercises, disentangled from the metaphysical turbulences such exercises could otherwise engender.

Riskier and more politically potent attempts have been articulated by
other allies, including Marisol de la Cadena and Mario Blaser, who call for
nothing less than a collective project in "political ontology," simultaneously
comprising "a certain political sensibility, a problem space, and a modality
of analysis or critique."[67] Not unlike the pluralistic realism I'm seeking to
activate, they too infuse their political sensibility with a trust in the possibility of responding to an insistent pluriverse that renders differences
irreducible and uncontainable, that renders divergent worlds partially
connected, ongoing and unfinished. And they too seek to reclaim such

forms of trust in the ruins of the modern operations of mass disqualification, of the earthly impoverishment brought about by world-monification, invoking political ontology "as the field where practices, entities, and concepts make each other be; and as the enactment within this field of modern politics itself, obliging what is and what is not its matter."[68] In deep affinity with them, this effort that I have decided to call "runaway metaphysics" is concerned with freeing thought and politics from the shackles of its modern foundations, with contending with realities that, despite their ongoing devastation, still feel like themselves, and insist and persist in spite of all. Of course, our words are relative to our practices, and there is no doubt that their efforts to politically pluralize ontology have proven generative in addressing conflicts that demand new tools of cosmopolitical translation. But the fact, in any case, is that no construction of a problem, however generous and generative, can forever ensure that others will meet us halfway. Each involves a speculative throw of the dice, a wager on the possibility that a certain formulation of a problem might interest others, infect our practices, shake our principles, lure us into the deep end.

It is just in this way that I here wager on the possibility of what might happen should we experiment with taking James's hypothesis seriously: that if reality feels like itself, the word *or* names not so much another ontology as a genuine *reality*.[69] Not because the problem of realism is universal, far from it. Rather, because if it is true that we tend to raise only the problems we can solve, as Pierre Clastres once put it, thinking of reality in the plural prompts us to inhabit a problem modern habits of thought cannot solve without undergoing a radical metamorphosis, one that is as much conceptual as it is existential.[70] "The word 'or' names a genuine reality" is an *outrageous* proposition, precisely in the sense that what it asks us to take seriously is nothing short of what modern realism has rendered impossible.[71] By inhabiting the problematic of the one and the many in terms that strike at the core of this tradition, such a proposition thus forces us to hesitate. And it is right in that moment of hesitation, which West had hoped anthropological theory might allay, that the problem we have sought to reformulate might implicate us. It implicates us because the outrageous character of such a proposition confronts us with what Isabelle Stengers, who insists that the smoke of the burned witches still hangs in our nostrils, has called our "curse"—a "curse upon anyone who thinks they are free to redefine, in their own terms, the way in which the 'other' inhabits this world, even when they are willing to tolerate them, even when they regret their own loss of innocence."[72]

Confronted with Lazaro Mmala's insistence that sorcery-lions are real, the task as I see it is not so much to develop an analytics that would disclose what conception of being or of reality the Muedans must implicitly exhibit for that proposition to begin to make sense (which implies: "given that it doesn't"). And it is not about engaging in the task of constructing a philosophy of sorcery, one that, in describing how sorcery practices conceptualize their world, would no longer make this insistence sound outrageous. The task is to contend with our own curse, to take up the challenge of thinking in the presence of what his insistence makes felt, without hastening to provide answers to the problems such insistence poses and that has forced us to hesitate. Honoring the moment of hesitation, the task is to ask what difference his insistence may make, should we take the risk of trusting it, to those of us who are heirs to the operations that tolerantly and silently whisper that there must be some explanation, that sorcery-lions cannot be real, not *really*. My attempt at a pluralistic realism, therefore, is not so much a matter of *translating* between worlds—let alone between worldviews—as it is one of "intranslating" one into another: an entirely non-symmetrical act, at once conceptual, political, and pragmatic, of "introducing" (*intraduire*) and precipitating generative vectors of alteration, curves of divergence, variations of interests, the many boiling over the one, a pinch of chaos in the cosmos.[73] Forging relays and partial connections that never crystallize into a stable cosmology or perpetual peace, what I call a runaway metaphysics, then, is an effort oriented at detoxifying the questionable tradition that in many ways, faithfully or unfaithfully, is *my own* —as well as that of those likely to read these pages—the tradition we have come to call modernity.

Situating myself speculatively in the interstices of this tradition, I call this a runaway metaphysics not least because I think that reclaiming a politics of the pluriverse simultaneously requires that we learn to honor metaphysical questions and that we do so with a bit of humor—escaping the habit of responding to those questions as many a metaphysician would have done, by way of abstract, general, and universal principles that must apply everywhere, to everything. This is not because of a distaste for the work of metaphysical abstraction as such—an extraordinary and outrageous activity of creation in its own right—but because I wager, speculatively, without guarantees, that no amount of principles will exhaust the responses to the question of what reality might be capable of. Indeed, "plurality" does not simply evoke a sense of the many but of *plus*, which is to say, of *more*. The pluriverse is not just more than one or more than a *universe*, but more than many—it's ongoing and unfinished. Thus, as helpful as they are in enabling us to come to terms with those aspects in which it does disclose itself as one, no amount of principles can exhaust the multifariousness of the world. Unless, of course, we create a principle for each event, a law for each experience. But even then, it is not just that principles and laws would cease having a purpose. They would still miss the mark, because each event is itself plural, a *multum in parvo*— intrinsically generative, generatively problematic. They mark a difference but they do not dictate what that difference is, as indeed "there can be no difference anywhere that doesn't make a difference elsewhere."[74] Instead, events are multiplicities, conjuring up manifold relations and partial connections to other differences, to other events. It is for those who come after them, those who feel their difference, to inherit, grasp, develop, evaluate an event, without ever being authorized by it.[75] This is why, in the previous chapter, I associated the work of this runaway metaphysics not with the ontological self-determination of others but with our own *metaphysical indetermination*.

To speak of "indetermination" is not to reclaim the negative operation of anti-realist deconstructions—no pluralistic realism can ensue from that. What is at stake is rather a speculative pragmatism, an ongoing experimentation with the differences that trusting these many strung-along realities may be capable of making to what we take reality to be (capable of) without attempting to solve once and for all the ongoing problematic of the one and the many that infuses pluralism with its own vitality and force. To labor toward our own metaphysical indetermination is to resist the metaphysics of ordinary nature that treats the universe as an unbending and homogeneous regularity, and lets its own impoverished account of some worlds in this world "appoint and decree what the others shall be."[76] It is instead to affirm, relaying James once again, that the "world is full of partial stories that run parallel to one another, beginning and ending at odd times," and that these stories diverge just as they "mutually interlace and interfere at points."[77] As such, it is to affirm that those realities that modern metaphysics cannot stomach and seeks to eradicate "have a certain amount of loose play on one another, so that the laying down of one of them does not necessarily determine what the others shall be."[78] It is to consent to the fact that, as yet ongoing and unfinished, the pluriverse is fundamentally vulnerable, its components susceptible to destruction, liable to expropriation and eradication—we are already witnesses to their ongoing devastation. But at the same time, ongoing and unfinished, its possibilities, against all odds, are real, and it is imperative that they're given a chance. For indeed, the pluriverse's "destiny thus hangs on an *if*, or on a lot of *ifs*—which amounts to saying (in the technical language of logic) that, the world being as yet unfinished, its total character can be expressed only by *hypothetical* and not by *categorical* propositions."[79]

Metaphysical indetermination, runaway metaphysics, after all, means simply this: insisting on the question "What is reality capable of?," inhabiting the problems it generates, and staying to hear the responses matters. Like Marilyn Strathern and Donna Haraway might say, it matters what realities we trust to trust other realities with.[80] And more, it matters *that* we pursue a politics of reality that is not the product of our sheer wariness about "reality" as such but the fruit of a living, generous, and generative trust that the word *or* names a genuine reality, that another world is both possible and underway: "On a quiet day, I can hear her breathing."[81] This is why a runaway metaphysics asks metaphysical questions and stays or moves around the day in eighty worlds, to hear the answers as they present themselves in manifold experiences. Because in so doing, it learns that the answers themselves are many, that there will always be *more*, that it must give up the monistic elegance of general principles and proceed in an errant, clumsy manner, "like a child stuttering out its most humble needs," as Deleuze wrote after and against Hegel.[82] Crawling and stuttering around the day in eighty worlds, inhabiting the problems its movement generates, a pluralistic realism might just open up an adventure in divergence that wagers that we "can and we may, as it were, jump with both feet off the ground into or towards a world of which we trust the other parts to meet our jump—and *only so* can the *making* of a perfected world ever take place. Only through our precursive trust in it can it come into being."[83]

CHAPTER THREE · Trust of a Held-Out Hand

Reality, life, experience, concreteness, immediacy, use what word you
will, exceeds our logic, overflows and surrounds it.

WILLIAM JAMES

With one last gasp of theological authority, let me therefore say unto
you—that for which God is a nickname cares not whether you believe
in God. Doesn't give a damn. Isn't in the damning business. What
matters, what might matter endlessly, is what we earth-dwellers now
together embody. Not what we say *about* God but how we *do* God.

CATHERINE KELLER

AS MUCH AS WE CAN SAY? · Reality feels like itself, and "that is about as
much as we can say."[1] Except it wasn't. Except it isn't. Except it couldn't be.
The ongoing problematic to which pluralism is a response generates a *plus*,
a more, an excess and overflow, an after to every ending. This feeling, that
which reality feels and makes feel, cannot be held down by the force of a
principle, not even by a self-referential tautology. Reality feels like itself, in
the plural. There's something else to be said, many other things that one,
or others, could say: what is reality capable of? Stuttering out its most curious question, its most humble needs, a runaway metaphysics would mean
nothing if not the generative experiment in carefully seeking to learn from
the manifold ways in which reality feels and makes feel. It means nothing if not an experiment in crafting arts of noticing as it passes on and

through, South and North, hearing the many ongoing and unfinished responses, until we fall asleep. For his part, James could not help this generativity any more than anyone can. In the same chapter of *The Principles of Psychology* where he penned that provocative phrase, he went on, attempting a provisional characterization of the perception of reality from the perspective of psychology—a characterization of "reality for ourselves."[2] As far as psychologists were concerned—which is to say, relative to the sense woven through the concern of their own practices—the feeling of reality is above all a matter of interest and importance, such that *"whatever excites and simulates our interests is real;* whenever an object so appeals to us that we turn to it, accept it, fill our mind with it, or practically take account of it, so far it is real for us, and we believe in it."[3]

That this proposition has not yet proffered the pluralistic adventure in divergence it nevertheless opens up, while at the same time James is lauded as the "father" of American psychology, seems itself to be a testament to more than the modern fascination with monistic origins. It simultaneously testifies to the very intimate affair *between* the proclamation of origins—always a question of *"father*hood," indeed—and the insinuation of endings. Which is to say, to the belligerent realism of the moderns. A modern realism that—more concerned with being able to draw a line between what is real and what is not than with the multifarious ways in which reality feels and makes feel; more concerned with uncovering an all-encompassing structure for reality than with passing on and through; patiently noticing the many ands that trail along modern edges—is anxious to let abstractions put everything in order, no matter the cost. As such, this realism remains content with reading such a proposition in a way that lets psychology—as it does at other times with physics, biology, or occasionally, sociology—*run amok*: becoming an imperial, destructive force capable of reducing a pluralistic realism to the inner byplay of the mind, of *reducing* reality to a psychological matter of belief. Indeed, this is what that native American—or Indian, as he called himself—thinker who knew the moderns so well, Vine Deloria Jr., captured in *The Metaphysics of Modern Existence.* He suggested that in the modern world, the reality of experiences, the fact that reality feels like itself but there is no one feeling of which reality is made, is itself *intolerable*: "the teachings of a life-time come thundering down," and reality ends up being reduced to "what you allow your mind to accept, not what you experience." The result, effectively, is that "a host of other beliefs rush in to cover up, confuse, and eventually eliminate the experience itself."[4] Little surprise that his publishers told him that "nothing would be done to give the book publicity 'because no one will buy a book on metaphysics written by an Indian.'"[5]

As such, the birth of scientific psychology would in this sense announce the end, perhaps even the stillbirth, of that radically pluralistic philosophy James nevertheless went on to articulate against all odds. That runaway metaphysics I am here seeking to relay while I still can. And it has to be said that the thundering down of modern-realist operations, the respective fates of psychology and of radical pluralism, so far, could only become effective by the systematic institution of principles of neglect—a neglect for the fact that, while psychology could become a practice concerned precisely with asking relevant questions about the various expressions of a "reality for ourselves," it had no right to claim all of reality *for itself*.[6] But also and at the same time, a rather embarrassing neglect for what James wrote in that very same passage above. For to suggest that "whenever an object so appeals to us that we turn to it, accept it, fill our minds with it, or practically take account of it, so far it is real for us" has nothing to do with saying that the reality of the object would *depend* upon our own psychological sense of interest and importance. Neither is it to say that things are real *only* insofar as we take an interest and represent them in our minds. This, once again, would be to hold Kant too close to our chests and to turn psychology into a de-realizing empire. It is *the object* that excites and stimulates our interests, reality that feels as it makes itself felt, that calls upon us to feel and pay attention, filling "our mind with it"—and not the mind that concocts by itself a world of objects to take account of.

Which is also to say that, rather than reducing reality to that which we allow our minds to accept, or to what we already *believe* to be real, James's proposition is markedly divergent: to the extent that reality, feeling like itself, manages to become *interesting*, "so far it is real for us, and we believe in it." This bears stressing: "*and* we believe in it." Belief, therefore, is a *function* of reality, and not the other way around. As he put it a couple of pages later, it is reality, "our own reality," which "is the ultimate of ultimates for our belief. 'As sure as I exist!'—this is our uttermost warrant for the being of all other things."[7] As sure as I exist! This Jamesian inversion is undoubtedly a blow to the Cartesian metallurgy by which modern forms of rationalism and realism became welded. What it opens up instead is the sense that, rather than extracting, from paranoid methods of radical doubt, an indubitably rational principle of truth, this manifold reality is distinctly *felt*, thoroughly *passional*: it exceeds our modern reasons, it overflows and surrounds them. Our involvement in it, then, is grounded not on the rationality of an "I think!" It is grounded on nothing but the multiple and immanent ways of "feeling our own present reality with absolutely coercive force," ways of feeling that we possess as they possess us.[8]

But there is more. If Descartes has now become a much-preferred scapegoat—although a deserving one—through which the moderns, particularly the self-critical among us, ask for forgiveness for our crimes, James's inversion, situating belief as a function of reality, also precipitates a possible *intranslation*, a pluralistic opening onto other worlds in this world. For it is in this case a different welding—or perhaps, here, a wedding—between the Protestant reformation and modern colonialism, which not only split the world into those who "know" and those who simply "believe," but which confined "religion," as Talal Asad has alerted us, to "a matter of symbolic meanings linked to ideas of general order," and refashioned "belief" into another universalizing, realist operation of *de-realization* of other realities, of other worlds in this world.[9] Traveling around the world as part of the abstract arsenal of colonial tools in the process of world-monification, the concept of "belief" became itself one of the very functions by which modern European empires sought to "secularize" the realities of gods and goddesses in and out Europe. Which is to say, as indeed Ashis Nandy says, to either "eliminate them" or at least "to tame them and make them behave."[10]

Ally day-travelers, like Nandy, Sanjay Seth, and others, have in this sense crafted generative stories-within-stories that tell us how "belief," as a modern-realist operation deployed in the colonial introduction of modern education and pedagogy as well as in the development of cultural politics and policies, sought to transform the realities of Hinduism in India into a two-pronged "religion" with a somewhat coherent set of beliefs: one resembling a "more-or-less monotheistic creed, with the profusion of Hindu gods representing different aspects of one God," and another disqualified as a "primitive, even 'animist' popular Hinduism, swarming with gods and spirits and idols."[11] But these are stories-within-stories, veritable counter-tales, for at the same time they make present the persistence of the reality of these gods, goddesses, spirits, idols, and ghosts in the face of these ongoing and *unfinished* assaults to turn them into a single theological order. And they rightly insist that indeed Hindus never *believed* in their pantheon of gods and goddesses, but *lived with* them, as they still do to this day. Indeed, "these gods and goddesses not only populate the Hindu world but regularly visit and occasionally poach on territories outside it"—their presence makes reality feel like itself.[12]

These modern operations of monification deployed through the turning of belief into an abstract weapon of de-realization are, nevertheless, still ongoing and unfinished. Alas, they did not just attempt, and partially fail, to poison the realities of Hindu gods and goddesses in South Asia. They went on. Indeed, "belief" is alive and well. And the fact that we still—whether conducting fieldwork in Africa, East Asia, Europe, or America, with Hindus, Muslims, or Christians—develop different modalities of the ways in which others believe and, like modern realist philosophers, debate intricate typologies of propositional versus indexical forms of belief, of whether it is a matter of belief *that* or of belief *in*, and engage in debates about whether or not "belief" is a matter of culture, these preoccupations make it clear that, necessary as it may be, no amount of Descartes-bashing will free us from our curse. If we are to go in search of possible alliances with other little hangings-together around the day in eighty worlds, with realities lost, suppressed, marginalized, and derided, a runaway metaphysics cannot let modern psychology, physics, sociology, or anthropology run amok. And it cannot let "belief" become a reality-principle, let alone one that only determines the reality of *others*.

In order to cultivate a pluralistic realism that is generous and generative, to develop arts of noticing that may enable us to learn from the manifold ways in which reality feels like itself, from how it feels and makes feel, until we fall asleep, an exercise in deconstructing the modern concept of belief won't suffice either. For these philosophies, sciences, and concepts, *as well as their critiques*, partake only in those dimensions of reality on which rationalisms of various kinds operate. And as James confessed, that part of reality "of which rationalism can give an account is relatively superficial. It is the part," he granted, "that has the *prestige* undoubtedly, for it has the loquacity, it can challenge you for proofs, and chop logic, and put you down with words." But despite the flame-keepers of modern rationalism in philosophy and elsewhere, there is more; reality exceeds our logic and overflows our reasons. Unless they themselves become felt, reasons "will fail to convince or convert you all the same, if your dumb intuitions are opposed to its conclusions."[13] To cultivate this anti-imperialist experiment in responding to the insistence of a pluriverse against all odds, despite our reasons, we will need to risk more than arguments. And we will need help from others, from other day-travelers, from other counter-tales, from other uses of our own poisoned words, to forge alliances with other worlds in this world. We will need, in other words, to hold out a hand and regenerate *trust*.

FEELING GOD · It is thus time we resume the arts of noticing by turning our attention to another world in this world, one which, once again, forms part of the ongoing and unfinished list sketched in the first chapter. And, it has to be said, this world is most *demanding*, a veritable test of generosity and generativity. Because like the counter-tales of Nandy and Seth, the story of this world, as it is told by ally anthropologist Tanya Luhrmann in her *When God Talks Back*, also concerns the felt reality of a god. And as such, it vectorizes a metaphysical indetermination of modern habits precisely there where, it often seems, they just won't give—namely, on their secular attachments. But if, through the tolerant gimmicks of "belief," and the renewed appeal for more-than-human agency, some have found interest in giving faraway animistic spirits, gods, and ghosts some credit, ontologically or just heuristically, *this* god is felt, and intensely so, in the geographical midst of the Western world. It is felt in California not least, and those who feel him do so by participating in a minor form of Christianity—namely, charismatic evangelism—some major factions of which are otherwise in profound affinity with the political right in the United States, even forming what pluralist political theorist William Connolly has dubbed "The Evangelical-Capitalist Resonance Machine."[14] Still, the story is worth relaying, and not just because the Vineyard, which is the name for the particular association of churches in which Luhrmann participated for two years, has a rather divergent, minor history within the US evangelical world—rather on the left, growing out of the hippie and counterculture movements of the 1960s and '70s.[15] Even if it weren't, one would be remiss to dismiss these worlds as mere fundamentalism[16] or ignore them as the mere byproduct of the new spirit of late capitalism.[17] The story is worth telling because, unlike some other forms of Christianity, what characterizes the relationship that the members of the Vineyard establish with their God is that it is personally intimate, and intimately experienced; indeed, these "evangelicals have sought out and cultivated concrete experiences of God's realness."[18]

For that reason, to ask whether, or even why, these congregants *believe* in God is to miss the point entirely. Or worse, it is indeed to eliminate the reality of their God, the relationship that they have sought to cultivate with him, and make everyone behave, monistically turning the pluriverse into a modern, secular universe once again. In this case, to ask whether or why these people believe is *dangerous*, but not because, like Hindus, they *don't* believe at all. After all, it is through Christianity, albeit of a different sort, that the Western secular notion of belief was formed.[19] It is dangerous, rather, because they do not *only* believe.[20] This is why, in addressing their world, we may rather have to take the risk of playing a variation on the words of James's student, Gertrude Stein, and affirm that indeed *there is a there there*.[21] The reality of this God feels and is intensely felt. As such, it belongs to a different set of questions altogether, more akin perhaps to what James, in *The Varieties of Religious Experience*, called "the reality of the unseen." For indeed it belongs to nothing less than "a feeling of objective presence, a perception of what we might call 'something there,' more deep and more general than any of the special and particular 'senses' by which the current psychology supposes existent realities to be originally revealed."[22]

If the "invitation," as Luhrmann calls it, the hand that the churches of the Vineyard hold out to those who participate in their practices, is "to experience God as if he were real in the flesh and standing by your side, with love," it is not for all that an invitation to play a hypothetical game of ideas.[23] To feel God *as if* he were real does not imply that he is *not*. The invitation is a held-out hand to the stretching out of another hand: it implies that the feeling of this reality is both ongoing and unfinished, already everywhere and yet to be discerned, such that coming to feel God's presence by one's side, with love, is something one can *learn*, not how to "believe" in, as if it were a matter of accepting doctrinal dogmas, but something one can learn to discern in one's experience, to appreciate as a distinct *there there*, "in the form," James would say, "of *quasi-sensible realities directly apprehended*."[24] This is a radically divergent invitation indeed, and consenting to it requires learning as much as unlearning. For just as the wedding between the Protestant Reformation and the modern colonial projects turned belief into a weapon of de-realization for non-Christians, in its alliance with the project of Enlightenment, the Reformation and Counter-Reformation transformed the dominant experience of Christianity in the West, too.[25] If before, the divine word—both spoken and written—"was necessarily also material," involving an entire acoustics, look, and feel, and as such was itself the object of reverence as well as the means of devotion, the Reformation conferred upon words an entirely different presence, as components of an abstracted language whose status, Talal Asad has argued, was itself "extra-real, capable of 'representing' and 'reflecting'—and therefore also of 'masking' the real."[26] Modern linguistics was born.[27] As such, where "*faith* had been a virtue, it now acquired an epistemological sense. Faith became a way of knowing supernatural objects, parallel to the knowledge of nature (the *real* world) that reason and observation provided."[28]

In case it needs restating, for the congregants at the Vineyard the proposition is not how to know and interpret a supernatural object, but to learn how to *feel* God as real, that is, how to discern his presence in the feeling of reality. This is why Luhrmann's question to their world is so relevant, so generous and generative. For it involves asking not whether, not why, but *how* they come to feel God: "how sensible, reasonable people, living in more or less the same evidential world as the skeptic, are able to experience themselves as having good evidence for the presence of a powerful invisible being who has a demonstrable effect on their lives and are able to sustain a belief in that presence despite their inevitable doubts."[29] By holding out her own hand to this world, she herself learned that learning to discern God was, above all, a *slow* process, "more like learning *to do* something than *to think* something," a process which required new habits of paying attention.[30] What's more, this involved the development of a whole new set of *practices*: of reading, of prayer, of worship, of hearing. For indeed, the corollary of the modern de-realization of language, and the turning of words divine into an epistemological problem, is not just the rise of visuality as a dominant form of perception, or indeed the modern association between "seeing" and "believing." The counterpart of this modern story involves also the gradual discovery that, to borrow Michel de Certeau's words, the "Spoken word" of the Holy Scripture "is no longer heard, that it has been altered by textual corruptions and the avatars of history. One can no longer hear it."[31]

Learning to pay attention, to discern the voice of this God, is something that these Christians have to become capable of, bit by bit. But the acquired modern inability to hear the Spoken word does not quite lead to mere "hearing loss." Like linguistics, modern psychology was born. The voice of God that they no longer hear has therefore already been replaced by other, secular voices, those of their own thoughts. And indeed, this compounds the challenge. For what is involved in becoming capable of hearing God's voice once again, of feeling his presence, which is to say, the *difference* he makes, is nothing less than taking the very significant risk of setting out "deliberately to overcome this fundamental human awareness that our minds are private." Seeking not to let psychology run amok, they have to learn how to "experience the mind-world barrier as porous, in a specific, limited way" in order to appreciate that "God participates in your mind, and you 'hear' what he says as if it were external speech."[32] Indeed, feeling this God's difference does not simply involve coming to accept the basic *idea* that one might possibly come to experience his presence, but the arduous development of an entire new set of tools and abilities, so that one can *confidently* experience aspects of one's own thoughts as being engendered by God. Which is to say that it is not enough for these Christians to "believe in God," as if it were a matter of including in their ontological repertoire the possibility of the existence of a God in the flesh. So long as *belief* matters to them, as Luhrmann suggests it does, it matters in a way that diverges from the modern history by which it came to designate an epistemological or propositional affair. Reality feels like itself, excites our interests, *and then* we believe in it. Indeed, if this God's reality feels like itself, and what is at stake for the Vineyard's congregants is learning how to let themselves be touched by it, to grant it the power to excite their interests and attention, to fill their minds with his presence, this has nothing to do with accepting the soundness of an idea.

In this sense, it may be worth recalling, rather, that the very notion of "belief" has a long and complex past, and before it was turned into a weapon of de-realization, into a term to describe the epistemological conundrum faced by those for whom faith became a problem of knowing, its uses in Vedic and Latin languages involved something else entirely, namely "the trust in the objectivity of some gesture."[33] Incidentally, I think it is also this sense of *believing*, not as a form of knowledge or ideation but as a matter of *trust*, that both James and Deleuze have in mind when they call for us to believe in another world in this world; when they suggest, as indeed James suggested quite a few decades before Deleuze, that "to believe in that world *may* be the most essential function that our lives in this world have to perform."[34] For whenever James is concerned, belief characterizes not a statement of knowledge with dodgy foundations, but an immanent, *"practical faith"* in light of which we *live*. "We cannot," James insists, "live or think at all without some degree of faith."[35] As such, this practical faith plays out as much in the active risks we take in living, as in the moments of doubt, skepticism, and disbelief. "Our only way of doubting, of refusing to believe, that a certain thing *is*, is continuing to act as if it were *not*."[36] Thus, I want to insist on this Jamesian concept of *trust* as a living attitude, because it may be capable of dispelling the modern confusion we experience with the notion of "belief," especially when it concerns the relations that these Christians establish with their God. But I insist on it, at the same time, because James's merit is to have turned "trust," such a seemingly innocent word, into a veritably speculative and pragmatic concept capable of precipitating a pluralistic variation of interests. Which is to say, with and beyond psychology, that James has managed to make the concept of trust capable of generating a transformation of our concept of reality and of precipitating an opening to our own metaphysical indetermination.

This is surely not without obstacles of its own. For in the modern world the notion of trust has by now become something of a hackneyed term—both conceptualized, and critically scorned, as a sort of mystical repertoire people draw on to act only when the rational and scientific foundations that would *justify* their knowledge are lacking. It is telling that modern characterizations of trust tend to coalesce around the idea of it emerging at a moment in which "disbelief" is "suspended." We are the deserving heirs of Descartes after all, taking those moments when we are corroded by radical doubt and paranoia as our most natural and most rational mode of living. It is perhaps no surprise that the modern West seems currently concerned with its own "crisis" of trust or that such conceptions of "trust" have become part of the new vocabulary of capitalist corporate ethics.[37] So long as our only way of effectively doubting that something is, is to act as if it were *not*, "it is often practically impossible to distinguish doubt from dogmatic negation."[38] And while the modern world may have equated rationality with corrosive skepticism and doubt, it seems rather the case that, as I have been suggesting in preceding chapters, all its trust, however little of it remains, is placed on what James regarded as one "singularly arbitrary caprice," that is, on the notion that trust "is only legitimate when used in the interests of one particular proposition—the proposition, namely, that the course of nature is uniform."[39]

In the face of the monism of modern principles, in response to the monifying and de-realizing notion of "belief," thinking with trust involves no disqualification of the reality of others, and neither does it constitute a way of making the unruly multifariousness of this world *behave*. Quite the contrary. What makes the word "trust" such a generative part of the runaway metaphysics I am relaying is precisely that it does *not* carry with it "license to define in detail an invisible world, and to anathemize and excommunicate those whose trust is different."[40] If trust is in some metaphysical sense an "ultimate," it cannot in any way be associated with a form of transcendence, of a general notion capable of judging the ways in which other realities feel like themselves, let alone capable of explaining them away. Trust is the *generic* name James gave to the feeling of reality in the plural, and, in this sense, it designates an immanent, living disposition that impregnates, always differently, the multifarious ways in which the inhabitants of the many worlds in this ongoing and unfinished world live, think, feel, and do. Which is to say that, like the congregants of the Vineyard, who seek to *confidently* experience aspects of their thoughts as being engendered by God, another name for trust is *confidence*. Not abstract notions of "market confidence," but a situated *com-fidere*, trust-with, feeling-with, the piecemeal cultivation of an art of feeling with one's world, of feeling with one's God. Making belief an immanent function of reality, James proposed trust as the vehicle for the cultivation of a pluralistic response to the nascent monification of the world, to its disqualifications, its dogmatic skepticism, and its systematic neglect. And as such, trust designates nothing if not the passionate, generous response to the passional and generative feeling of reality—feeling itself, like itself, in the plural. Trust, in short, characterizes a living attitude of *consent* to the world. Once again, in confidence: con-sent, *consentire*, feeling with, trusting another world in this world.

LEARNING TO TRUST · The pluriverse, I argued with James in the previous chapter, hangs on a lot of *ifs*. And what makes trust both generous and generative is that, as a living attitude in light of which one acts, as a passionate response to the feeling of reality, it does not simply subtend the manifold relationships people establish with their worlds in this world, but opens these relations up, and creates the possibility of extending them, to a whole array of "ifs" and "maybes." Indeed, you may "make one or the other of two possible universes true," James proposed, "by your trust or mistrust,—both universes having been only *maybes*, in this particular, before you contributed your act."[41] James's famous example is that of the inexperienced climber in the Alps, who due to ill luck has worked himself "into a position from which the only escape is a terrible leap." Having no recourse to similar experiences, he has no evidence of his ability to perform the leap successfully. Nothing can guarantee that a successful leap is possible or that he'll make it to the other end. And yet there he is, inextricably confronted with a maybe, forced to take the risk. Were he to let "the emotions of fear and mistrust preponderate," he'd waver for so long that eventually, "exhausted and trembling," upon taking the risk in a moment of despair, he'd miss his "foothold and roll into the abyss." But there's a chance that, were he to *trust* the possibility of carrying himself to the other side, he might succeed in attuning every nerve in his body to the "if" of a successful leap, thereby realizing what otherwise "would perhaps have been impossible."[42]

This, it seems to me, is the precise meaning of the Vineyard's invitation to experience God "as if" he were real and standing by your side, with love. For just as falling down the abyss cannot, practically speaking, realize itself unless it effectively de-realizes the *thereness* of the possibility of reaching the other side, so congregants seek, by *trusting* the reality of God's presence, to make that reality felt. This is to say that, rather than simply designating some underlying, homogenous, passional essence sustaining our world as the actual, irremediable fact that it is, trust is also generative: it can be generated and cultivated anew. If trust is the oxygen from which the "As sure as I exist!" takes its breath, it can also, in turn, breathe new life into other modes of existence—one can and may *learn to trust another world in this world*, to trust that reality may well be capable of more than modern realism deems possible. This, though, is never an easy task. It is neither without risks, nor is it a matter of good will. Remember part of the challenge that such a task involves for the congregates of the Vineyard: to learn to hear their God's voice, his presence, the difference he makes, just as they must resist the thundering-down of modern lessons, as they must unlearn the instruction to relate to their own thoughts as a purely private affair. That said, for all its difficulties, what matters is that it is not *impossible*. At least not as a matter of principle. To our critical, epistemological pluralists who, through their warnings of incommensurable "cultures" and "epistemologies," assure us that we can never hope to step outside our own, we might reply that they are right: one may not be able to make two different worlds commensurate—for that would be tantamount to canceling out their radical forms of divergence. But being unable, thankfully, to create an equivalence between them such that an adequate translation could be provided does not mean that one has to mistrust the very possibility of holding out one's hand and seek a possible *intranslation*, of precipitating our own metaphysical indetermination, of noticing the transformation of our world as the feeling of other realities passes into our experience.

This, too, is what these Christians have learned: not to believe that they can translate God, but to trust that they can learn to trust the reality of God standing by their side, with love. Luhrmann recalls the story of Sarah, for whom, before joining the Vineyard, "religion had been a social obligation," spending much of her youth in a "nondescript fifty-minutes-and-you're-out Methodist church, and converted to Catholicism, her husband's faith, when they married. She was never, she said, a good Catholic." Indeed, although she did believe in God, she did so "in an abstract, distant sort of way, but the rituals didn't move her":

> Yet the first morning Sarah attended a Vineyard service, she wept uncontrollably. She told [Luhrmann] that she cried because for the first time in her life she was singing directly *to* God, not *about* God, a love song to a living person—a man, even—who loved her openly and unconditionally, and it made her sob. For the first three months, she cried in every service.[43]

Sarah decided to stay. But the intensity of those first experiences did not immediately assuage the uncertainty around "how on earth she was supposed to get into a relationship with an invisible force whose face she could not see, whose voice she could not hear, who's hand she could not shake, but with whom she was supposed to have an intimate and ongoing dialogue about the small details of everyday life."[44] Learning to trust the reality of God, or that of another world in this world, may well constitute a terrible leap, but it is not for all that a matter of instantaneous conversion. It is instead more akin to the piecemeal, experimental, and situated process of cultivating an art—curiously noticing, errantly looking for signs, developing an entire new mode of appreciation for that which, generously and generatively, is in the process of making itself felt.

As Sarah continued to partake in the activities of the church, she joined a "prayer group," and "they taught her how to pray."[45] Prayer, Luhrmann tells us, is primarily how congregants of the Vineyard learn to discern God's presence in their life, how they learn to trust the reality of their God. It is the art of talking to God—and it is hard work. Guided by teachers and books that seek to develop the arts of prayer, "congregants begin to search for God's voice by," for instance, "holding conversations with him in their heads, modelled on the kinds of conversations they have with friends." But that particular friend which this God progressively becomes has, like any other friend, singular demands of his own. And as such, it is important that those who hold their hand out to him, those who are learning how to trust, create a space that is quiet enough "to listen for God's response."[46] Some prayer books recommend the arrangement of a "prayer closet," a place "where you can go, unplug the phone, and be fully undistracted." And indeed, she met congregants "who had the equivalent of closets, quiet rooms where they could go at certain hours and shut the door," as well as many who kept a "prayer journal" to write down not just what they thought or said in their prayers but also—*pace* modern psychology and linguistics—to write "what God had replied in return."[47]

It took Sarah "six to nine months before she felt that she understood how to develop a personal relationship with God." While she read the Bible often, she didn't consider that praying. And although she would find herself entertaining ideas about people she saw on the street—"that this man would develop a back problem he'd have to deal with today, that the kid with the skateboard had trouble brewing at home"—she did not then recognize those thoughts as God's.[48] Indeed, it appears that when it comes to learning to trust this God, and more, to learning to be *trusted by him*, establishing a purely individual relationship with him is not quite enough. In developing the art of praying *for others* who may be present or absent, through practices that require one to stand before the person they're praying for and to put "one's hand on their arm or shoulder," or on the shoulder of another person touching them, or indeed to hold out one's hand "facing them," it is through these ministerial and "intercessory" arts of prayer that Sarah—and many congregants of the Vineyard—began to discern the presence of God, as the thoughts that came to their minds during the prayer seemed "uncannily appropriate for the person about whom they prayed." So much so that the thoughts could, in fact, "be identified as extraordinary."[49] To Sarah, this happened on an occasion when she was "praying for the church":

> It was the first year that I [Sarah] was with the church and the first year I was really praying for the church. The Vineyard Association was having their national meeting in California, and they asked for intercessors to be praying regularly for that. I took it very seriously, and I prayed every morning. And one morning I was just sitting in my prayer chair, I had just finished and I was thinking about a picture. I thought my mind was wandering. I kept on seeing these boats. And I was thinking about that, and the phone rang, and it was the pastor. He was at the meeting, and he was calling about something completely different—and it was really silly for him to be calling. And after we went through with that, I just waited, and then felt moved to say, "Why did you call me?" And he said, "I don't know. I just felt like I was supposed to call you." And it clicked then, that the picture I had seen *wasn't* a distraction from my prayers but was *connected* to my prayers. I told him about this picture that I'd gotten. And he told me when he came back that several people had gotten the same picture, and that it was about Jesus with his hands on the wheel of a ship! It sounds like lunacy, I know. And yet that's how it works.[50]

Learning to trust the reality of God is not only something these Christians *do*. It is also something that *happens* to them *as* they do it. As they, through their arts of prayer, become capable of learning how to feel-with their God, of trusting the reality of a God standing by their side, with love, so perhaps "God himself"—James suggested once, as these Christians continue to do—"may draw vital strength and increase of very being" from their trust and become capable of replying to their prayers.[51] This is what James meant by trust being *precursive*, namely, that "often enough our faith beforehand in an uncertified result *is the only thing that makes the result come true*."[52] To say that it is *the only thing* that makes the result come true is not the same as saying that it is the *cause* of its verification. These Christians do not perform, enact, or construct God. Their arts of prayer do not make God up. Their prayers may occasionally avail nothing, just as the Alpine climber may face the abyss despite his best efforts. The result is indeed uncertified, and it "is only by risking ourselves from hour to hour that we live at all."[53] If the risks they take in their praying enable them to "clearly experience themselves as getting better at picking out God's voice from the everyday flow of inner speech," the risk of failing to establish such a relationship never recedes, and "they also clearly experience the process as inherently ambiguous, and they hesitate to assume that their interpretations are accurate." Sometimes, when they "think it's the spirit moving," a congregant told Luhrmann with humor, "it's just our burrito from lunch." Indeed, the more developed their art of discerning God's presence, "the more uncertainty you invite about any particular claim to God's presence."[54] With their inherent hesitation, their practices nevertheless "do God" in one precise sense: namely, in the sense that they generate the oxygen required to inhabit their world "as if God were real," to live in light of his presence, to trust the reality of this God standing by their side, with love.[55] Without them, without their trust, they might not be able to discern his presence, to discern the difference he makes, to make that reality feel like itself. God may be "eternal, almighty, and unchanging, but he gets hurt when you don't come out to play."[56]

TRUST OF A HELD-OUT HAND · This is to say that trust is precursive, but not *only* precursive.[57] It is generative, but also generous. If the trust of a held-out hand involves a risk, a wager on a "maybe," if it involves a generous jumping-off of our modern grounds toward the possibility of another world in this world, it is not because this is a "leap of faith," piously surrendering to a divine command to lose one's ground regardless of the consequences. If the holding out of one's hand involves a wager, it is not a leap or a jump "*of* faith," as if one could jump without it. As with the Alpine climber, it is the *jumping itself* which is practically and immanently faithful, or indeed, *trusting*—the risk of jumping toward "a world of which we trust the other parts to meet our jump," to borrow James's words once again.[58] In other words, for the congregants to feel God standing by their side, with love, God has to *meet their jump*. The response to a held-out hand, is another hand stretched back out. Not *just* "back," but back *and* out. This is why, when these Christians read their Bibles, they do so "in a conversation with God as if both they *and* the Bible were changing" in tone, in relevance, in the poignancy of the words. God talks back indeed, and congregants "look for the way God answers, inspires, consoles, enlightens by changing the way that the text reads."[59] God talks back, and his response is itself an *inspiration*, an incitation to respond to him in turn, to live in the light of his response.

This, in other words, is a veritable *relationship*. And because they are in a relationship with their God, because they learn to trust the reality of God, these Christians also know that "failure to recognize God's voice—or even worse, in recognizing him, the failure to respond—is understood to carry real-world consequences."[60] In an arresting moment, Luhrmann recalls the story of a now pastor who once had "a dream about someone in the church who was trying to become pregnant. She didn't know the woman terribly well," Luhrmann continues, "but it was a mildly troubling dream." This woman proceeded, therefore, to report the dream to her own pastor, "and thought she'd done her job. But then she learned that the woman had in fact been pregnant at the time of the dream . . . and that she had lost the baby. The woman telling the story said that she was devastated, and she spoke to us as if God let the baby die because she hadn't prayed."[61] A troubling episode, no doubt. The Evangelical-Capitalist Resonance Machine looms large. And indeed, for Luhrmann this was a disturbing idea, "that this God—the perfectly tolerant source of unconditional love—would hang the balance of a child's life on a near-stranger's prayer."[62] This is surely a difficult story to relay, for one can already sense proud, modern atheists sharpening their knives, lurking impatiently for their "gotcha!" moment, when the contradiction inherent in the proposition of an unconditionally loving God that can interrupt the coming life of a baby yet to be born on the failure of a prayer would finally reveal the reality of this God as pure delusion. As if reality was free from paradox. As if the ultimate metaphysical principle had to be a logical one, the law of the excluded middle.

Modern logicians and psychologists may well build an alliance, as they often do, and disqualify these Christians' experience on the basis of its failure to live up to the commandments of logic. But from the perspective of a runaway metaphysics, such an operation is out of the question. To the extent that their God is felt, to the extent that he makes a difference, this difference cannot be dismissed by the logic of modern realist of operations—it cannot be neglected, thrown under the bus driven by logical principles. This has nothing to do with abstract principles. The "unseen region in question" that is the presence of this God directly apprehended as a quasi-sensible reality "is not," James would surely agree, "merely ideal, for it produces effects." So let me borrow James's own words from *The Varieties of Religious Experience* again, where, in addressing such unseen regions as Gods, spirits, and other realities divine, mystical, or "supernatural," as he then called them, he insisted that "that which produces effects within another reality must be termed a reality itself, so I feel as if we had no philosophic excuse for calling the unseen or mystical world unreal."[63] The only excuse offered is the mistrust bred by the operations of disqualification of modern realism. And that is no excuse. Reality is capable of more than their logical rules. For the feelings of reality are "as convincing to those who have them as any direct sensible experiences can be," and they surely are "much more convincing," James insisted, "than the results established by mere logic ever are."[64]

What's more, such "gotcha!" moments create a pragmatic problem, which is that, while they rest in the comfort of their scavenging logic, something important about this story is missed. The key is in how Luhrmann relays the story, choosing her words carefully: "she *spoke to us*," the attendants to the regional meeting, "as if God let the baby die because she hadn't prayed." Whether their God did or did not let the baby die *because* she hadn't prayed, nobody—neither the woman, nor Luhrmann—can effectively confirm. Indeed, the point of the retelling of this story lies rather in *how* the woman spoke. That is, in her own relationship with God, and, by implication, in the cultivation of the congregants' respective relationships with him, rather than in God's relationship with the baby. It concerns the fact that the feeling of God's presence makes a difference, one that those who feel it are to learn to become responsive to. Like other friendships with humans or animals, one's relationship with that God must be honored, too. This is God's own stretched-out hand to the hand held out. And it seems this is just how another attendant at the meeting understood the story. He told Luhrmann after the meeting that "he didn't really know why God acted like that, but he thought that God behaved with his worshippers the way a parent works with a child to help the child grow into adulthood." That is, if "a father is at the beach with his son," he could "make a sand castle" himself, and "it would be a more beautiful and perfect sand castle if he made it by himself. But no father does that. A father puts up with the messiness and does it with his son. His relationship with his son, the man went on, is much more important than a sand castle, which after all the waves will wash away."[65]

This interpretation explains nothing, of course. But it is precisely in those moments of uncertainty, Luhrmann suggests, that congregants of the Vineyard "made God real." In other words, "when the world they thought God had created was senseless."[66] As such, these Christians may get "mad at God or sad at God" but they "do not turn" their "back on God."[67] The story of this failure to respond to God's presence, to the difference he makes to these Christians, discloses something important about the response, to their held-out hand, from God's hand stretched out. This is that *trust* is not only precursive but *recursive*, such that, as James speculatively suggested, "a social organism of any sort whatsoever, large or small," human or not, "is what it is because each member proceeds to his own duty with a trust that the other members will simultaneously do theirs."[68] And it is worth stressing: it is recursive, not *reciprocal*. Reciprocity, the hand stretched *back* to the held-out hand, would here imply a contract of exchange, demanding from the other the equivalent of what one has given in turn, making one's relationship with the other conditional on criteria that they *must* follow in response *or else*. And such conditions, the mutual submission of both parts to a contract of exchange laying down what may be given and what would be expected in return, would curb the radical and irreducible *difference* that persists between the held-out hand and the hand stretched back out, that divergence which makes trust a thoroughly risky affair through which worlds in this world sometimes partially connect — that ongoing generativity of the many ways in which reality feels like itself.

The recursivity of trust is made all the more present in another story, about the way in which the Cree of northeastern Canada, a group of hunter-gatherers, relate to the reindeer that they hunt.[69] There's no doubt that hunting reindeer involves *killing*. And yet, Tim Ingold notes, hunters are "well-known for their abhorrence of violence in the context of human relations" as well as in "their relations with animals," such that "the encounter, at the moment of the kill," must be "non-violent."[70] How is that possible? The nonviolence of the encounter stems from the fact that, where the Cree are concerned, the reindeer *offers itself to the hunter*. Reindeer—or caribou, as they are called in North America—have a distinct way of responding to their pursuit by their predators: instead "of running away," a reindeer stands "stock still, turns its head and stares you squarely in the face." Biologists suggest this gesture is the result of an evolutionary adaptation to their predation by wolves, such that "when the reindeer stops, the pursuing wolf stops too, both of them getting their breath back for the final, decisive phase of the episode when the deer turns to flight and the wolf rushes to overtake it."[71] The reindeer and the wolf generate, together, a fleeting moment of trust. But, *pace* evolutionary biologists, the former also generates a different form of trust with the Cree. To be sure, when pursued by the Cree hunters, the difference that the standing still of the reindeer makes is no longer the creation of a moment of repose for both, but the potential occasion for the hunter to strike and kill it. Whenever the Cree are concerned, however, this is still a moment of trust, for in standing still and staring at the Cree hunter squarely in the face, the animal effectively "offers itself up, quite intentionally and in a spirit of good-will or even love towards the hunter. The bodily substance of the caribou," Ingold remarks, "is not taken, it is *received*."[72]

By going in pursuit of the reindeer, the Cree practically and immanently hold out a hand to it, adapting their own bodies and developing the art of the hunt in relation to the demands of the encounter. To this held-out hand, the animal responds in turn as it offers itself to the hunter, with love. But the caribou's response is itself a hand stretched out. The animal trusts not that it will be killed or eaten, but that in so doing the Cree will treat it *well*. Thus, while the Cree may consume its flesh, the reindeer's soul is to be "released to be reclothed with flesh." Treating reindeer badly, breaking their trust, would involve "failing to observe the proper, respectful procedures in the processes of butchering, consumption and disposal of bones, or by causing undue pain and suffering to the animal in killing it. Above all, animals are offended by *unnecessary* killing: that is, by killing as an end in itself rather than to satisfy genuine consumption needs. They are offended too," Ingold tells us, "if the meat is not properly shared around all those in the community who need it." And it has consequences: "animals will not return to hunters who have treated them badly in the past."[73] What is formed between the held-out hand of the hunters and the hand stretched back and out of the reindeer, then, is not a relationship of reciprocity, no kill and be killed, but a precarious yet generative *ensemble of relays*. For it is not enough for the hunters to trust the reindeer to stand still and stare back. The hunters have to trust the reindeer's trust to trust them to treat it well, to trust *it* to reclothe its soul anew with flesh and return.

The trust that the members of the Vineyard weave together with God is in many ways radically different, specific to the form of their own encounters and relationships. But in their relationship, a precarious yet generative ensemble of relays is formed as well. This is that to trust the reality of God is not simply to trust that he'll be good or just; it is not even, I'd suggest, to trust *him*. It is also, crucially, to trust in the reality of his hand stretching back and out. It is to trust in God's trust that the ones who engage in the art of prayer will trust their own openness not to confuse his voice with the stream of their own private thoughts, but trust God's standing by their side, with love, in confidence, trusting those praying to trust his reply so as to pay attention to it and act in response. Rather than a contract of reciprocity, then, trust involves a generous engagement, without guarantees, in the recursive relationship between a held-out hand that calls for a response from a world it trusts it will meet its hand and the stretched-out hand from another world in this world, which calls for *another* response in turn. What is generated, in confidence, between the held-out hand and the other hand stretching back out is no give and take, but a swirl of gestures, of openings to one another where *the trust of our held-out hand is a trust in another hand's trust, a trust in another hand's trust in our trust in theirs*. All the way through.

A complex weaving indeed. In each case, through the specific gestures of their own situated encounters, what is sparked is a *pluralistic event*: the partial, fragile, ongoing, and unfinished weaving of a tremorous form of togetherness that obtains thanks to, and not in spite of, divergence. It is precisely the establishment of such fragile and trembling relationships dancing together on the pin of a "maybe" around the day in eighty worlds; of reality feeling like itself in the plural, overflowing and surrounding our logic; of a multiplicity of worlds in this world hanging on a lot of "ifs"; it is precisely that which modern realist operations interrupt, and it is that which is at stake in this ongoing and unfinished experiment in learning that a runaway metaphysics involves. This is why James once proposed that the pluriverse, ongoing and unfinished, expressed never in categorical and always in *hypothetical* propositions, underway and yet to be made, could be "conceived after a *social* analogy, as a pluralism of independent powers. It will succeed," he wrote, "just in proportion as more of these work for its success. If none work, it will fail. If each does his best, it will not fail."[74] Laboring toward our own metaphysical indetermination, which is to say, toward the verification of this many-storied universe around the day in eighty worlds, we cannot fabricate such a loosely connected universe at will. Instead, "we must recognize that, even though we do our best, the other factors also will have a voice in the result. If they refuse to conspire, our good-will and labor may be thrown away. No insurance company," James remarked, "can here cover us from the risks we run in being part of such a world."[75]

If *believing* in another world in this world matters, if trusting other worlds around the day in eighty worlds makes a difference, it is precisely so as to reactivate the generative systems of relays that might, perhaps, make the pluriverse true. It is in this sense that trust can be called an "ultimate." As James said, there is no self-fulfilling logic here, and no "'vicious circle,' unless a circle of poles holding themselves upright by leaning on one another, or a circle of dancers revolving by holding each other's hands, be 'vicious.'"[76] What this does present, however, is *a genuine option*: consent to the world, to the terrible leap; learn to feel-with this world *and* that; build alliances and relays with realities scorned, fantastical, and derided; and perhaps reality may become capable of more; perhaps we may, together, render each other capable of making a pluralistic transformation of our world effective. Mistrust it, mistrust the thereness of its reality in the plural, the thereness of its response, the thereness of your response to the world, and there will be no there there.

CHAPTER FOUR · Worldquakes

Philosophy, like life, must keep the doors and windows open.
WILLIAM JAMES

I don't understand what I saw. And I don't even know if I saw it,
since my eyes can't differentiate themselves from the things they see.
Only an unexpected tremor of lines, only an anomaly in the uninterrupted
continuity of my civilization, made me experience for an instant
vitalizing death. The fine death that let me brush up against
the forbidden fabric of life.
CLARICE LISPECTOR

THE TREMBLING OF TOGETHERNESS · Muddled, messy, gripping, and tangled, the pluriverse could not afford the hollow elegance of an inaugural "bang!" There is no absolute beginning. Ongoing and unfinished, its composition is piecemeal, always in the making, bursting at the seams, growing by its edges. "There are novelties; there are losses," and this many-storied universe "seems, on concrete and proximate level at least, really to grow."[1] One and many, it enjoys no foundation, no inauguration, but a permanent buzzing of myriad little brushings and transitions, slippages and fractures, turbulences and frictions—tremors between so many divergent modes of trust around the day in eighty or a thousand worlds. The pluriverse trembles in the interstices between the one and the many, between a before and an after. It *insists* on their turbulent togetherness, precipitating divergences, transitions, and transformations.[2] And so "life," its ongoing and unfinished life as much as ours, is "in the transitions as much as in the terms connected." Indeed, James observed that it often seems "to be there more emphatically, as if our spurts and sallies forward were the real firing-line of the battle, were like the thin line of flame advancing across the dry autumnal field which the farmer proceeds to burn."[3] It is the trembling itself, the partial connections between its different little worlds, that makes the insistent possibility of a pluriverse felt. On a quiet day, one can hear it breathing.

Might this be why, when James visited Stanford in the spring of 1906, he had such an unusual reaction to the trembling of the Earth under his feet?[4] He was thrown down on his face as a mild earthquake began "shaking the room exactly as a terrier shakes a rat. Then everything that was on anything else slid off to the floor, over went bureau and chiffonier with a crash, as the *fortissimo* was reached, plaster cracked, an awful roaring noise seemed to fill the outer air." And then, in an instant, "all was still again, save the soft babble of human voices from far and near that soon began to make itself heard, as the inhabitants in costumes *negligées* in various degrees sought the greater safety of the street and yielded to the passionate desire for sympathetic communication."[5] Yet he experienced no panic, but a feeling of "glee and admiration; glee at the vividness with such an abstract idea or verbal term as 'earthquake' could put on when translated into sensible reality and verified concretely; and admiration at the way in which the frail little wooden house could hold itself together in spite of such a shaking. I felt not trace whatever of fear; it was pure delight and welcome. '*Go* it,' I almost cried aloud, 'and go it *stronger!*'"[6]

His buoyant delight at the trembling of his world is perhaps unusual, but it might have presaged something of this very pluriversal trembling which his nascent pluralistic metaphysics would seek to honor ever since. For it wasn't just the room that was trembling: the earthquake threw his entire world into transition, jolted his thought, confronted him with the force of an irresistible call, with the demand of an imperative. Indeed, it is not that reality is raw material for our cognitive mediations. Reality, rather, "falls in passing into conceptual analysis; it mounts in living its own undivided life—it buds and bourgeons, changes and creates."[7] Forced into thinking by the shaking of reality itself, James discerned certain peculiar ways in which the earthquake had altered the stream of his thought, ways that "were quite spontaneous and, so to speak, inevitable and irresistible."[8] The tremor made itself felt to him in the concrete, with an "overpowering dramatic convincingness," as a personified thing, a "living agent" that had "been lying low and holding itself back during all the intervening months, in order, on that lustrous April morning, to invade my room, and energise the more intensely and triumphantly."[9] It was *his* room that it invaded, for the earthquake came "directly to *me*. It stole in behind my back, and once inside the room, had me all to itself, and could manifest itself convincingly. Animus and intent were never more present in any human action, nor did any human activity ever more definitely point back to a living agent as its source and origin."[10]

The quivering of the Earth constituted, therefore, a very singular form of trembling. For it precipitated a veritable *worldquake*, the insinuation of another world underway, of a buzzing multiplicity of other worlds in this world, of the feeling of another world passing into one's experience. All the other witnesses he talked to agreed that "'It expressed intention,' 'It was vicious,' 'It was bent on destruction,' 'It wanted to show its power,' or what not"; one of them interpreted it as the very end of the world and the beginning of the final judgment, and did not in fact "think of its being an earthquake till after she had got into the street and someone had explained it to her."[11] For his part, the earthquake made James "realize now better than ever how inevitable were men's earlier mythologic versions of such catastrophes, and how artificial and against the grain of our spontaneous perceiving are the later habits into which science educates us." It was impossible for people untutored in modern science "to take earthquakes into their minds as anything but supernatural warnings or retributions."[12] But sensing earthquakes as anything other than the intrusion of a living and concrete difference in their world was not just impossible *for them*. In the midst of the experience, James himself thought that whereas for modern science "earthquake is simply the collective *name* of all the cracks and shakings and disturbances that happen," for him "*the* earthquake was the *cause* of the disturbances, and the perception of it as a living agent was irresistible."[13]

Which is to say that the gathering on the street of those yielding to the passionate desire for sympathetic communication was not just a coming together of people who had survived the tremors. It was also a shimmering togetherness of a different kind: of a plurality of divergent stories and feelings of the worldquake in the concrete, as it had passed into their experiences, making the scientific foundations of modern geology burst at the seams. A buzzing and bubbling *multum in parvo*. In its multifariousness, the quake precipitated a cascade of intranslations, generating a divergent opening to other worlds in this world, underway and yet to be made. It was the worldquake that made the pluriverse felt. Indeed, nowhere is the feeling of reality in the plural made more present, more dramatic, more exhilarating, more shocking, than at those moments when one brushes against the feeling of difference in the concrete and the trembling of togetherness strikes our experience. And this matters. For if by cultivating the arts of learning to trust another world in this world, of trusting in the possibility of an *additive* operation that enlarges what reality may become capable of, the work of a runaway metaphysics can lay siege to the empire of modern realism, it is precisely because other worlds can never simply "add" themselves to ours without simultaneously posing problems that are liable to shake our own world to its core. Others cannot meet our jump without, in some way, making the ground from which we've jumped tremble. If this pluralistic realism I'm seeking to cultivate with allies while we still can involves a consent to the "terrible leap" of going around the day in eighty worlds, trusting that other worlds in this world can be "as acceptable, possible, and real as having soup at 8 p.m.," it must also come to terms with the fact that soup will never taste the same as a result.[14]

Trust, therefore, constitutes neither a solution nor a safe path through the problem that differences pose. It is not the vehicle of some perpetual peace or of a new cosmopolitanism. Generating trust, instead, is what the problem of a trembling togetherness itself requires. As the world quakes, there is no stable, equal footing on which everyone can stand in spite of their divergences. The jump, which we trust others might meet, is one we take at our own risk. It is a non-symmetrical gesture whose effect is, above all, to provoke our own metaphysical indetermination: a metamorphosis precipitated by the trembling of togetherness, shaking our world as the feelings of other worlds pass into our experience. As such, what trust makes possible is an opening to another kind of problematization: that of the always problematic coexistence of a multiplicity of divergent worlds, together in the concrete, even when their togetherness *falls* upon our conceptual analyses like a shock of incompossibility, infecting thought with a vertiginous perplexity.[15] It is this worldquake, this moment when the insistence of a living pluriverse becomes felt, that turns pluralism into an anti-imperial political insurrection, seeking not to compose a new postcolonial ecumene, but to dramatize the fragility of the many partial and loose connections that, in spite of all, have so far allowed the possibility of a pluriverse to scat the eschaton, and resist complete monification. Pluralism, in this sense, is a way of honoring the moment in which we brush against the feeling of difference in the concrete, making present that philosophy, as much as politics, must always keep the doors and windows open to the presence of others who, without being required to partake in the reformulation of our problems, create an insistence no generative formulation can ignore.

TOLERANT OPERATIONS, AND OTHER STORIES · Worldquakes—they've been happening all along, around the day in eighty worlds: learning to trust the presence of a God standing by their side, with love, the congregants of the Vineyard wavered before conferring on their experiences any particular interpretation; the local ethnographers on the Mueda Plateau hesitated before translating sorcery-lions into anthropological theory; the story of the first circumnavigations, of the modern birth of the world's monification, could only become perceptible in the resonating frictions of its competing versions. It would be tempting to ascribe those moments of hesitation, wavering, and friction to an affectation of the writing hands that tremble, of the speaking voices that stutter, of the indecisive minds that hesitate. But such an ascription would also be regrettable. For it would turn the pluriverse into a stable, homogenous, all-inclusive whole, and thus take the trembling as a mere psychomotor imperfection. And yet, ever not quite! This living pluriverse, ongoing and unfinished, insists and persists in and through divergent modes of trust around the day in eighty or a thousand worlds. It is the feeling of difference in the concrete, of reality in the plural, that bursts our world open at the seams and throws it back at us once again as "one great blooming, buzzing confusion" that trembles as it brushes against the presence of another possible world.[16]

Needless to say, modern realism has always fought the tremors. It might perhaps have been created precisely to resist them at all costs, going to any lengths to hold its world fast, deploying its weapons of de-realization to countervail the quickening of its own foundations. What are the inventions of "belief" and "superstition," of "symbols" and "cultures," of "representations" and "epistemologies," of "growth" and "development," if not abstract tools the modern project has deployed on the turbulently expanding edges of empire to hold its world fast precisely on those occasions when its foundations tremble? What are they if not the means by which we can secure our foundations when the presence of another world in this world insinuates a possible intranslation, shaking our thought with the force of a worldquake? And yet these tools have never been enough. The feeling of reality in the plural has a way of boiling over every metaphysical determination, and it doesn't much care whether the trembling happens in the colonies or at the heart of Empire. Thus, modern realism could not rest content with the disqualification of other worlds, but had to develop an entire artillery of operations to fend against its own tremors, and therefore secure the stability of its expanding territory. Even more than in modern philosophy, where it's never been more than an a belligerent operation, modern realism spread its mistrust everywhere: in the sciences, which, with their law-abiding, evolutionary naturalisms, degraded the "preternatural" into the "paranormal";[17] in medicine, which in its obsession with distinguishing between rational doctors and irrational healers turned the healing powers of trust, faith, and hope into clandestine, placebo effects, into suspect somatizations;[18] in psychology, where its imperative of "mourning" sought to turn the togetherness of the living and the dead into a temporary affliction against which everyone shall work;[19] and also in literature, where the birth of a literary realism in the nineteenth-century novel denigrated the multifariousness of reality to the ordinariness of bourgeois life and, like Cortázar's classmate, derided other styles as "too fantastical," dangerous, and immoral.[20]

This is to name but a few of its forms of operation. There are many others. At the same time, these tools have never completely succeeded. Thankfully, the pluriverse insists and persists, and other worlds in this world have kept making themselves felt in and out of Europe. Peoples around the day in eighty worlds still brush against the presence of holy, ghostly, and extraordinary others in the concrete. In the interstices and cracks, they still cultivate their own forms of togetherness. Indeed, even at the height of the modern imperial project, resistance in the colonies found alliances and relays in a Western "metropolitan anticolonialism" that, as Leela Gandhi has superbly shown, wove together the disparate energies of Marxism, utopian experimentation, mysticism, and continental anarchism to make common cause with anti-colonial efforts elsewhere, thereby temporarily precipitating the "mutation of 'internationalism' into a series of countercultural revolutionary practices."[21] James's work itself—Gandhi remarks in a most unusual gesture among postcolonial theorists—with its damning of great empires, with its rejection of the annexation of the Philippines[22] and its "refusal of secular rationality and transcendental subjectivity,"[23] is to be counted among those radically disparate yet "quintessentially political and anticolonial" efforts to cultivate ways of living and dying well in this world as "a function of being in relation to others."[24] Ongoing and unfinished, the pluriverse is yet to take its last tremorous breath. There is still an after to that ending.

Nevertheless, the numbing effects of modern operations cannot be underestimated either. For if nobody can predict, let alone prevent, when the next pluriversal worldquake might strike, what modern realism has achieved is a significant *quieting* of the tremors. Indeed, what James said of our intellectual habits more generally, namely, that "by far the most usual way of handling phenomena so novel that they would make for a serious rearrangement of our preconceptions is to ignore them altogether, or to abuse those who bear witness for them," is, I think, especially true of modern habits.[25] For these are very particular habits, ones that give to general principles the power to determine what can and cannot be, the power to legislate fact from fiction, knowledge from belief, reality from illusion, irrespective of what a particular encounter with difference in the concrete might make felt. As such, these habits have turned those who are heirs to the modern project into a particular kind of people: the ones who, traveling around the world in eighty days or twenty hours—with their reasons and their laws, with their distinctions and their explanations— will not let themselves be perplexed. Nothing new, nothing different, nothing other, will be allowed to provoke a radical rearrangement of their mode of inhabiting the present. Of course, differences keep pressing on. But thanks to the tools at their disposal, these moderns have become extremely tolerant. Indeed, what is the meaning of "tolerance" if not the capacity *not* to be put at risk by the difference that concrete differences make? What is it if not the capacity to withstand the tremors they cause? Guided by principles of Progress, Reason, Humanism, Democracy, or Peace, modern tolerance shuns perplexity, for it prevents the *percepts* of another world in this world to make our *concepts* tremble, to trouble the visions of human and more-than-human flourishing we hold most dear, to throw the dice and open up the question of what reality may become capable of once again.[26]

Traces of this modern habit of preventing the tremors of togetherness from falling into our conceptualizations are everywhere to be found. But it is perhaps in those instances where it is the opposite gesture that was genuinely sought, where it is the *difference* of another world that is purposefully being addressed, that they become most acutely visible and the effects of this modern habit appear most strikingly disabling. Postcolonial thinker and historian Dipesh Chakrabarty dramatized this tension like no other in a most generative essay that has deservedly become something of a classic among postcolonial scholars, and that has for long been a personal source of inspiration for me. In the context of a discussion around the challenges modern history faces in addressing "subaltern pasts," Chakrabarty revisited an account by the founder of the Subaltern Studies group, Ranajit Guha, that constituted a rightly celebrated instance of the group's more general aim: to "make the subaltern the sovereign subject of history, to listen to their voices, to take their experiences and thought (and not just their material circumstances) seriously."[27] Focusing on the rebellion of the Santal, a tribal group in Bengal and Bihar who rebelled against both the British and nonlocal Indians in 1855, Guha's essay dramatized the task of subaltern studies in that it attempted to make the "insurgent's consciousness the mainstay of a narrative about rebellion."[28]

Yet this instance, Guha's "The Prose of Counter-Insurgency," simultaneously disclosed something troubling, something that made Chakrabarty suspect that "the problem of subaltern pasts" had been "dogging the enterprise of *Subaltern Studies* from the very outset."[29] In the course of studying and relaying the story of the Santal rebellion, Guha "unsurprisingly came across a phenomenon common in the lives of the peasants: the agency of supernatural beings. Santal leaders," recounts Chakrabarty, "explained the rebellion in supernatural terms, as an act carried out at the behest of the Santal god Thakur."[30] The disclosures of such pasts may have been "unsurprising," but when the ones supposed to be sovereign subjects of history assign their historical subjectivity to a god at whose behest they had acted, the critical historiographical project is certainly faced with a perplexing problem. The constraint of the subaltern studies project meant that, of course, in order to address it, Guha could not put the Santal account into question. But the historiographical constraint meant that he could not trust it either. Thus, he readily and generously affirmed the Santal story as "the truth and nothing but the truth for the speakers." *For the speakers:* the Santal's truth could not be History's truth. Not, in other words, without displacing *their* truth under the more abstract truth of a tolerant, modern principle—embraced by historians since their craft became modern in the late eighteenth century—that it is *humans*, and not gods, that make history.[31] To withstand the effects of the real agency of Thakur without simultaneously contributing to a Eurocentric history that would have disqualified the Santal altogether, the truth expressed by the Santal had to be translated into *their* truth—transposed in such a way that the Santal's ascription of agency to the god Thakur was in turn ascribed to the Santal's own agency and worldview, to the particular "logic" of their own "consciousness."[32] Thakur was at the center of the Santal's story, but if their rebellion was to serve the modern, "historical cause of democracy or citizenship or socialism,"[33] he had to be, at one and the same time, inscribed in the Santal's worldview and exorcised from History.

If Chakrabarty's reading of Guha's reading of the Santal is so generative, it is because he makes this problem dramatically felt. For him, the very problem that had been dogging subaltern studies from the outset is precisely that subaltern pasts "are pasts that resist historicization, just as there may be moments in ethnographic research that resist the doing of ethnography."[34] Indeed, the very realization of such a problem at the heart of a project he was a part of generates, halfway through his essay, a truly vertiginous intimation: that the togetherness of subaltern pasts with our modern present does not merely pose a methodological or epistemological problem; that the worldquake the Santal story is liable to generate would make not only history-writing, but our concept of time itself, tremble "like stubborn knots that stand out and break up the otherwise evenly woven surface of the fabric."[35] Throwing time out of joint, the Santal's story would, Chakrabarty writes, prompt one to stay "with heterogeneities without seeking to reduce them to any overarching principle that speaks for an already given whole." And this radically pluralistic gesture might, in turn, be liable to implicate us in another project altogether. In one that, instead of seeking to include the subaltern in the historical cause of democracy, citizenship, or socialism, would have us "struggling, or even groping, for nonstatist forms of democracy that we cannot yet either understand or envisage completely."[36]

A metaphysical indetermination begins to insinuate itself here. And yet, at that very moment when the Santal's past becomes alive and present, when our heterogeneous togetherness renders them "our contemporaries," disclosing "a plurality of times existing together, a disjuncture of the present with itself";[37] at that moment when we, as Chakrabarty's readers, begin to feel the world quake, and sense the *and* that trails along modern edges, the essay comes subtly off the ledge, and the tremors are almost imperceptibly quieted. And they are relieved by a strange proposition, that subaltern pasts cannot but remain "signposts of this border" at the edge of our present, ones that mark "the limit" of "the practices and discourses that define the modern."[38] Chakrabarty's suggestion, in other words, is that subaltern pasts put the historian in a bind of sorts: "they enable history, the discipline, to be what it is and yet at the same time they help to show what its limits are."[39] As such, he proposes that we could indeed "look on the Santal as someone illuminating possibilities for our own life-worlds,"[40] but that they "do not give the historian any principle of narration that can be rationally defended in modern public life."[41] Instead, the intolerable character of the Santal's story makes us aware of the deeply provincial character of modern habits—it marks the limits of historicizing itself and halts the modern impulse to historicize at all costs. For as far as history itself is concerned, "one can see that this requirement for a rational principle . . . marks the deep connections that exist between modern constructions of public life and projects of social justice."[42]

Chakrabarty's invitation, then, is to acknowledge the limits of our practices and modes of abstraction, and to acknowledge the intimate connections that modern habits of knowing establish with our most cherished political ideals. By turning them against themselves, Chakrabarty uses those deep modern connections as tools to sensitize us to the existence of this border, to the importance of acknowledging its existence, and even to entertain the possibility of peeking through it to a shared and "unhistoricizable" togetherness. As such, to write the history of the Santal is to tell the story of the depletion of our own history.[43] The invitation is welcome. But surely this is not the only story we could tell.[44] The past isn't dead, and the pluriverse is still, in spite of all, teeming with stories that *make present* that we, humans, are not alone in the world, and that we do not, in spite of all, singlehandedly make history. To respond to the insistence of this ongoing and unfinished pluriverse while we still can, therefore, we need to consent to taking a different kind of risk: the risk of troubling those very modern connections so as to become capable of giving to the *feeling* of this porous border the power to make our modern habits tremble; the risk of allowing the problems that the Santal's story poses to transform the ways in which we pose *our own* problems. It is by interrupting the intimate affair between modern habits and public life that we might perhaps become capable of imagining more generative and generous forms of justice, of envisaging democracy otherwise. It's not that I think Chakrabarty would disagree. And yet, while immensely generative, his essay sets welcome limits to history but stops short of allowing the worldquake to reverberate, to experiment with what, if anything, history and its reasons might become were they to consent to the metaphysical indetermination that the Santal's story (almost) precipitates. What if Thakur, on that occasion, were indeed a subject of history? How might we tell what has happened to us? What is reality capable of?

After all, the Santal's story may *sound* intolerable to us, but as James once wrote, "the immediate facts don't sound at all, but simply *are*, until we conceptualize them or name them vocally."[45] As such, "the contradiction results only" from our own abstract operations, "from the conceptual or discursive form being substituted for the real form."[46] We are "so subject to the philosophic tradition which treats *logos* or discursive thought generally as the sole avenue to truth," James went on, that falling "back on raw unverbalized life," or consenting to the trembling of our habits as they brush against the Santal and their god in the concrete, "comes very hard." For indeed, we might need to give up on our secular historicism but also on our habit of thinking in general terms, terms which lead us to denounce any attempt at situating our stories as a relativist ploy.[47] We would need to revise our criteria of relevant evidence and cultivate ways of learning about the ways in which the Santal established a relationship with Thakur. We might need to collectively reimagine what we mean by, and how we and others pursue, the always fragile possibility of justice. The modern territory of politics itself would have to be redrawn as we discover that, to recall Marisol de la Cadena's experiences in the Peruvian Andes, subaltern and "indigenous politics may exceed politics as we know them."[48] We would have to learn how to cultivate other values for collective existence, to tell other stories, and to tell our own stories otherwise, to create other ways of telling what has happened to us.

This would no doubt be immensely difficult, trying, and demanding. It may even be frightening, for we would be "putting off our proud maturity of mind and becoming again as foolish little children in the eyes of reason."[49] There are no guarantees that we'd come out of it any better for doing so. But perhaps, just perhaps, that is a risk worth taking. Perhaps consenting to the tremors might enable us to trust that other forms of democracy and justice we can dimly envisage and do not yet understand are nevertheless possible. Perhaps brushing against the difference of the Santal in the concrete, contending with the problems it poses to us, might help us not only appreciate that ours is not the only way of relating to the past, that time is not homogeneous, that gods and spirits might be capable of putting our political categories and ideals at risk—that our stories, in short, cannot be the only stories through which the pluriverse is to be made. It may also enable us to appreciate that other worlds are not only possible, but underway; that there are ways of inhabiting our present otherwise, making our togetherness with Thakur and the Santal something other than a double bind; that there may be forms, yet to be invented, of living and dying *well* with others in ways that make the pluriverse felt.

IN THE COMPANY OF SPIRITS · One thing, nevertheless, is clear. Consenting to the tremors, letting the worldquake *fall* into our conceptualizations, would, at the very least, make present that it is not so much that there "are pasts that resist historicization, just as there may be moments in ethnographic research that resist the doing of ethnography,"[50] but that there are pasts and moments which modern habits actively *resist*. That there are felt differences modern operations do everything to tolerate and withstand. Indeed, even among those allies in contemporary anthropology who, thanks to their renewed appetites for metaphysical experimentation, have taken the pluralistic arts of noticing to new horizons, the generous relaying of worldquakes remains a rare occurrence.[51] What's more, when the trembling of togetherness is occasionally allowed to reverberate, to fall into our conceptualizations and throw them out of joint, "the discipline publicly objects or theoretically dismisses."[52] The language of ontology doesn't quite help, for if it was initially meant as a philosophical reverberation of the worldquakes occasioned by ethnographic differences in the concrete, its generalization has rapidly turned it into its own antidote, a new mode of analysis that allows analysts to become *more tolerant*, which is to say, better able to withstand the tremors that such forms of togetherness make felt.[53] If, for a while, the language of ontology did raise the conceptual stakes of the feeling of difference in the concrete, its generalization turned it into a problem we already have the tools to handle,[54] into an "equivocation" we can learn how to "control," even when the act of controlling it is deliberately designed to jolt our forms of representation, even when it controls the tremors only "in the sense that walking may be said to be a controlled way of falling."[55] Having learned how to walk the tightrope of multiple ontologies, we are in danger of returning to the habit of not letting ourselves be perplexed, of not encountering anything capable of making us fall.

This is why, as we resume our wandering around the day in eighty worlds, the following story seems all the more precious, all the more generative and generous. This story, much more complex than I can here convey, has been recounted various times, always slightly differently. And it is relayed not by the father of the symbolic anthropology with which, in a previous chapter, Harry West sought to address the Muedans and their sorcery-lions, but by *another* Turner: his wife Edith, who after Victor Turner's death decided to return to the same place in Zambia where they had done fieldwork together in order to learn more about a particular kind of healing practice known as Ihamba.[56] The practice of Ihamba consists of treating an affliction, by the same name, that is produced when a patient has been "bitten by the tooth of a dead hunter, an object normally kept as an amulet helpful for hunting. When the tooth is neglected," Turner recounts, "it enters someone's body and travels along the veins, biting and inflicting a unique disease. The thing is both a spirit and a tooth," and it is "removed by means of cupping horns after a lengthy ritual."[57] Turner went back to the village in Zambia where she had lived with her partner thirty years earlier, but as she partly knew, and quickly found out, nothing returns save difference itself. This time, she was returning without "Vic," the partner through whom her "academic world" had been mediated for so long, yet who also had indeed, Edith recognized, "treated Ihamba as a ritual of psychology" that was "performed under the aegis of an African traditional doctor extremely skilled in social psychology."[58] It is not that Victor was immune to worldquakes. But neither could he resist the temptation to withstand the tremors. His "thought often changed," Edith wrote, and "he used to be on the watch for psychologically derived behavior, yet had his own visionary experiences that he could not help but trust."[59] For her part, she was neither able nor "willing to push what happened to one side," and found herself involved, quite irresistibly, in a very "different kind of anthropology" that would need to "regard the field subjects' criterion of truth" not simply as their own, but "as a fundamental one."[60] And she did so precisely so as to be able to relay the story of what happened to her: the felt togetherness with a visible spirit from among the Ndembu of Zambia.

It wasn't just her own personal situation that was different, however. In the intervening thirty-odd years since her previous visit, Zambia was a different place as well. In the 1950s the Ndembu were under the "absolute" rule of the British colonial government, "headed locally by an English District Commissioner and implemented by the traditional chiefs under a cunning system of 'indirect rule.' Medical facilities were exiguous, and the infant mortality rate stood as 250 per thousand."[61] While the radical neglect of the British Empire for its own colony had paradoxically "enabled the system to continue much as it had done for thousands of years, thus keeping the ecological balance," what the British "bequeathed to the Zambians before they left was their 'civilized' value system so that in both urban and rural milieux an overriding desire for Westernization took hold of people."[62] Independent Zambia fell prey to the neocolonial capitalist supply chains that captured so many countries in the Global South that relied on a single main form of production, consisting of supplying raw materials to the North: "that of collapsed prices resulting in economic disaster." In Zambia, Turner writes, "what happened was partial layoffs in the copper mines and the closing of many of the factories that produced consumer goods, while on the farming front there were insufficient funds for fertilizers with which to replenish the depleted arable soil to supply the cities with food."[63] The rippling effects of the copper crash resulted in uncontrolled processes of deforestation, even higher rates of both mortality and birthrates, and generalized food shortages.

When Turner returned in 1985 alongside her assistant, Bill, some of these transformations had affected the Ndembu's practices of healing as well. Marginalized by the missions and government schools, they "persisted in an underlevel of the community" in which healing rituals were increasing "despite the fact the assisting ancestor spirits had been branded as demons by the missionaries (who were wondering why the young no longer respected authority)." Indeed, Turner notes that "indigenous doctors had been improving their techniques during these years, gauging well which cases would respond to African treatment and which would not, and were curing a greater proportion than formerly. Perhaps owing to lack of laws and control, there was a chance for these skilled people to experiment, develop, become more sure in their spirit work,"[64] while people "sought treatment in the village or hospital according to the kind of disease, 'African' or 'European,' without much soul-searching about what was 'right,' just what would work."[65] Unlike modern medicine, whose foundation as a rational practice instills in it the expectation that what works somewhere must work everywhere, these practices of healing did not disavow their own situated efficacy.[66] Even when they were dealing with spirits, Turner suggests, the rituals were thoroughly pragmatic, and they "were popular because they worked."[67]

The transformations of Zambia and its healing practices during that time did not, however, corrode the trusting relationships that had been cultivated between herself and the Ndembu in the past. A shared memory wove them together: "Their past was my past."[68] If anything, their relationships were now "more normal, less constrained by imperialism than in 1951."[69] Thus, when the moment came a few weeks into her stay, and she met Fideli and Singleton, the two Ihamba doctors whose practices she hoped to "sense and perhaps at last to describe them for what they were,"[70] they asked her not simply to be an observer of their practices but to actively participate together with them, as another *chiyanga*, or doctor. A veritable ensemble of relays was formed between them. What's more, during both her earlier and later visits Turner had borne witness to several Ihamba rituals, and those earlier experiences had of course raised their own problems and demanding questions, not least concerning the curious nature of the ihamba itself: intractably ambiguous, at once a spirit belonging to a dead hunter and a material tooth capable of navigating through the patient's bloodstream, hiding under their fingernails, afflicting their body with pains and aches, potentially flying out during an extraction ritual and affecting other people unless caught by the doctors. A spirit that can be *persuaded* to come out, that can "*smell* castor oil leave and mukosu soap tree bark, and *doesn't like* them and *fears* them"; that "*wants* to be fed on blood"; that "*tends* to fly away, and therefore, the doctors take trouble to make it *honest*" so that "it *permits* us to catch it."[71] An ihamba, she thought, "has its own personality, like that of a different species—wild, unpredictable, grotesque, and dangerous."[72] Turner had indeed engaged in a kind of ontological experimentation *avant la lettre*, wondering whether the very "waywardness" of this being "makes it the very embodiment of the uncertainty principle."[73] She observed the extent to which the West's "logicality of officialdom and its law of noncontradiction has ridden roughshod over many delicate intuitions and modes of thought that hinted that ambiguous definitions *were* possible."[74]

The conceptual elaboration of the ihamba's fundamental ambiguity wasn't pointless. It allowed her to cultivate a certain disposition that added to the generative weaving of trust between them. Indeed, both Singleton and Fideli were quite aware that Turner *knew* their practices worked. But at the same time, this remained an abstract ambiguity, allowing for the conceptual *possibility* of a spirit-being about which she had heard but whose mode of existence could not easily be accommodated within a modern ontological framework, save perhaps for some metaphorical borrowings from quantum physics. And yet, as she very often points out, practices are "effective when performed, not read as in this passage."[75] Indeed, none of those ontological adjustments, quantum metaphors, and written passages could have prepared Turner for what she experienced during the second ritual in which she participated in 1985. As she put it, on the day that Fideli and Singleton told her they'd be performing an ihamba on Meru, a fifty-five-year-old woman who was suffering severely from pains associated with ihamba, Turner didn't know—indeed, couldn't have known—what she "was in for."[76]

As was common, they began early in the day, summoning the spirits while foraging for the right medicines, a task which massive deforestation of the Zambian bush had significantly complicated. What's more, this had to be done *well*, weaving a complex ensemble of relays that involved not only doctors and patient, not only the others that gathered together to accompany the ritual, but also the plants, roots, trees, the resounding drums, the spirit in question, as well as other doctor ancestors without whom the practice of extracting the ihamba would not be possible. Plants had to be cut with great care, not to let leaves fall on the ground, and the site of the ritual had to be arranged in a very particular way. Thus, when they eventually found a *mufungu* tree,[77] Singleton "squatted down before the base of the tree trunk and took out his mongoose skin bag from which he drew a lump of red clay; he rubbed this in a broad vertical line," Turner writes, "down the west side of the trunk, then in a line from the foot of the tree to himself, and then on the east side of the tree." He drew those lines "to call ihamba to come soon, directing it along the lines,"[78] as when this is performed the persuadable ihamba knows that it is soon going to be out of the patient.[79]

After a few hours of searching for and collecting the medicines, marking the *mufungu* tree, and making all other necessary preparations, Meru was taken to the designated site, and a crowd began to form around it. The drums started playing, and with them the ritual commenced. The first step was to medicate the doctors with some of the herbal tea they had prepared, to protect them from the ihamba in case it managed to fly out of Meru's body and enter one of them. They then made some small cuts into Meru's back, from which the ihamba was to be extracted with the help of cupping horns. A long and difficult time followed, during which Singleton and Fideli, with the help of Turner and the other doctors, sought unsuccessfully to extract the ihamba from Meru. It just wouldn't come out. Unsure of what was wrong, Singleton and Fideli started to get anxious. Hours into the process, the group had increased to a crowd of about thirty people, and a "young woman with an armful of school books passed behind the crowd, saw what was going on, and gave a sniggering laugh. She went right on walking. Anger rose within me. Snob! I thought."[80] Tensions were high. The crowd had started to get tired, and their singing was waning. After painstaking efforts that availed nothing, Singleton realized they had made a mistake: the ihamba was supposed to leap out of the body like the sun rises from the east, and yet "Meru had been put facing west, and she still was." Quickly, they rearranged the whole site, sitting her facing east, and moving the spirit house, basket pans, mortar, and receiving cans to the other side, such that "the scene was exactly the same only in reverse."[81]

That changed everything. The drums thundered, the ritual grew to its maximum potency, and, overwhelmed by the intensity of the situation, Turner began to cry:

> And just then, through my tears, the central figure swayed deeply: all leaned forward, it was indeed going to be it. I realized along with them that the barriers were breaking—just as I let go in tears. Something that wanted to be born was now going to be born. Then a certain palpable social integument broke and something *calved* along with me. I felt the spiritual motion, a tangible feeling of breakthrough going through the whole group. Then Meru fell—the spirit event first and the action afterward. . . . Suddenly Meru raised her arm, stretched it in liberation, and I *saw* with my own eyes a giant thing emerging out of the flesh of her back. This was a large gray blob about six inches across, a deep gray opaque thing emerging as a sphere. I was amazed—delighted. I still laugh with glee at the realization of having seen it, the ihamba, and so big! We were all just one in triumph. The gray thing was actually out there, visible, and you could see Singleton's hands working and scrabbling on the back—and then the thing was there no more.[82]

Turner sat back, breathless. She had brushed against the presence of the ihamba in the concrete, and "it was something not coming from me, not coming from them, but happening to all of us together."[83] The worldquake was irresistible. There were no modern tools capable of withstanding the tremors such a form of togetherness precipitated. No amount of concepts, gestures, and operations could accommodate, rationalize, or tolerate the sensible perception of a six-inch gray spirit coming out of Meru's back. Its presence could not be mediated away. For indeed, the "perception was, unmediated, immediate, direct,"[84] and it fell upon Turner's conceptualization very much like those other worldquakes fell upon James's, with a mix of glee and admiration at their very happening, and an inescapable sense that "this department of nature" was meant "to remain *baffling*."[85] Her world trembled like the moon on water. The day had gone quiet, and, through her tears, she could hear the insistence of pluriverse beating.

A metaphysical indetermination indeed. Prompted by an immediate and irresistible difference, the worldquake generated problems rather than solutions. For the feeling of another world as it passes into one's experience "leaves a door unlocked."[86] Of course, modern lessons came thundering down, doing their best to keep the door shut. Turner experienced a disturbing sense of distress, and wrote in her notes at the time that something "is trying to stop me. The devil disguised as Christianity is furious that I have found him out. 'We are not ready for your universalisms,' he says. 'It is not time. Quick! Back to your old beliefs. You never saw a spirit.'"[87] But she *did*. What she had experienced, she had experienced. This difference had made itself felt with a force no devil, Christian or modern, could resist. Unable to put what happened to one side, Turner quickly became aware that what was at stake in such an event of togetherness could not be dealt with by an effort to perfect "the method of symbolical analysis, the meaning of the ritual, not even the style of the report itself." Her modern, secular, Christian world was quivering as it brushed against the feeling of difference in the concrete. And this worldquake posed a baffling question: "What is actually going on here?"[88] What is reality capable of? The ihamba could not be consulted on it, for very quickly "the thing was no more."[89] As such, it would not take part in *her* problem, but its irresistible presence was one that no formulation of the problem, and no answer to it, could ignore. The reality of a visible, six-inch spirit that is both gaseous and material, spirit and tooth, and can be persuaded to come out of someone's back, one moment here the other gone, may certainly sound irrational. What's more, it may seem *impossible*, for its intranslation creates a radical indeterminacy: a trembling of togetherness from which nothing follows as a matter of logic or necessity, but which confronts everything with the imperative of a response, the need to contend with the difference that this irresistible difference has made.

Which is to say that a worldquake dramatizes the *radical contingency* of any and all responses to the feeling of difference in the concrete. "After all that reason can do has been done," James wrote, "there remains the opacity of the finite facts as merely given, with most of their peculiarities mutually unmediated and unexplained."[90] An ever-trembling stream of differences all the way down. Quivering at their core, there are no principles capable of providing a foothold, of restoring to reality a unity other than that of its partial and loose, manifold connections. This is why the only "rational" explanation that could be given to the feeling of reality in the plural, the most "parsimonious" one, as Turner says, would be none other than that which puts modern rationality out of its depth and affirms that, indeed, "it is what it is,"[91] that these "spirits actually exist."[92] A parsimonious explanation it would certainly be, for it "would account for the importance placed upon the rituals by [Turner's] consultants and it would also account for [her] own experience."[93] But this most radically empirical of explanations would also turn the very *function* of a rational explanation on its head, providing no intellectual satisfaction, no reordering of differences within a more encompassing whole. What it precipitates instead are the indeterminate effects of a pluralistic intranslation: the introduction of a generative divergence, the turbulent feeling of reality feeling like itself. These spirits actually exist: what is reality capable of?

The trembling of togetherness, in other words, does not tell us how to respond to the feeling of difference in the concrete. It implicates us in a living moment whose function is as perplexing as it is intense: that of confronting us with the pragmatic problem of "granting consent to one possibility and withholding it from another, to transform an equivocal and double future into an inalterable and simple past."[94] It situates us, those who are hesitating, in a such a way that a response is at once imperative and radically contingent, without warrant or foundation. The question is not, cannot be, whether to respond or just to "tolerate," for tolerance is itself a response, one that seeks to withstand the tremors and withholds consent from the insistent possibility of the pluriverse itself. With tolerance, there will be no there there. But neither can it be a matter of "translation," for what is there to translate when the impossible implicates the translator herself? The imperative of translation may indeed be a modern, disciplinary one, but here it would be not a case of *"traduttore, traditore,"* a choice between betraying either the language of origin or of destination. At best, it might be a choice between translating and *intranslating*: making language—the only one she has—stutter, allowing it to grow from the middle of the worldquake like "a pure dance of words" that activates "an affective and intensive language, and no longer an affectation of the one who speaks."[95] Hence the need for Turner to briefly ruminate on another question: "Have I left the field of anthropology entirely by asking the first question?"[96]

But it is not simply the field of anthropology that is at risk. For addressing the feeling of this difference in the concrete can neither be simply a question of coming up with an equanimous response, one that might finally succeed in conceptualizing the nature of reality *in general* in such a way that puts us all, analysts, Ndembu, and spirits, on equal footing. Rejecting the colonial, geopolitical asymmetries of modern realism does not automatically make "symmetry" a shared endeavor.[97] Learning to trust requires that these asymmetries be rejected, so that the trust of a held-out hand may become capable of repatterning our connections along pluralistic lines. But those asymmetries cannot be rejected *in the name* of those with whom we would dream of being connected otherwise. While the worldquake is generated by our experience of togetherness, that doesn't make it *their worldquake*. They do not become our shareholders, nor do we become their spokespersons. And learning "to recognize and value such difference," Helen Verran suggests and I agree, "learning to refuse the step which requires a colonising reduction to a shared category, an acceptance that we may not be metaphysically committed to a common world"—and also that we may not be equally committed to metaphysics—"is what is involved in a postcolonial impulse."[98]

This is what is involved in a pluralistic impulse, too. Indeed, if pluralism dramatizes the moment in which we brush against the feeling of difference in the concrete, it makes present that, whatever its eventual formulation and whatever its contingent answer, the problem of what is going on, of what reality is capable of, has to be posed "in company with the spirits who are comrades in proposing ideas and marching ahead of us."[99] Thus, to grope for another way of posing the problem in their company, in response to our togetherness, is to affirm that no pluralistic response can ignore their presence. The spirits' propositions fall upon our conceptualizations in the form of problems with which *we*, those who are left trembling as they pass, are moved to experiment. Doing so in their company, therefore, is to expose our decisions to their presence. It is to attempt to make our language stutter so as to convey, in a dance of words, what our stories and concepts may do to their ongoing insistence. Which is to say that when a worldquake makes us tremble, experimenting with all doors and windows open means giving to the trembling of togetherness the power to transform our concepts, to render us capable of telling our stories otherwise. For it is the feeling of reality in the plural that "brings an element of concrete novelty into our experience."[100] And it is that element of concrete novelty that, if allowed, might inspire a conceptual invention capable of *dramatizing* our tremorous experience, of bringing "far bits together and separat[ing] near bits," of jumping "about over its surface instead of plowing through its continuity." It is that trembling togetherness that may enable us to make the insistence of the pluriverse felt and to ask it to "tell us whither it is bound."[101] And if stories and concepts "not only guide us over the map of life, but we *revaluate* life by their use,"[102] allowing this trembling togetherness the capacity to have us inventing them anew may in turn precipitate new transitions, generate other connections and alliances, and transform the kinds of relations we are and could be in—it may perhaps help us cultivate ways of inhabiting our present otherwise.

But it is an experiment indeed, without warrants or guarantees, and without any form of authority capable of legitimizing the adventure or ensuring how its consequences may be received. Alas, it may fail. What's more, there is no way of telling, in advance, "how much more outcry or how much appeasement comes about."[103] The ongoingness of the pluriverse itself will be at stake, and just as there are novelties, there will be losses. There's something tragic in every decision, and "shipwreck in detail, or even on the whole," James wrote, "is among the open possibilities."[104] The pluriverse is no ecumene, and something will always be left out—ever not quite. Which is why a runaway metaphysics cannot but keep stuttering out its most humble needs like a foolish little child in the eyes of reason, groping for possibles we dimly envisage but do not quite understand, until we fall asleep. Its last question, the final test of each of its experiments around the day in eighty worlds, cannot but be, again and again, a radically *pragmatic* one: what differences does this response make? With our conceptual additions, does the pluriverse "*rise or fall in value? Are the additions worthy or unworthy?*"[105]

CHAPTER FIVE · Pragmatism in the Wake

The really vital question for us all is, What is this world going to be?
What is life to make of itself? The centre of gravity of philosophy must
therefore alter its place. The earth of things, long thrown into shadow
by the glories of the upper ether, must resume its rights.

WILLIAM JAMES

Using all your sensitivities, melting together you spin tales for the
future. "Don't think. Feel!! Creation and Act!!"

REVEREND TAIO KANETA

TO BELIEVE IN THE WORLD · In this tremorous cosmos, worlds hang by
a thread. Indeed, this many-storied universe might itself be likened to an
unfinished fabric of which each thread tells a separate tale; where each
thread leans on other threads, which on the whole amount to no whole
and lean on nothing. The threads interlace and interweave with one another; they form knots of various degrees of strength and propagate vari-
able forms of influence and power through and over others. But a knot is
a weaving-together of divergent threads. And just as they knit and tangle themselves together, just as new threads develop and spin themselves
through the fabric of things, the weavings tremble, the seams burst. Just
as there's weaving, there's tearing—threads are added and are knitted in,
and others are strained, snapped, and lost. If each thread tells a story, it
is also the case that in "point of fact all stories end," and since there is an

after to every ending, "here again the point of view of a many is the more natural one to take."[1] The buzzing and bubbling of reality feeling like itself in the plural is what worldquakes make felt. They dramatize the fact that novelty and loss often come in one and the same breath—the quivering of our world as the feeling of another world passes into our experience.

Countering the hubris of our modern tales of progress and triumph while simultaneously messing up our narratives of romantic resistance and cosmopolitan reconciliation, worldquakes dramatize the tragic fragility of the pluriverse's threads: the inextricable fact of chance and contingency, of paradox and ambiguity, of generative yet unwieldy worlds gone and to come; the fact that no world is immune to destruction, to the vicissitudes of its unwritten fate, to the differences it has made and have been made to it in turn; the fact that between knowledge and ignorance, between action and passion, between achievement and failure, between possibility and catastrophe, there is no opposition but multiple *appositions*—ongoing and unfinished variations, stories within stories, vertiginous risks. It's the risks, after all, that make the runaway experiment in going around the day in eighty worlds a veritable adventure in divergence. Bar the possibility of going astray, and you wish the adventure away.

What is the world going to be? At each turn, this ongoing and unfinished pluriverse brushes against its bygone and possible ends. A more hazardous cosmos has never been invented, not least because the pluriverse is no armchair metaphysician's invention but the name for a bubbling and buzzing problematic that pushes the very meaning of "cosmos" over the brink, into an irrepressible plurality of partial and fragile connections and disconnections, folds and snags, achievements and tragedies. Indeed, were the pluriverse a proposition put forth to us by some mythical author, the proposition might, James speculatively suggested, sound something like this:

> "I am going to make a world not certain to be saved, a world the perfection of which shall be conditional merely, the condition being that each several agent does its own 'level best.' I offer you the chance of taking part in such a world. Its safety, you see, is unwarranted. It is a real adventure, with real danger, yet it may win through. It is a social scheme of co-operative work genuinely to be done. Will you join the procession? Will you trust yourself and trust the other agents enough to face the risk?"[2]

No romanticism, no promise of salvation, and no guarantee of safety or peace can protect us from the risks we run in consenting to join in the adventure. If it requires a terrible leap into a world in which we trust others to meet our jump, then falling down the abyss is entirely within the possible outcomes. And yet, the alternative is a reality given entirely in advance, a reality so ready-made, so perfectly self-contained, that no difference can be felt, and no difference can be made. What to do save risk ourselves, trusting that something might be gained? "Would you say that, rather than be part and parcel of so fundamentally pluralistic and irrational a universe, you preferred to relapse into the slumber of nonentity from which you had been momentarily aroused by the tempter's voice?"[3]

What's more, today the stakes seem especially high. At this time that is ours, the ground beneath our feet is already beginning to crumble. Piling on the rubble of the colonial ecumene, on the belly of the ship, the present is now marked by poisonous patterns of ecological devastation accomplished in a "terrifying communication between geopolitics and geophysics" that, as Déborah Danowski and Eduardo Viveiros de Castro have rightly observed, "contributes decisively to the collapse of the fundamental distinction of the modern *episteme*: the distinction between cosmological and anthropological orders, for so long (that is, at least since the seventeenth century) divided by a double discontinuity, of both essence and scale."[4] Which is why, as the modern world begins to crumble under the pressure of its own imperial weight, the pluralistic proposition demands to be relayed today once again, while we still can (jump)—not as a vanguard project, but as a genuine option, a generative if risky opening, proffered in the ruins of a postcolonial present whose dreams of innocence and redemption are now put tragically to the test, with no standing place outside the challenge this all-too-probable ending creates.[5] Yet if the proposition may still insist in the ruins, if it demands to be relayed in spite of all, it is also because pluralism cannot constitute an opening without simultaneously accepting an inexorable constraint—that of learning to affirm the precarious fragility of any "after" it may perhaps manage to precipitate, of consenting to the generative weavings *and* the devastating disasters that contingently bind human purposes to more-than-human problems no utopian ideal can effectively dissipate. Ever not quite!

Damning all great empires, including that of the Absolute, "ever not quite" is the cry, the deep howl that precipitates, again and again, the stuttering of the question *What is reality capable of?*, and propels a pluralistic realism to stay to hear the multifarious responses around the day in eighty worlds. And it is the generative echoes of this cry that make James's and Deleuze's proposition *to believe in the world* reverberate through our al-

liances as a veritable call to pluralistic arms: a call for a runaway metaphysical and political experimentation to be done, in the company of other
worlds, with the trust of a held-out hand. But no triumphalism, no striving
for transcendence, is ever implied. "'Ever not quite,'" wrote James, "has to
be said of the best attempts made *anywhere* in the universe at attaining
all-inclusiveness."[6] If this goes for modern monification, it also goes for
those who dream of a Great Community to come, of a good common world
we might all one day call home.[7] As such, "to believe in the world" is not
to believe in some messianic world that might save us from the one we've
got. By contrast, to believe in the world is above all to believe in *this* world,
in the many and the one, in other worlds in this world, in their intensities
and possibilities, in what it may still be capable of in spite of all. Rejecting
all transcendental horizons, it is the name for an immanent, *interminable
task*, the most essential task "that our lives in this world have to perform."[8]
And if to believe in the world is simultaneously the most difficult task, as
Deleuze reminded us, it is also because this immanent task *binds* us to this
world, to its gains as much as to its losses, to its achievements as much as
to its failures, to its possibilities as much as to its tragedies. To believe in
the world, therefore, is the task that those who seek to inhabit our world
otherwise carry out *in the wake*: in the wake of the world we have lost, of the
worlds we have brought to an end as a result; in the wake of the devastation
that our modern dreams of progress and our imperial projects of world-
monification have brought about; in the wake of the dreams that have
never come to pass; in the wake of the worldquakes that make our desolate
world quiver, that make us hesitate, that make our reasons tremble; in the
wake of realities fantastical, divergent and abandoned, risking ourselves
from moment to moment, casting our lot with the fragile indeterminacies
opened up by divergent worlds in this world.[9]

To believe in the world, in other wor(l)ds, is therefore the name for a
pragmatic wager we might make from the rubble, at our own risk, while we
still can: a wager on the chance of snatching a possibility from the claws of
catastrophe, of rendering one another capable of spinning our tales otherwise, of generatively reweaving the threads, of composing worlds otherwise in the wake. I call this wager pragmatic because pragmatism, that
"oddly-named thing" that James associated with his philosophic method,
has in fact *always* been proffered in the wake.[10] Despite what many of those
who have come after James would have us assume, it is not simply out of
some capricious instrumentalism, out of some philistine disdain for the
philosophical "glory of the upper ether," that one asks of every idea and of

every concept that it consents, that it subjects itself—its very meaning, significance and truth—to the question "*What difference will it make?*"[11] To seek to cultivate pragmatism as an art of consequences, as an attitude "of looking away from first things, principles, 'categories,' supposed necessities" and "towards last things, fruits, consequences, facts,"[12] constitutes neither a gratuitous move, a clever game, nor merely a matter of reminding philosophy—though it may well need the reminder now and again—that it bakes no bread.[13] Rather than an arbitrary philosophical choice, I suggest that pragmatism cannot be dissociated from the dramatic force that brings it into existence as a "way of just seeing and feeling the total push and pressure of the cosmos," of responding to its "problematic thrill," of sensing "the presence of its vastness" in the wake.[14] For this problematic thrill was and still is generated by nothing other than a series of worldquakes, by seeking to think in the presence of an insistent pluriverse that witnesses the Earth—one collective name for our multiple and divergent modes of togetherness—resume its rights, and pressures thought to take the risk of believing in the world otherwise.

Philosophically, James suggested, pragmatism was born in the wake of "the break-down" which the end of the nineteenth century "brought about in the older notions of scientific truth." It was the truly effervescent plurality of scientific hypotheses and experiments, the profusion of "so many geometries, so many logics, so many physical and chemical hypotheses, so many classifications, each one of them good for so much and yet not good for everything," that precipitated a running of the tremors through any and every sense that it was the one Christian "God that geometrizes," having Euclid as his mere scrivener; that there was "an eternal and unchangeable 'reason'"; that there were invariable laws of nature or perennial natural classifications; that the "anatomy of the world is logical, and its logic is that of a university professor."[15] The many brought *that* rationalistic story of unshakeable truth to an end. But the worldquake was more than philosophical; it was political as well. As others have shown, the progressive constitution of the American empire, its tragic annexation of the Philippines, its role in the Spanish-American War, and its reaction to the Dreyfus affair all weighed heavily on James's thought and heart.[16] And as he said of "the army of suicides" when considering the question of whether life is worth living, the presence of all those others that have been lost, their realities and differences and worlds, is one that those who take the risk of believing in the world must honor in their wake—they "forbid us to forget their case."[17]

It is in the wake of this tragic push and pressure of a wide-open and tremorous pluriverse, therefore, that James turned away from any dream of a modern philosophy that would come up with words capable of speaking in the universe's name. For if pragmatism asks of our ideas to take the risk of attending to the difference they make, it is because in a tragically fragile and unfinished universe ideas do not simply mimic, represent, or give an account—they enjoin the adventure. As such, nothing can erase the debt that binds our choices and propositions to the consequences they might be capable of precipitating. Giving to what makes our worlds tremble the power to make us think, to craft our stories otherwise, we risk ourselves at every twist and turn, with every speculative throw of the dice, spinning tales for the future without being able to tell, in advance, whether these futures will prove themselves worthy or unworthy; whether these intranslations, these metaphysical indeterminations, will regenerate our imaginations or compound the devastation of a reality felt like itself, in the plural. But risk themselves they must, regardless. The Earth has resumed its rights, and it's beginning to rumble.

A METAPHYSICAL INCIDENT · It is almost never noted but perhaps not all that surprising that James's lectures on *Pragmatism* begin and end with stories about death.[18] Pragmatism is always in the wake. It surges there where metaphysics and experience join hands, where the question of what reality may become capable of, of what its differences may render possible in the concrete, is no longer a mere expression of idle curiosity but a response to the push of an insurgent political and cosmoecological imperative— to risk it all, wagering on the possibility that not all, in spite of all, will be lost. This, I suggest, is what James means when he writes that, as far as pragmatism is concerned, reality "*is still in the making, and awaits part of its complexion from the future.*"[19] For if reality, feeling like itself, in the plural, is still in the making and may perhaps remain unfinished for as long as it remains ongoing, it is also "at all times subject to addition or liable to loss."[20] Concerned with crafting concepts and stories capable of rendering the future generative of ways "in which existing realities may be *changed*," pragmatism cannot but take these as anything other than *Denkmittel*, as James called them, borrowing from the German: not objects of admiring contemplation, or faithful copies of that to which they refer, but generative *tools* which plunge ourselves "forwards into the river of experience with them," looking for differences, seeking to cultivate the possibility of probing and composing worlds otherwise by their means.[21]

In so doing, pragmatism strips all philosophical principles from their commanding authority. It "unstiffens all our theories, limbers them up and sets each one at work"[22] as vectors of a radical metaphysical adventure: what "afters" might you be liable to generate in the wake of this breakdown? What realities could you be capable of cultivating? What difference will you make? What, through your additions to it, is this world going to be? For this reason, to characterize pragmatism as a mere method of philosophizing, or a quirky theory of truth, is frankly to do it a disservice. When worlds are at stake, pragmatism is above all the name for an *art of living and dying with others in a tremorous cosmos*, in the aftermath of a devastated world, spinning our tales otherwise in appreciation of the precarious fragility both subtending and upending a divergent plurality of worlds. As such, an exploration of the importance of pragmatism in this radically pluralistic adventure cannot but be performed with allies, in the presence of practices that dramatize this art of living and dying with others by having experimentally developed a specific version of it in the wake of a disaster. It is time, therefore, that the arts of noticing resume their work once again, by turning our attention to one of the most dramatic worldquakes this ongoing and unfinished pluriverse has witnessed in recent times, as well as to the pragmatic forms of experimentation that were generated in its wake.

The event in question is one that has come to be known, rather appropriately, as the Great East Japan Earthquake and Tsunami. Striking off the coast of Tōhoku, in northeastern Japan, on March 11, 2011, the earthquake is the biggest to have struck Japan, and the fourth most potent in the history of seismology. Achieving the maximum value of 7 on the Richter scale (and 9.1 in Momentum Magnitude Scale), the earthquake was so powerful that it knocked the Earth 6.5 inches off its axis, and moved Japan thirteen feet closer to America.[23] In the tsunami that followed, an entire area of 217 square miles was flooded, ravaging everything touched by the wave: almost 20,000 people were killed, the lives of countless other critters were brought to a sudden end, and over 45,000 buildings were destroyed. Among those who survived, 4.4 million households were left without electricity, over 340,000 people were displaced and suffered from food, water, shelter, medicine, and fuel shortages for a long period of time afterward, even when enormous material efforts were deployed to restore collective life in the wake.[24] Disclosing the oneness and manyness of the

Earth precisely at the moment when it quakes, the tsunami propagated waves throughout the Pacific Ocean, precipitating other tsunami warnings across at least twenty different countries.[25] What's more, in the days that followed, the wave's effects precipitated the infamous Fukushima Nuclear Disaster, which has tragically poisoned natures, cultures, and a lot more besides until today.

It is in more than one sense, therefore, that this tsunami constituted a veritable worldquake. In his extraordinary study of the aftermath of the tsunami, ally day-traveler Richard Lloyd Parry recounts the story of Ono, a local builder who at the time of the earthquake was working on a house at some remove from the coast. While he did have to cling to the ground for as long as the tremors lasted, the wave didn't reach the area he was working in or the town where he lived with his family, and so he didn't quite become aware of the effects of the tsunami until a few days later, when the television had finally been restored and he was able to watch "the endlessly replayed image of the explosive plume above the nuclear reactor, and the mobile-phone films of the black wave crunching up ports, houses, shopping centres, cars and human figures."[26] The devastation captured by those images was disconcerting for they depicted places "he had known all his life, fishing towns and beaches just over the hills, an hour's drive away." And yet his life had relatively quickly returned to normal, or so it then seemed. No one he knew was dead or hurt, and as such his experience was as much marked by the intimate connections he held with the affected area as by the radical sense of detachment that accompanied his belated witnessing of its devastation. Ono couldn't quite believe what his eyes were seeing, and as he put it, "I hadn't seen the tsunami myself, not with my own eyes, so I felt as if I was in a kind of dream."[27]

This almost oneiric state lasted for about ten days, until Ono decided to drive with his wife and his mother to the affected area, to see for themselves. "For most of the way," Lloyd Parry relates, "the scene was familiar: brown rice fields, villages of wood and tile, bridges over wide, slow rivers." At a certain point, however, everything around them changed. There "was no advance warning, no marginal area of incremental damage. The wave had come in with full force, spent itself and stopped at a point as clearly defined as the reach of a high tide. Above it, nothing had been touched; below it, everything was changed." Ono himself was radically transformed by this experience of finding himself in the ruins, amid the rubble, a witness to the devastation of his world: "It was such a shock to see it," he told Lloyd Parry. "It's difficult to describe. It felt dangerous. My first thought was that this is terrible. My next feeling was, 'Is it real?'"[28] Indeed, what *is* reality capable of? Of what novelties, of what losses, of what transformations? Ono's story makes present that the effects of the tsunami far exceeded the visible, material destruction it brought about. The wave also generated a whole series of metamorphic processes which—to borrow the words of a collective of Japanese activists and scholars writing in the wake of the tsunami and the nuclear disaster—amounted to a "metaphysical incident." Processes whose almost invisible, atmospheric consequences have affected "the very fabric of our reality" and transformed the composition of their world and its modes of habitation: "How to compose a collective after such an event? How is the relationship with the cosmos affected? How to go on living in such a catastrophic environment?"[29]

These were questions asked by many in the wake of the tsunami, as much by the living as by the dead. For one of the transformations that the tsunami left in its wake was the profusion, in increasingly large numbers in the six months that followed the wave, of a multiplicity of stories and experiences of ghost sightings, hauntings, and even possessions in and around the devastated area. "A young man," Lloyd Parry tells us, "complained of pressure on his chest at night, as if some creature was straddling him as he slept. A teenage girl spoke of a fearful figure who squatted in her house. A middle-aged man hated to go out in the rain, because of the eyes of the dead, which stared out at him from puddles."[30] Upon returning from the devastated area, Ono himself woke up the morning after to discover—amid threats of divorce from his wife and visible signs of anger from his mother—that in the intervening night he "had jumped down onto all fours and begun licking the tatami masts and futon, and squirmed on them like a beast."[31] Indeed, it was not just the spirits of humans that started lurking around the area, but also those of dogs, cats, and other critters that had drowned with them as well. Meanwhile, in the city of Tagajo, calls to a fire station were repeatedly made from places where everything had been destroyed by the wave. And yet the firefighters "went out to the ruins anyway"—praying for the spirits of the dead—"and the ghostly calls ceased." In Sendai, the capital of the Miyagi prefecture in the Tōhoku region, a taxi driver "picked up a sad-faced man who asked to be taken to an address that no longer existed." The driver set off with the passenger until, halfway through the journey, he "looked into his mirror to see that the rear seat was empty." On he went nevertheless, "stopped in front of the levelled foundations of a destroyed house and politely opened the door to allow the invisible passenger out at his former house."[32]

This profusion of ghosts in the wake of the tsunami was all the more disturbing in that, according to those polls that social scientists carry out in the hope that they may finally browbeat religion into telling them something about society, Japan features as one of the most "secular" or "ungodly" countries in the world.[33] Indeed, Japan had its own "modernizing process" during the Meiji period, which extended through the second half of the nineteenth century and into the turn of the twentieth. This era, anthropologist Marilyn Ivy writes, was not only marked by an ambitious financial and infrastructural development program, as well as by Japan's own imperialization, but also by a "widespread appreciation of western knowledge," a "single-minded incorporation of western structures and institutions and a bureaucratization of power based on norms of objective rationality; the formation of national compulsory education and conscription incorporated the newly emergent national citizenry (*kokumin*) into ever-widening circles of standardized participation and co-optation in establishing the body politic."[34] If this can be characterized as the "becoming-modern" of Japan, however, it is also because the Meiji period simultaneously involved the invention of a belligerent operation, a new realism that turned ghost stories into signs of superstition and irrational backwardness, into obstacles that the modern project had to eliminate through education and even state legislation, and eventually incorporate into the global political economy of Orientalia.[35]

And yet, it would be wrong to understand this modern-realist operation as the creation of a new state-sanctioned secularism that merely brushed aside religious practices and ghost stories as remnants of a bygone, feudal, and pre-modern past. Talal Asad already warned us of the distinctly Eurocentric character of the concept of religion itself, which performs a universalizing operation of *de-realization* of other worlds, turning them into mere matters of "belief," an anthropological figment of the faithful imagination.[36] In Japan the concept of "religion" was itself *invented and introduced* during the Meiji government, which indigenized this previously nonexistent notion in the course of its ongoing political and trade negotiations with the West. According to religious scholar Jason Ānanda Josephson, this newly invented and indigenized concept made a crucial diplomatic difference to these international negotiations, lubricating trade and foreign relations with the West by enabling, under the guise of a discourse of rights and tolerance, the controlled readmission of Christianity in the island, which had been previously outlawed as a heretical form of Buddhism since the sixteenth century.[37] But this was by no means the only difference that the Japanese notion of religion made. For its reinvention also led to the entangled creation of two other world-altering notions: that of a Shintō-infused secularism—regarded by the Meiji government as something more akin to a science than a faith—which provided the enlightened foundations for a modern model of statecraft,[38] and that of a marginalized category of "superstition," which designated a host of new practices and orthodoxies previously associated with heresy.[39]

It (almost) goes without saying that ghosts—their presences, their realities, their stories—were to be placed in the latter category and therefore became subject to operations of disqualification and psychologization. It is not that ghost stories were outlawed. Rather, they were refashioned,[40] de-realized, turned into symptoms of nervous disorders which, even when capable of producing frightening experiences, were ultimately "fears that could be explained and thus controlled with a newly coined language that represented a newly constructed knowledge." As a result, historian Gerald Figal writes, these techniques of "managing popular beliefs and spirits afforded the 'professors of civilization' a source of power to redefine the psychic as well as the physical reality of the populace, a crucial step in the production of a modern nation-state."[41] As in other "modern" states, care practices were therefore removed from the hands of local practitioners and became centralized, administered by government authorities who would take over the task and promise of guaranteeing the well-being of the individual and the health of the population.[42] As a consequence, the production of a modern nation-state coincided with the ravaging of both local knowledges and their practical arts of living and dying with others, arts and knowledges by means of which people had previously contended with the unsettling presence of ghosts in their midst.[43]

It is thus that, six months after the tsunami, once survivors had managed to settle into temporary housing and became able to face their experiences of loss and the presences, hauntings, and possessions of those who had been lost to the wave, many consulted medical, psychological, and social work practitioners to provide the support they desperately needed. Yet while various kinds of financial and material assistance to survivors were made available by the government, "there was little in the way of formal counselling or mental health-care."[44] What's more, whatever support was provided was indeed approached as "mental health-care," through a host of psychological explanations that sought to treat ghosts as symptoms of post-traumatic disorders or of emotional distress caused by grief. To no avail: despite the modern investment in centralized forms of government and in the rational sciences of health, these modern practitioners could not effectively care for those living with ghosts in the wake.[45] There was no guarantee of well-being in the end. After all, like James said of philosophic rationalism, modern realism "is far less an account of this actual world than a clear addition to it, a classic sanctuary in which the rationalist fancy may take refuge from the intolerably confused and gothic character which mere facts present."[46] And sometimes the mere facts irrepressibly flood the place. Sometimes their confused and gothic character starts boiling over, shaking the sanctuary's foundations, making it quake. Having unraveled vital threads, sometimes modernity itself, alas, comes at a tragic expense.

PRAGMATISM IN THE WAKE · Strained by the making of the modern state and torn by the wave, the remote, marginal, and slightly melancholic region of Tōhoku was left striving in the muddy, ghostly ruins. But while the tsunami brought many stories to an end, no end is absolute—*ever not quite!* The word "and" trails along even the sharpest edges. Ruins always remain, and as James once put it, civilization itself "is founded on the shambles."[47] Even before the tsunami, the region of Tōhoku had a long history of taking care of the dead. And despite the becoming-modern of Japan, the region remained "poorer, hungrier and more backward than anywhere else," characterized by "an impenetrable regional dialect, a quality of eeriness and an archaic spirituality that are exotic even to the modern Japanese."[48] Given the failure of modern healthcare practices to adequately respond to the swarm of ghosts, regional priests of various denominational traditions began to be regularly called upon to quell unhappy spirits. Though their responses were marginally better than those of doctors and psychologists, as at least some priests felt compelled to offer survivors whatever help they could, that was not a very high bar to set. Indeed, many of them did not know how to care for ghosts or for those who bore witness to them, and some simply didn't care.[49] All sorts of scholarly and theoretical discussions ensued among religious practitioners and scholars as to whether or not ghosts *truly* existed, to what extent these may correspond to the Buddhist realm of the hungry ghost, whether these experiences were *really* the spirits of the dead, or whether in fact these stories might be but the product of superstition, manifestations of the Devil, or apparitions of the Holy Spirit. The collective preoccupation, in other words, revolved largely around theological concerns, focused on finding an explanation capable of uniting the profusion of unruly ghosts with the theological order of the One.[50]

Yet it was also from these ruins, in the midst of the rubble, that a divergent collective of priests of various of faiths—Zen Buddhist, Shintō, and Protestant—were forced, gropingly, into developing what deserves to be regarded as a radically pragmatic form of experimentation. For instead of "turning their face towards the absolute," looking for a proposition that could be deemed true insofar as it would "come nearest to symbolizing its ways of uniting the many and the one," they put themselves at risk, experimenting with a reality their efforts could perhaps manage to become true of. This group of priests, in other words, undertook the immanent task of believing in the world, in the intensities and possibilities that fester in the ruins, so as to develop tools with which to "dip back into the finite stream of feeling and grow most easily confluent with some particular wave."[51] The point, as Reverend Taio Kaneta put it, was that the wave had changed everything. Whatever the theological justification for the profusion of ghosts, "what matters is that people are seeing them," and "in these circumstances, after this disaster, it is perfectly natural. So many died, and all at once. At home, at work, at school—the wave came in and they were gone. The dead had no time to prepare themselves. The people left behind had no time to say goodbye." As such, it is "inevitable that there are ghosts."[52] Reality felt like itself, differently, in the wake. Which is why Kaneta and his colleagues had to risk a pragmatic hypothesis, that "there is no difference of truth that doesn't make a difference of fact somewhere":[53] that there is no difference in deciding whether or not these ghosts are real unless, wagering on one option or the other, one becomes capable of crafting responses that are worthy of the new arts of living and dying with others that had to be cultivated in the wake of the disaster, in appreciation of the tragic fragility subtending and upending the worlds of the living and the dead.

They did not come to this hypothesis easily. Indeed, if I say they were *forced* into developing a pragmatic form of experimentation, it is because, once again, pragmatism is always in the wake, and here too it was precipitated, not only in the aftermath of the tsunami, feeling the total push and pressure of a ravaged world, but also as a direct result of the priests' own theological worldquake. After dealing, by whatever means they had available, with an increasing number of people possessed by ghosts, Kaneta gathered a group of fellow priests to perform a ritual march to Shizugawa, "a town almost completely obliterated." As they walked, they bore witness to a landscape that was "broken, and corrupt with decay. Bulldozers had cleared ways through the rubble, and piled it into looming mounds of concrete, metal, wood and tile. The heaps," Lloyd Parry writes, "had been incompletely searched; cadavers were folded inside them, unrecovered and invisible, but obvious to everyone who passed." The whole area smelled of dead bodies and of mud. Multiple mementos of people's lives were scattered around, and the priests had to watch where they stepped "to avoid trampling on photographs." The procession of conspicuously dressed priests treaded carefully through the ruins, "holding aloft a placard bearing characters meaning 'Consolation for the Spirits.'"[54] As they marched, machines were clearing the rubble; workers picked at the debris and waved them brusquely away from the tractor tracks. "The men of religion began to feel self-conscious. They began to suspect that, rather than helping, they were an unwelcome obstruction to the clean-up operation." But the workers weren't alone. Ordinary people were there as well, looking for the bodies of those they had lost. And as they saw the priests passing by, "they turned and bowed their heads. They were praying desperately to find their loved ones."[55] The priests' plan was to chant sutras and sing hymns while they marched. But once there, "their voices failed them. 'The Christian pastor was trying to sing hymns,' said Kaneta. 'But none of the hymns in his book seemed right. I couldn't even say the sutra—it came out in screams and shouts.'"[56] When finally, after four hours of marching, they got to the sea, they just couldn't face it. "'It was as if we couldn't interpret what we were seeing.'"[57]

It was then that they realized that, in the wake of the tsunami, under the full pressure and push of that unwieldy situation, ready-made theological reasons would not help them. For "all that we had learned about religious ritual and language," Kaneta said, "none of it was effective in facing what we saw all around us. This destruction that we were living inside—it couldn't be framed by the principles and theories of religion." More than inadequate, the strictures, religious principles, and theories were *unworthy* of the situation to which they were seeking to respond. Indeed, the priests realized that these principles constituted "an armour which we wore to protect ourselves, and that the only way forward was to take it off."[58] Of course, for this collective of priests, taking the armor off was not a matter of abandoning either their respective faiths or their practices. Though they did come "close to the fear that people express when they say, 'We see no God, we see no Buddha here,'"[59] it wasn't a moment of secular reckoning, when one wonders how a devastated world like this could simultaneously be the creation of an all-loving and fundamentally benevolent deity, and starts treating cases of ghost possessions or sightings as nothing but symptoms of pathological grief. That, indeed, was the medical response already.

But if it wasn't a question of abandoning faith, neither was it a matter of engaging in a form of theological revisionism, asking, like religious scholars had done, what theological principles might justify the devastation or make sense of what these ghosts *really* were. Instead, taking the armor off belonged precisely to the challenge of allowing that disastrous situation to enable them to believe in the world again, to enable them to fabricate a generative response. It was a question of developing means of learning, practically, how to take care of the possible that insisted in its wake, of approaching this ghostly reality as awaiting part of its complexion from a future that could still, in spite of all, be generatively and generously woven, from a world-to-be-made that could still be otherwise composed.[60] Perhaps. That, in any case, was the risk they had to take. They had to risk taking the armor off so as to experiment with arming themselves with something else, with stories, concepts, and practices that would *become* true only insofar as they succeeded in recomposing their world, only so long as they contributed to the cultivation of the arts of living and dying with others that had been lost to modernity and the wave. Consenting to the reality of ghosts, as these priests learned to do, was therefore not a theological revelation, but a pragmatic constraint. It was not a proposition with which one would close some principled quest, but a metaphysical "program for more work," as James would say—an opening and a task, by whose guidance they could enter "the particulars of experience again and make advantageous connections with them."[61] It was a trusting hypothesis whose truth-value had to be borne in the consequences their practices might be liable to make.[62]

It is thus that Reverend Kaneta and his fellow priests set out, practically, to invent means worthy of the plights of the living and of the dead. What to do? "Make a space where people can relax in the midst of the rubble!"[63] They decided to set up an itinerant café which they named Café de Monku, playing on a triple pun: *Monku* is the Japanese word for "complaint"; "monk" is the English term for priest; and it was the improvisational jazz of Thelonious Monk that accompanied their pragmatic experimentation. "It was," Kaneta said, "the perfect music for the occasion."[64] The Café de Monku collective would travel around the devastated area, providing a space for survivors to gather together around tea, coffee, and cakes, to remember the dead and to share their sorrow and their stories with one another. The survivors, then living in temporary residences, would gradually arrive, and once they had gathered, Kaneta would stand up and address the room, welcoming everyone, introducing his helpers, and making some jokes: "'Mr Suzuki is here to give you a massage round the shoulders, if you want one,' he would say. 'Ah, what a massage! You should try it. His massage is so relaxing that you may actually find yourself slipping into the next world. But you needn't worry, if that happens—we have lots of priests on hand.'"[65]

But massages and humor were only *some* of the things on offer. "Pragmatism," after all, "is willing to take anything, to follow either logic or the senses, and to count the humblest and most personal experiences. She will count mystical experiences if they have practical consequences."[66] And so music would be playing, flowers were laid, the scent of incense was in the air. Sutras and hymns would be sung for those who welcomed them; colored cord and beads of glass were provided, and the elderly would be invited to sit on the floor to string Buddhist rosaries; the priests inscribed and blessed memorial tables bearing the names of the dead, for those who had lost both their memorials and their dead to the wave; images of Jizo, a much loved Buddhist divinity whose statues are often found around graveyards, would be made and lined up with a message that read, "We offer these to those who lost somebody dear in the tsunami." On occasion, they would perform the rituals and techniques needed to care for those who had been possessed. Crucially, what began to be cultivated in their pragmatic experiments was a practice of "listening to the heart," a practice of paying attention to the tales of suffering of the survivors, understanding their meaning for each person, and allowing these tales of suffering to render one another capable of crafting "tales for the future."[67]

Café de Monku proved immensely effective. Indeed, in the aftermath of the tsunami, once the victims had been fed, sheltered, and provided other material means, their "spiritual care practices" became an essential emergency measure, not only responding to the overwhelming loss that accompanied life after the wave, but also helping prevent a second catastrophe of less visible consequences associated with increasing experiences of anxiety, depression, and suicide. With the priests' experimental and down-to-earth propositions, the good that the café did "to the tsunami refugees was obvious from their faces. Requests were coming in from all over Tohoku; Kaneta and his priests were setting out their tea and biscuits once a week or more."[68] Eventually, their experiment attracted the interest of the University of Tōhoku itself, which, with the help of Kaneta and others, set up a program in "practical religious studies" that now trains interfaith chaplains in a variety of listening and caring practices oriented toward the specific and situated challenges associated with disaster relief response.[69] But the difference Rev. Kaneta and his colleagues made was far more profound as well. It was at once ecological and cosmological, simultaneously pragmatic, pluralistic, and metaphysical: they began to reweave an art of living and dying with others in the wake.

Their practices of listening to the heart not only involved becoming attentive to people's sorrows, but also understanding "these sorrows from a cosmic perspective." A Buddhist concept, *jita funi*—meaning "self and other: undivided"—allowed this double perspective to generate compassion, feeling-with, and brought them into trusting, practical relationships with the worlds of the living and the dead. "'This universe wraps everything up inside it, in the end,'" Kaneta explained. "'Life, death, grief, anger, sorrow, joy. There was no boundary then, between the living and the dead.'"[70] This and other concepts, deployed as *Denkmittel*, as pragmatic tools, enabled the priests to learn a great deal about ghosts, and about the relationships between the living and the dead, allowing them to reweave new relations between them. For instance, they learned in very concrete terms how certain forms of dying pose their own risk: "When people die violently or prematurely, in anger or anguish, they are at risk of becoming *gaki*: hungry ghosts, who wander between worlds, propagating curses and mischief."[71] And they learned that it is the ghosts themselves that often speak through the suffering of the living, such that in order to address them one must truly learn how to hold a conversation with the dead.

Indeed, some of the ghosts did not even know they were dead. Nowhere was this more evident or more demanding than in Kaneta's experience with Rumiko Takahashi, a young woman who suffered repeatedly from ghost possessions, to the extent that, over the course of a few weeks, Kaneta consoled twenty-five ghosts that had taken hold of her. One of the first ghosts Kaneta had to care for was a middle-aged man who, speaking through Rumiko, "despairingly called the name of his daughter. 'Kaori!' said the voice. 'Kaori! I have to get to Kaori. Where are you, Kaori? I have to get to the school, there's a tsunami coming.'"[72] Kaori had been at school when the wave came. Her father had left work in a hurry and was driving along the coast road to pick her up when the water overtook him. He was intensely agitated, "impatient and suspicious of Kaneta":

The voice asked, "Am I alive or not?"

"No," said Kaneta. "You are dead."

"And how many people died?" asked the voice.

"Twenty thousand people died."

"Twenty thousand? So many?"

Later, Kaneta asked him where he was.

"I'm at the bottom of the sea. It is very cold."

Kaneta said, "Come up from there to the world of the light."

"But the light is so small," the man replied. "There are bodies all around me, and I can't reach it. And who are you anyway? Who are you to lead me to the world of light?"[73]

The conversation went on for two hours, with Kaneta trying to persuade the ghost to come up. Eventually, he asked the ghost to consider the suffering of his living host: "'You are a father. You understand the anxieties of a parent. Consider this girl whose body you have used. She has a father and mother who are worried about her. Have you thought of that?'"[74] After a long pause, the ghost moaned deeply and finally said, "'You're right.'" Kaneta then began chanting the sutra. "He paused from time to time when the voice uttered choked sounds, but they faded to mumbles and finally the man was gone."[75]

This ghost was only one of many, however. Indeed, though most of the spirits taking hold of Rumiko were ghosts of the tsunami, not all were. For the wave had not only devastated the lives of the living, but also the afterlives of ancestors who in March 2011 lost their living to the wave, and as such were cut loose from the care their living descendants regularly provided, snapped from their moorings in their own afterlives. That's why what Kaneta and his colleagues also learned was that caring for the survivors of the tsunami, seeking to recompose their devastated worlds in the wake, required caring for the possibility of caring for the dead as well, of enabling them, through the various practices they wove together, to find a safe path toward the afterlife and to help them recompose their worlds in turn.

Which is to say that, by risking themselves and putting their practices to the test, the collective of priests pragmatically approached their reality from the perspective of what it could still be capable of in the wake. Reweaving the threads of care that the modern state had damaged and the wave had shaken, they confronted the metaphysical and theological conundrum of the reality of ghosts, of the truth of the survivors' experiences, with a pragmatic test, experimenting on their reality while trusting that, were these experiences true, something might be achieved, some consolation might be brought for the spirits of the living and the spirits of the dead. In their itinerant, immanent experimentation, in other words, they therefore dramatized the fact that truth "*happens* to an idea. It *becomes* true, is *made* true by events. Its verity," James proposed, "is in fact an event, a process, the process of verifying itself, its veri-fication."[76] None of this makes sense, of course, so long as we persist in the habit of a modern realism that must torture reality into confessing the *one* true and complete description of the way the universe is. But in a tremorous cosmos, before the insistence of the pluriverse, reality feels like itself, in the plural, always differently in the wake. It grows in spots, here and there, around the day in eighty worlds, and so with it "truth grows up inside of all the finite experiences." One cannot demand one true and complete description of the pluriverse, in other words, because the pluriverse is more than one—a *multum in parvo*, always ongoing, permanently incomplete. Which is why, in the same way, the pragmatist "account of truth is an account of truths in the plural,"[77] of truths in the concrete, of truths in their immanence. Nothing outside of the weaving and tearing, of the tangling and unraveling, can secure them. What is true *of* the pluriverse, what is true *in* it, is whatever enables it to take another breath, allowing the *and* to keep trailing along its shifting edges, enabling us to believe in the world in turn, to trust it in the wake.

Thus, whenever pragmatism is concerned, the function of truth is *existential* before it is cognitive.[78] Indeed, truth means nothing if not the name for "*a leading that is worth while.*"[79] It designates whatever proves itself generative and generous, whatever succeeds in becoming worthy of a reality felt like itself, in the plural, always differently in the wake. So much so that any "idea that helps us to deal, whether practically or intellectually, with either the reality or its belongings"; any idea, in other words, "that adapts our life to the reality's whole setting," that gives to it the power to transform our habits and reweave its threads in the wake, "will agree sufficiently to meet the requirement. It will hold true for that reality."[80] Hence James's insistence that true ideas aren't paper copies of a reality to which they would be said to correspond, but wholehearted additions to it. For the *happening* of truth does not obtain without a transformation of the world, without the *co-responsive* weaving of a reality which these additions could be true of.[81] Which is to say that the art of pragmatic truth-making belongs to the always unstable, pluralistic, and experimental task of weaving together the multifarious "feelings of *and*" with the speculative "feelings of *if*." It is the art of learning to inhabit the problem of the one and the many, in its viscosities and its openings, in its losses and its novelties, so as to intensify the possibles that, like throbbing pulsations of an ongoing and unfinished reality awaiting responses from the future, fester in its interstices and insist therein.

The priests, for their part, understood this well. They understood that there is no point in pondering over the reality of ghosts, or on the truth of ghost stories, unless one also becomes capable of crafting responses that could render the living and the dead capable of response in turn, unless one becomes capable of crafting stories for a future worthy of new arts of living and dying with others in the wake of the disaster. They understood, therefore, that because the function of truth is existential before it is cognitive, the true is *"one species of good*, and not, as is usually supposed, a category distinct from good, and co-ordinate with it."[82] Indeed, by experimenting with the reality of ghosts, with the truth of stories told both by the living and by the dead, Kaneta and his colleagues sought to experiment with their own feeling of *if*: the possibility of spinning tales for a worthy future, tales worthy of the care required by the living and the dead, worthy of the collective effort to compose a world in the wake. And in so doing they *made* those possibilities true. They *verified them* in the differences that these concepts and practices managed to make. They engendered them, with the trust of a held-out hand, in the composition of a world to be made.[83]

It is precisely in this sense, therefore, that we may finally understand James's seemingly glib assertion that pragmatism is "primarily a method of settling metaphysical disputes that otherwise might be interminable."[84] For the "dispute" is no longer a matter of academic discussion among armchair metaphysicians, or even among religious scholars. It is not a question of coming up with a general justification for the reality of ghosts, or for the truth in ghost stories. What's worse, it is the modern habit of approaching these questions as shadows of some theoretical concern that *makes* the dispute interminable. But a pluralistic, runaway metaphysics cannot not speak in the universe's name. Unhinged from general principles, attentive to the feeling of *and*, it proffers itself outward, from the ruins of a devastated world, with the trust of a held-out hand. Thus, if pragmatism can be said to settle the dispute, however momentarily, it is simply because what it wagers on is that, in the face of a devastated world, metaphysics is a *radically practical affair*. The pluriverse, in other words, must be *made*. It grows and unravels as a plurality of divergent practices continue to intervene experimentally in it. And once they have done their task, it insists therein: creating openings, posing problems, intimating possibles unforeseen. Indeed, it is *because* worlds are experimentally done and undone, rather than merely posited or refuted, that they remain fragile, awaiting to receive their ongoing and unfinished touches at the hands of all those who compose them while they still can. The touches may fall short, they may fail, they may contribute to their falsification and unraveling, hindering verification and flourishing. No general principle can protect us from the risks we take. "This is consolation. This is understanding. We don't," Kaneta said, "work simply by saying to people, 'Accept.' There's no point lecturing them about dogma. We stay with them, and walk with them until they find the answer on their own. We try to unthaw the frozen future."[85]

The priests jumped, then, into a world of ghosts they trusted would meet their jump. Sometimes they succeeded, sometimes they failed. At every moment, with every touch, the pluriverse's fate is decided in the risks they take. Which is to say that metaphysical disputes are not over words but over worlds in the wake. They're eminently political, for our arts of living and dying with others are at stake. And they're *metaphysical* precisely in the sense that our political choice, our practical decision, the risk we and others take, "is no longer a question in the theory of knowledge, it *concerns the structure of the universe itself*."[86] What is this world going to be? In the aftermath of the tsunami, many people felt "as if they have staggered into a fantastic land of disaster and pain." Yet the collective of priests was keenly aware that "it is not a place of fantasy. It is the universe we inhabit, and the only life we have on these islands."[87] Fractured by the wave, their task was to experiment, pragmatically, with giving to the disaster the power to enable them to trust the possibility of crafting their stories otherwise. And in so doing, their stories engendered nothing less than what, with James, deserves to be regarded as "one moment in the world's salvation."[88] It is one moment only, of course, without perfect reconciliation or total preservation of all that was. The dead won't come back to life, and neither will the living go back to theirs. There are real losses, and as the Earth continues to rumble, there will be many more. But even without any assurance that it will last a second longer, even when only fleetingly grasped in the course of an interminable and always unstable task to be done, that moment matters. It is for those moments, for their intensities and potentialities, for the differences they might make, that we might risk believing in the world today. For "if reality genuinely grows," may those moments not contribute to its growing? May "it not grow," asked James, "in those very determinations which here and now are made?"[89] It will be said that, in the aftermath of its devastation, experimenting with crafting our tales otherwise will not save the world. Perhaps not. But perhaps, just perhaps, these stories may resonate amid the rumbling noise, "stealing in through the crannies of the world like so many soft rootlets or like the capillary oozing of water."[90] Perhaps they may weave regenerative threads through the desolation of the present, creating an after to this ending, animating other ways of living and dying well with others in the wake.

CHAPTER SIX · The Insistence of the Pluriverse

The worth and interest of the world consists not in its elements, be
these elements things, or be they the conjunctions of things; it exists
rather in the dramatic outcome of the whole process, and in the
meaning of the succession stages which the elements work out.

WILLIAM JAMES

Before going back to sleep I imagined (I saw) a plastic universe,
changeable, full of wondrous chance, an elastic sky, a sun that suddenly
is missing or remains fixed or changes its shape.

JULIO CORTÁZAR

IN THE STILL OF THE NIGHT... · He may have been obsessed with punctu-
ality, and did sustain a pious relationship to the unforgiving machinations
of the clock, but Phileas Fogg learned that weird things happen to time
when one attempts to go around the world in eighty days.[1] To be sure, his
mathematical calculations were nothing if not exact: every potential delay,
every unexpected event, every possible setback, were all accounted for. He
had, after all, bet half of his considerable fortune on the very possibility of
carrying out the trip successfully and getting back to London in time. It
did not matter one bit, therefore, that the train from Bombay to Calcutta
in fact did not—despite what the *Daily Telegraph* had stated—cover the
whole distance, forcing him and Passepartout to travel the missing fifty-
mile stretch from Kholby to Allahabad on an elephant's back. His calcula-

tions had such an eventuality factored into them already. Neither did the fact that he took it upon himself to prevent Aouda, a young Indian woman, from undergoing *sati* make any difference to his estimations.[2] Nor did any of the numerous other obstacles on his way to Yokohama, San Francisco, New York, and Liverpool manage to throw his precisely timed adventure into disarray. Had he not been temporarily jailed, by mistake, upon arrival on English soil, he would've still had enough hours left in his day to reach London in time.

This is perhaps what's extraordinary about the pen of Jules Verne. Were it not for his inimitable storytelling, the reader might have quickly gathered the impression that *Around the World in Eighty Days* was in fact a sort of anti-adventure: an ode perhaps to the modern dream of rational mastery and technical prowess, where every risk can be preempted, where exact calculations triumph with both hands down over the unruly character of worldly events, where we remain entirely unaffected by a world that bears us and through which we pass. It had to be the law, unjustly administered and improperly applied, that finally got in Fogg's way and made him arrive five minutes late. Or so he had thought. Because of course, once released from prison and back in London, he discovered with much astonishment that, *despite* his calculations rather than thanks to them, he wasn't late after all. Nor was he just on time. He had arrived much earlier than his clock-based predictions had assured him he would. It was not, as he thought, the 22nd of December, but the 21st. A whole day had simply vanished. Yet what had interfered here had been neither common law nor the law of numbers but the ongoing push and pressure of the cosmos: the whirl of the Earth in its relations with the sun conspired to make it such that, traveling eastward, he had witnessed eighty sunrises and sunsets where his colleagues in London had only seen seventy-nine.

If by going around the world in eighty days Fogg learned that, unlike him, time is not governed by the needles of the clock, that sometimes it can be both yesterday and tomorrow, consenting to go around the *day* in eighty worlds yields an altogether different set of lessons. In this other direction, in this other sense, it is not the hours but the worldly threads that begin to proliferate, expand, tangle, snap, complicate, and conspire. Going around the day in eighty worlds one learns that other worlds are not only possible but underway, that on a quiet day one might hear them breathing. By contrast to Fogg, one learns that unexpected events, radical differences, extraordinary realities are not mere obstacles that a tightly timed plan can overcome. Whereas "philosophers have always aimed," James protested, "at cleaning up the litter with which the world apparently is filled," these other worlds are "the first sensible tangle," they are precisely that through which one must pass on and through, looking for treasures, for the feelings of difference in the concrete passing into our experience and transforming our world as we pass.[3] They are one and many worlds that lure us into a reality that feels like itself, in the plural, which no abstract principle can ignore; they are the stories through which an indetermination of our modern metaphysical foundations may be brought about; they are the very places where things happen, and from whose interstices a politics of the pluriverse becomes perceptible as a felt possibility in view of which we might speculatively throw the dice. Which is why, in relay and return, one learns to honor the questions and problems without which the adventure would become but an errand that an armchair metaphysics could run. One learns to affirm the openings and worldquakes thanks to which one is always forced to begin again or not at all, looking for an after to every ending, running after every hesitant beginning. Days are much too short, sleep befalls us all, and in the end not one, no one, neither Columbus nor Magalhães, not even Fogg, "ever carried out a plan foretold in all its details," just as no "consciousness ever embraced in a single act of thought the whole."[4] Ever not quite!

And so the formula "The world is One!" turns out to be less an innocent cosmological depiction of the whole than a belligerent "sort of number worship" which this questionable tradition we learned to call "modern" has turned into a machine of war, a belligerent operation with which it disqualifies everyone and everything that would insinuate the possibility of an "or" naming a genuine reality, of an "and" that might just trail along the edges of the One.[5] Trusting the "ors," "ands," and "ifs," risking ourselves with them at every turn, is precisely the challenge. But if it is a matter of taking these feelings seriously so as to make perceptible that nothing makes the "'one' more excellent than 'forty-three,' or than 'two-million and ten,'"[6] in going around the day in eighty worlds one also learns that it is not simply a question of reveling in a celebration of the many, nor one of determining whether this world is *really* forty-three, eighty, one thousand, or two million and ten.

Indeed, it is not even a question of denying that certain forms of oneness do exist. As James noted, there is some *discursive* or abstract oneness by which we can hold "the universe" such that, in name at least, nothing be left out; there is some *continuous* oneness, too, in the sense that we can pass from one place to another without falling off a cosmic cliff; there are some practical forms of oneness that establish "lines of influence"—gravity or heat conduction, say—as well as forms of "generic unity" through which we can, however imperfectly, class things into kinds. Some oneness in things is expressed, for better and ill, by "networks of acquaintance-ship" among people and other beings, forged as human and more-than-human efforts, and "colonial, postal, consular, commercial systems" unify parts of the world and "propagate themselves within the system but not to facts outside of it."[7] In some respects, in some planetary respects, we're all in the same storm, to swim or sink together. But divergence is the very stuff of togetherness, and though we're together in many ways, nothing dominates over everything. As such, there "is no pragmatic meaning in claiming either absolute oneness or absolute manyness for our world. It is partly one and partly many, in the generic sense. We must discriminate the aspects, and follow the unity or the differences alternately, according as our practical interests seem the better served."[8] Monism falls apart at the slightest insinuation of difference, at the slightest challenge to its in-difference. Thus, it is the fact that there is *some* difference that makes *all* the difference.[9]

One *and* many, ongoing *and* unfinished, "the worth and interest of the world," James wrote, "consists not in its elements, be these elements things, or be they the conjunctions of things." *Pace* many a contemporary realist, the adventure consists not in determining whether, in the end, the world is made of substances or of processes, of things-in-themselves or of relational networks, of human significations or of objective determina-tions. The worth and interest of the world exists rather, James insisted, "in the dramatic outcome of the whole process, and in the meaning of the suc-cession stages which the elements work out."[10] Will it rise or fall in value? Will the stages be worthy or unworthy? Stuttering its most humble ques-tion, pursuing its most unprincipled quest, this pluralistic adventure in divergence consists in generatively and generously following the threads of such dramatic process through their myriad folds and snags; it consists in staying with the trouble they generate, with the way in which threads weave and tear, with partial connections made and unmade.[11] It consists in giving to what makes our foundations tremble the power to craft our stories otherwise, in doing one's best to enable the process to take another breath. It consists in risking it all while trusting that differences might be made, that even on a day when we have learned to expect nothing perhaps the sun might set on a place that would no longer be west.

And while moments of salvation and recuperation are indeed possible, there is no promise of perpetual peace in the end. Rejecting all transcendental horizons, the adventure must be carried out immanently, with the trust of a held-out hand, "affirming and adopting a thought which, left to itself, would slip away," but keeping on affirming it at our own risk, while we still can, without seeking justification in the messianic promise of what that other hand stretched back out might yield, or what it might demand of us in relay and return.[12] Indeed, this might well be the challenge of that living pluralistic attitude that James called *meliorism*, which "treats salvation as neither inevitable nor impossible," even when it is never total, even when it is never final.[13] For while the possibility of composing another world *requires* our precursive trust in its making, while it requires our will and energy and effort and our held-out hands, nothing, not all our goodwill nor our best endeavours, will ever bypass the *ifs* and *maybes* that keep this unfinished universe "with doors and windows open to possibilities uncontrollable in advance."[14]

Ongoing and unfinished, the fact is that the experiment of *Around the Day in Eighty Worlds* recalcitrantly escapes every attempt at a conclusion. For as Benjamin Paul Blood—the pluralistic mystic James held in such high regard—once asked: "What has concluded, that we might conclude in regard to it?"[15] Something always escapes in the still of the night. Other worlds are always lurking in the interstices, insinuating myriad metaphysical indeterminations yet to be sensed, troubling every attempt at attaining closure. It is these that prompt us to begin again as they remind us that *beginnings* derive not from origins but from openings, from the gaping open of a many-storied universe that harbors a multitude of endings but resists finality and escapes totality.[16] In the end, in the beginning, the "facts of struggle," wrote James, "seem too deeply characteristic of the whole frame of things for me not to suspect that hindrance and experiment go all the way through."[17]

And if hindrance and experiment go all the way through, weaving multiple stories that begin and end at odd times, the stubborn facts of struggle yield what is perhaps this adventure's most demanding lesson. What they perhaps intimate is that that which, after James, we call a "pluriverse" is not after all the name for an ideal form of togetherness to be attained, the image of a perfected cosmos, of the good common world our collective efforts might eventually make manifest. Perhaps the pluriverse is, in the end, in the beginning, the nickname for a certain "perhaps," for this very *gaping open* at the edge of our present, for this irrepressible swirling and precipitating of differences all the way down and through. Perhaps it is the name for this ongoing and unfinished *insistence* of a possible that remains impossible for us to envisage yet demands a response and keeps us and others in its hold, keeping on together, keeping differences proliferating, pouring over, flooding in. Perhaps it is the name of an insistence that calls for an interminable task, for an ongoing and unfinished *activity* that needs to be done with others, without guarantees, while we still can.

NO WORLD COMES WITHOUT ITS OTHERWISE · This, for now, is the possible in whose hold I dwell. And I dwell in it because I sense that that's what James himself discovered in 1896, in the wake of his own adventure in and out of the Chautauqua Assembly—an educational retreat on the bank of Chautauqua Lake in New York. His was a discovery whose reverberations might well be read today as a little parable on the pluriverse's unrelenting insistence. James had gone "in curiosity for a day," yet ended up staying "for a week, held spell-bound by the charm and ease of everything, by the middle-class paradise, without a sin, without a blot, without a tear."[18] Upon setting foot in that "sacred enclosure," he wrote, "one feels one's self in an atmosphere of success. Sobriety and industry, intelligence and goodness, orderliness and ideality, prosperity and cheerfulness, pervade the air."[19] James was truly enchanted by what seemed like nothing less than "a foretaste of what human society might be, were it all in the light, with no suffering and no dark corners."[20] In Chautauqua, he wrote praisefully and at length:

> You have a town of many thousands of inhabitants, beautifully laid out in the forest and drained, and equipped with means for satisfying all the necessary lower and most of the superfluous higher wants of man. You have a first class college in full blast. You have magnificent music—a chorus of seven hundred voices, with possibly the most perfect open-air auditorium in the world. You have every sort of athletic exercise from sailing, rowing, swimming, bicycling, to the ball-field and the more artificial doings which the gymnasium affords. You have kindergartens and model secondary schools. You have general religious services and special club-houses for the several sects. You have perpetually running soda-water fountains, and daily popular lectures by distinguished men. You have the best of company, and yet no effort. You have no zymotic diseases, no poverty, no

drunkenness, no crime, no police. You have culture, you have kindness, you have cheapness, you have equality, you have the best fruits of what mankind has fought and bled and striven for under the name of civilization for centuries.[21]

James mingled with the crowd, took lessons on bread-making, on walking, on storytelling, attended a variety of sermons, a balloon ascension, a theatre-play. He sailed around the lake and engaged with the monkeys, bears, foxes, and other animals that populated the rich environs—it was all "a real success."[22] Economically equal, socially experimental, intellectually generative, politically peaceful, spiritually ecumenical, ecologically generous, and radically relational, Chautauqua would in many ways constitute a sort of microcosmic omen of a pluralistic "Utopia."[23]

Yet all stories come to an end. Once the visit was over, James hopped on the train back home, and upon "emerging into the dark and wicked world again," he caught himself "quite unexpectedly and involuntarily saying: 'Ouf! what a relief!'"[24] This sigh of relief induced a new experience of astonishment, throwing the very dream of what a world-to-come might be back at him in the form of an insistent problem that refused to go away.[25] There he had been, a witness to "the realization—on a small, sample scale of course—of all the ideals for which our civilization has been striving: security, intelligence, humanity, and order,"[26] only to discover himself longing for nothing other than a crime, a massacre, the "flash of a pistol, a dagger, or a devilish eye, anything to break the unlovely level of 10,000 good people."[27] His experience of astonishment owed precisely to the fact that this wasn't one of those abstract dilemmas one encounters in moral philosophy, where the achievement of collective flourishing is said to rely on the unmitigated suffering of a few, and one is asked to explain what the moral justification for one's choice would be. James was astonished precisely because here there was no moral dilemma, and no justification for his irrepressible desire "for something primordial and savage."

Nothing, no awful injustice, no foundational exclusion, no intrinsic violence lay underneath the constitution of the Chautauqua Assembly, no stern reminder that its accomplishment was but a mirage, an illusion disguising a fundamental atrocity at the heart of civilization. "At Chautauqua," he noted, "there were no racks, even in the place's historical museum; and no sweat, except possibly the gentle moisture on the brow of some lecturer, or on the sides of some player in the ball-field."[28] The ten thousand good people, the animals, the ideas, the atmosphere of inspiration gathered there were by all measures *lovely* indeed. But still, what he felt relieved to abandon was precisely the thorough *absence* of the "heights and depths, the precipices and the steep ideals, the gleams of the awful and the infinite." It was "the atrocious harmlessness of all things," the entirely gracious form of coexistence of everyone and everything in "this city simmering in the tepid lakeside sun." It was, in other words, the thoroughly *unproblematic* togetherness of a community "so refined that ice-cream soda-water is the utmost offering it can make to the brute animal in man."[29]

His own reaction had him hesitating. It forced him into thinking by the shock of his own sense of relief upon finding himself back again "in the big outside worldly wilderness," pondering over what other versions of the good common world, what other forms of togetherness, what other modes of living, might be capable of redeeming life from the insignificance to which the harmlessness of Chautauqua seemed to relegate it. At stake, in other words, was the need to identify a way of living that would consent to the heights and depths, to the drama, to the expressiveness and struggle that he so craved for. One that would allow him to reclaim "the element of precipitousness, so to call it, of strength and strenuousness, intensity and danger."[30] And alas, reclaiming this element of precipitousness required coming to terms with the fact "that life is hard," that there are novelties and there are losses, and that given our "planetary conditions"—his as much as ours—there "is nothing to make one indignant" of that fact.[31] He wasn't joking, therefore, when he suggested that pluralism is "a turbid, muddled, gothic sort of affair, without a sweeping outline and with little pictorial nobility."[32] But the success of Chautauqua could not simply be dismissed, and his acceptance of the dangers of our earthly living bred neither resentment nor the kind of cosmic nihilism that revels in a sense of inescapable suffering. Meliorism, he was keen to stress, is not another word for pessimism. That this is a dangerous planet few could deny, but this observation takes nothing away from the fact that what is indeed "capable of arousing indignation" is the fact that certain ways of ploughing the world have lead so many beings, human and not, "by mere accidents of birth and opportunity," to "a life of nothing else but toil and pain and hardness and inferiority imposed upon them."[33] How to characterize this element of precipitousness, then, without "the need of crushing weaker peoples?"[34] How to do it without sanctioning—let alone celebrating—the suffering of those who are remanded in a life of nothing but suffering?

James developed his meditation errantly, groping experimentally in the dark for other world-visions and modes of living that might be capable of reclaiming that most important element of precipitousness which, he reckoned, would redeem life from its insignificance. And he first found one right there, in the wicked world itself, looking out the window of the speeding train heading toward Buffalo. James was struck by the sight of frantic urban and industrial development, and impressed by the heroism of workers "doing something on the dizzy edge of a sky-scaling iron construction." Recalling his "feeling of awe and reverence in looking at the peasant-women" in Vienna many years before, he began to entertain the hypothesis that the problem with Chautauqua might have been its sheer benevolent gentleness, its middle-class mediocrity. He therefore experimented with the idea it is neither the middle-class paradise of Chautauqua, nor the generals and the poets, that should be lauded for the realization of the ideals of civilization, but "to the Italian and Hungarian laborers in the Subway, rather, ought the monuments of gratitude and reverence of a city like Boston to be reared."[35] And yet, after a long excursus exploring Leo Tolstoy's own romantic ode to working-class life, James couldn't remain quite content with that alternative. The problem insisted and persisted. For any such romanticism, he thought, makes one's "love of the peasant so exclusive, and hardens his heart toward the educated man as absolutely as [Tolstoy] does."[36] After all, though the people of Chautauqua exhibited no sweat and minimal muscular strain, it could not be concluded that they were, for all that, deprived of other, less visible "vital virtues not found wanting when required." James thus concluded that perhaps Tolstoy's ode to the worker's life remained something of a "false abstraction," neglecting the importance of the way in which the element of precipitousness expresses itself in "books" as much as in "dirty boots."

It is thus that he moved to a more generic proposition. That is, the idea that what brings forth the element of precipitousness, in whatever guise it may happen to appear, is above all the cultivation of modes of living, of forms of togetherness, in a manner that is geared toward the striving for some *ideal*, no matter how intellectual or mundane. For indeed, "there is nothing absolutely ideal: ideals are relative to the lives that entertain them."[37] In other words, because the "ideals of other lives are among those secrets that we can almost never penetrate,"[38] James ruminated over the possibility that what at least was not apparent in Chautauqua in spite of all its relational goodness, and what needed not be present in the strenuous lives of the subway laborers by default, is the sense of either an individual or a collective life—with its inner joy, its courage, its pluck and endurance— enjoyed in the entertaining of some novel outlook toward which our actions might be lured. Yet once again he found that this proposition offered no solution to the insistence of the problem that had him ruminating in the first place. For indeed the "more ideals a man has, the more contemptible, on the whole, do you continue to deem him, if the matter ends there for him, and if none of the laboring man's virtues are called into action on his part,—no courage shown, no privations undergone, no dirt or scars contracted in the attempt to get them realized."[39] Alas, it turns out that, on their own, "mere ideals are the cheapest things in life."[40]

Just when this groping experiment appeared by all accounts to be leading nowhere, James turned to his audience with some trepidation, precipitating a radical transvaluation of the terms of the problem itself. As he put it:

> With all this beating and tacking on my part, I fear you take me to be reaching a confused result. I seem to be just taking things up and dropping them again. First I took up Chautauqua, and dropped that; then Tolstoï and the heroism of common toil, and dropped them; finally, I took up ideals, and seem now almost dropping those. But please observe in what sense it is that I drop them. It is when they pretend *singly* to redeem life from insignificance. Culture and refinement all alone are not enough to do so. Ideal aspirations are not enough, when uncombined with pluck and will. But neither are pluck and will, dogged endurance and insensibility to danger enough, when taken all alone. There must be some sort of fusion, some chemical combination among these principles, for a life objectively and thoroughly significant to result.[41]

The answer to the question of what makes life significant, in other words, cannot be found any single mode of living. If what was at stake in his sense of relief after leaving Chautauqua was that element of precipitousness that makes our collective lives a blend of intensity and danger, of hindrance and experiment, one cannot ask "*which* version of the good common world? *whose* mode of living?"—for that chemical combination is not to be found in any single form of individual or collective life, nor in any single vision of the common world to be realized. If his experience at Chautauqua led not simply to a moment of relief but managed to precipitate a new experience of astonishment, it was because the issue was not simply with the particular constitution of Chautauqua, one that some other mode of collective life, be that of the subway laborers or those who hold ideals dear, might allay. The problematic persisted, it insisted in each and every one of those versions. Because while there is no question that some versions of the world to-be-made may be better than others, while there is no doubt that the colonial, capitalist, extractivist, and desolate nature of the modern world we inhabit not only causes indignation but is itself unworthy of the ways of living and dying with others we could be implicated in cultivating with the trust of a held-out hand, it is also the case that *no world comes without its otherwise*. As such, no realization of *the* significant life, of *the* good common world, can avoid the risk of passing into its opposite, of turning the world thus realized into a single, impeccable, all-pervasive cosmos, with neither risks nor possibles, with neither conflicts nor pragmatic experiments in crafting our stories otherwise.

And so it turns out that the element of precipitousness that James had sought to reclaim, the very chemical combination that *must* be but cannot be identified with what already is, is but the very hold of a perhaps, of the immanent and almost imperceptible movement of an indeterminate otherwise insisting on the edge of cosmos, trailing after every world-vision, staring "back at us without perhaps being able to speak to us."[42] To speak of "perhaps" here is not just to theorize a moment of undecideablity that would constitute the condition of possibility for every decision, interruption, revolution, responsibility, or truth.[43] In its plurality, this reality that feels like itself *implicates* the perhaps as an iridescent indeterminacy, where what *is* mingles with the felt difference of what could be otherwise still. Whenever James is concerned, to speak of "perhaps" is to intensify the feeling of what *insists and persists* in every moment of decision, in every operation of addition, calling forth a *plus* whose contours we may not be able to determine but in whose hold we keep experimenting, in the dark, out of bounds, all the way through. "Perhaps," therefore, belongs to a certain experience of activity, to a precipitous *going-on* in the midst of what has been settled, to a tingling feeling of difference and possibility that knocks at the door, poses a problem, and calls for a response. And as James insisted, that "sense of activity" which I'm calling "perhaps" is "in the broadest and vaguest way synonymous with the sense of 'life.'"[44] For without the feeling of difference and possibility that insists in every pulsation of experience, there would be no feeling at all. Even in a completely locked-in and determined universe, even in a cosmos that is through-and-through *one*, our "own reaction on its monotony would be the one thing experienced there in the form of something coming to pass." Which is why, if without feeling there is no world, and no feeling without an insistent otherwise, even the best of all possible worlds is always more than one, always unfinished, always in the hold of an indeterminate perhaps.

PLURALISM IN THE HOLD OF PERHAPS · James's demanding lesson upon leaving Chautauqua belongs therefore to the sense that trusting the possibility of another world underway and yet-to-be-made is vital, perhaps even the most vital function that our lives in this world might have to perform. But it also makes present that doing so authorizes *nothing*. It provides no definition of how the good common world ought to be, and it warns us against giving in to the temptation of dreaming of a world that, once made, would bring the facts of struggle to an end. The pluriverse must be made, even when it won't get made. Indeed, it is almost as if the vital task of composing other worlds in the wake of what has happened to us would only succeed, as sheer activity, by espousing as a political vocation the indefinite failure that simultaneously upends and subtends its project. As if taking the risk of setting out to fail might one day, by apposition rather than opposition, turn failure into its opposite, linking the imperative of struggling for another possible world with the very insistence on staying alive to an ongoing experimentation with worlds in the making.[45] Such is the insistence of the pluriverse in the still of the night, gaping open the world on the edges of every world-vision, drawing it into the hold of perhaps.

But just as this lesson is demanding, creating an after even to the endings we might collectively seek, it also is extremely timely, or more precisely, radically *untimely*. For the gapings of other worlds in this world are still going on, ongoing in spite of all, amid all endings—insisting in the interstices of our times, calling for other times to come, perhaps. They forbid us to forget their case. And thankfully, those who seek to honor and stay alive to them are themselves increasingly plural. Interrupting the intimate affair that the modern proclamation of an origin of all origins establishes with the catastrophic insinuation of an end to all endings, a host of ally day-travelers have of late been behind a certain resurgence of the "pluriverse" as a notion capable of capturing something vital of the facts and hopes of myriad ongoing pluralistic struggles by peoples and other beings in and out of Europe—struggles that are irreducible to the politics of identity and rights, of economic development and state democracy, not least because it is the very modern territory of politics that they must question before they themselves can become perceptible.[46] In other words, the question at heart of these subtly divergent and untimely proposals is precisely that of a political ecology of practices which, as Mario Blaser and Marisol de la Cadena have recently put it, "make worlds even if they do not satisfy our demand (the demand of modern epistemology) to prove their reality (as they do not leave historical evidence, let alone scientific)."[47]

One common cause frequently pulsating throughout such resurgence of the notion of pluriverse—quite independently of James's pluralistic experiments—is the effort to relay the echoes of the collective cry and call proffered from the Lacandon Forest in Chiapas in the late 1990s by the Zapatista Army of National Liberation, who, "born of the night" and insisting on living in it still, did much more than affirm the possibility of composing another world. Seeking to gather "the minorities of the world" in transversal encounters where their divergent struggles could be generously shared and generatively connected in a global ensemble of revolutionary relays, they also, at the same time, insisted on the fact that "many worlds are made" and "many worlds make us," that "many words are walked in this world." And given that "in the world of the powerful there's only room for the bigwigs and their servants," they called upon allies to compose a world "where everyone fits"; to compose, as they famously put it in their fourth declaration, *"a world where many worlds fit."*[48]

Many others have rightly highlighted the way the political ethos cultivated by the Zapatista uprising prefigured and influenced much of the defining political strategies of contemporary revolutionary movements around the world today.[49] But it also has to be said that one of the achievements of their revolutionary call for political and cosmological recomposition has precisely been to enable its own echoes to reverberate in multifarious ways, in fuzzy resonances with manifold worlds in the making and myriad projects made by these worlds in relay and return. These resounding echoes have therefore been relayed in disparate affinity, animating a multitude of divergent world-visions and proposals for composition which together dramatize some of the stakes of a political cosmology today, stakes that James's pluralism might, in the hold of a perhaps, help us expand, complicate, and reclaim.[50]

Some, it must be said, have sought to turn the notion of the pluriverse into a decolonial cosmopolitanism which, by encompassing projects of deracialization and depatriarchization, food sovereignty, reciprocal economic organization and definancialization, spiritual liberation and aesthetic decolonization, would enshrine a communal principle of planetary connection between local cosmopolitanisms "in which all will participate, in which every cosmo-polis (local histories) will join as a project in which the pluriversal will be the universally agreed-upon goal."[51] While they are at pains to rescue (or decolonize) "cosmopolitan ideals" from the racist and imperial geographies in which they are inscribed, thereby making modern cosmopolitanism accountable for its crimes, to those efforts that conceive of "pluriversality as a universal project that can be imagined in the name of democracy," the insistence of an otherwise might perhaps function like a cautionary tale.[52] It might make perceptible the possibility that it is the very ideals of cosmopolitan redemption themselves that have a ready-made definition of the cosmos built into them, a regulative cosmos—whatever constellation it might take—in which everyone is exhorted to take part, or risk being cast aside. It might help us envisage that the moment the insistence of the pluriverse is turned into a series of substantive values that everyone must espouse, indeed into a universal condition of pluriversality, we're no longer in the hold of a perhaps but in under the tight grip of a categorical imperative.

Yet not all contemporary versions of the pluriverse seek to shape it into a universal cosmopolitan project. For a collective of allies who are striving to think in the wake of the way in which the modern colonial project has ploughed the world and devastated the Earth in the name of progress, relaying the Zapatistas' call to build "a world where many worlds fit" involves reclaiming the pluriverse as a cosmological manifold that can host a multiplicity of alternative political practices and projects in its midst. Inspired by "cultural groups across the world that still enjoy a collective existence" and make possible transitions for living well with others outside the modern coordinates of "development,"[53] these allies have been involved in a plethora of efforts devoted to crafting compositions capable of giving shape to a political cosmology of divergent projects across heterogeneously and partially connected worlds. Some of these efforts have been ethnographic, paying attention to the ways in which in certain situations divergent worlds negotiate "their difficult being together in heterogeneity."[54] Arturo Escobar, for his part, has recently been revisiting certain aspects of the history of design practices in the hope of wresting their transformative potential from the modern functionalist, industrialist, and rationalistic orientation with which they have been largely inscribed. At stake here is therefore an experiment in harnessing the potential of design practices and traditions so as to precipitate environmental, epochal, and civilizational transitions into other-than-capitalist, ecological forms of togetherness.[55] And resonant impulses have also led a collective of scholars and activists to engage in the production of a dictionary—which is to say an ongoing and unfinished list—of alternative visions and projects from

South and North for crafting minor futures outside the coordinates of modern progress, including entries on *Degrowth*, *Buen Vivir*, *Ubuntu*, and *Swaraj*, but also *Kyosei*, *Islamic Ethics*, *Tikkun Olam*, *Permaculture*, *Queer Love*, *Nayakrishi Andolon*, *Ecofeminism*, *Earth Spirituality*, and many others.[56]

This multiplicity of efforts matters, because together they help us envisage, they make resonate, that it matters what worlds we think to think the good common world with. They are important for in their divergences they *make* matter, they intensify, not only the existence of other worlds in this world but also something of what these other worlds could make perceptible, of the possibles they themselves create in spite of our desolate present. They matter because they make present *ifs* and *maybes* underway and yet to be made, proposals which, from an otherwise our tradition has derided and disqualified, generatively hold out a hand to our impoverished imaginations and insist on the possibility of proffering a response in relay and return, of wagering that world-monification is not the obligatory starting point for an experiment in other ways of composing togetherness in the wake. As James said of other utopian dreams of social justice, they "help to break the edge of the general reign of hardness and are slow leavens of a better order."[57] And as the Earth continues to rumble, we will need every help we can get. For that and more, I salute them. Yet once again, alliances are build thanks to divergences, and while here it is not another cosmopolitanism that is at stake, it is nevertheless clear and open that another well-defined cosmological image takes shape, one which James's difficult lesson at Chautauqua prompts us to complicate. For what comes into view as one attends to their efforts is a concerted attempt to conjoin the "pluriverse" with a quite definite sense of what the world to-be-made would be made *of*: namely, a non-dualist, radically interdependent and interconnected web of relations.[58] Escobar puts it in the clearest and most honest terms when he hypothesizes that the process of attending to and mapping manifold projects of ecological, social, and pluralistic justice "amounts to *a political activation of relationality*."[59]

Needless to say, when the recomposition of worlds in the wake is at stake, this activation is not just political; it becomes "ontological" as well. The struggle here becomes one of bringing down the "ontological dualisms" that are said to underpin the modern colonial project of world-monification and its geopolitical hierarchies, and to bring them down precisely by simultaneously rediscovering and reactivating a relational ontology for which "life is interrelation and interdependence through and through, always and from the beginning."[60] It is by embracing not only the situated relations that any of these projects might weave but also a broader image of a radically relational pluriverse that, we are told, we may become capable of cultivating the values of reciprocity, mutuality, care, and respect that resisting and counteracting the deleterious histories of colonialism, capitalism, and extractivism would appear to demand. Some, adds Michael W. Scott with humor, "are even saying that the Earth can be saved from cataclysmic climate change only if Cartesian dualists can somehow reset their mode of being to relational non-dualism—and do so quickly."[61] Scott's humorous characterization matters because it is neither caustic nor merely ironic. It matters because it reminds us that the task of trusting the possibility of another world is a task we carry at our own risk, in response to problems no version of the world-to-be-made can single-handedly dissipate.[62] I for one take no issue with the possibility that, in the end, in the beginning, a relational ontology of other worlds in this world might turn out to precipitate one moment in the world's salvation.[63] At the very least, this seems at present to be a *live* hypothesis.[64] It's a risk one may rightfully take while one still can.[65]

But perhapses, as Nietzsche once said, are *dangerous*.[66] They demand a response but do not provide instructions as to what that shall be, and they never say what might lie on the other side. They are dangerous because no cosmological composition can anticipate what would happen if the world it dreams of would materialize. One may well seek to nurture the values, ontologies, projects, and modes of living together that might foster more just and peaceful alter-globalizations, more equal worlds to be shared, but there's no telling what consequences the requirement to engage in such relational projects might bring about. One is reminded, just for example, of Falk Xué Parra Witte's rendering of the fundamentally essentialist and universalist environmental politics of Kogi cosmology, which regards the Sierra Nevada de Santa María in Colombia as the very "heart" of the world at large and Kogi ecological principles as possessing universal validity.[67] Or indeed, Philippe Descola's account of the Achuar, unconcerned "to represent themselves as a political body, forgetful of their past and indifferent to their future, quite unable to imagine the possibility of delegating one's own free will to people authorized to speak on one's behalf, mindful of their personal reputation, and quick to desert those who seek too much commitment from others." One is reminded of those who, for their own reasons, would reject relational connections; of those, in other words, who "cannot envisage a world where one can become part of a whole."[68] Relationships matter, as we have seen, and one might decide that Earth-wide relationality is worth the price.[69] By recalling that no world comes without its otherwise, I'm not arguing for the imperative to include what has been neglected. I am seeking to reclaim the generativity of what escapes even the most generous arrangements. For if it is not a matter of denying that the world might in some sense be one, or that it may turn out to be relationally connected, neither is it a case of regretting the fact that there are as many disjunctive relations as there are conjunctive ones, that there are "in reality infinitely more things 'unadapted' to each other in this world than there are things 'adapted'; infinitely more things with irregular relations than with regular relations between them."[70] What is reality capable of?

All this is to say that the activity of political cosmology is always beginning again or not at all, that it is always without end or it is not. Because whatever form it takes, every vision of the world to be made strives to bring about what it envisages, but it cannot quite envisage what its bringing about generates.[71] It can conceive of everything except "how much more outcry or how much appeasement comes about."[72] It is done and undone, troubled and animated, problematized, in one and the same breath, by the precipitous call of the otherwise. For there "is no complete generalisation, no total point of view, no all-pervasive unity, but everywhere some residual resistance to verbalisation, formulation, and discursification, some genius of reality that says 'hands off,' and claims its privacy, and means to be left to its own life."[73] It is this fugitivity, this runaway character of reality at once metaphysical, political, and ethical, that situates us in the hold of perhaps. And in this way, James's difficult lesson, that no world comes without its otherwise, is one that lures us, perhaps, to reclaim the proposition of "a world where many worlds fit" in its most paradoxical dimension. To assert, that is, that a world where many worlds fit is also—by accident or definition, by fate or fiat, by a throw of the dice—a world where many divergent worlds begin and end at odd times, where many worlds strive and experiment, where many worlds connect and disconnect, where many worlds overflow and surround, where many worlds are made and unmade, where many worlds escape, where many worlds *never quite fit*, perhaps.

"Not unfortunately," wrote James, quoting Benjamin Paul Blood, "the universe is wild—game-flavoured as a hawk's wing. Nature is miracle all; the same returns not save to bring the different. The slow round of the engraver's lathe gains but the breadth of a hair, but the difference is distributed back over whole curve, never an instant true,—ever not quite."[74] Interstices proliferate in the midst of every cosmological arrangement, whether modern or not, drawing every cosmos into the hold of an indeterminate perhaps. And it is in and through those interstices that, perhaps, a certain runaway experimentation might get fugitively underway, a counter-composition that does not make a cosmos and does not seek to make one, but is intent on reclaiming a buzzing present teeming with what has managed to escape, with what has managed to persist in spite of all, making present what with James C. Scott we could well call multiple *shatter zones*: worlds-within-worlds through which something escapes, stories-within-stories where tales are told otherwise.[75] Shatter zones may be found wherever the eschaton is scatted; wherever empires are damned; wherever reality feels like itself, in the plural; wherever world-monification is confronted by the cry of a "hands off!" by the worldquake of an unsuspected otherwise. They proliferate around the day in eighty worlds "wherever the expansion of states, empires, slave-trading, and wars, as well as natural disasters, have driven large numbers of people to seek refuge in out-of-the-way places,"[76] wherever people and others have been driven to reweave their arts of living and dying well with others, to believe in other worlds in this world and insist on and persist from there, trusting that there's a there there, that beginnings can and do happen even amid all endings.

Emerging there where worlds don't quite fit, shatter zones are signs that keep alive and keep us alive to the possibility that, perhaps, "profusion, not economy, may after all be reality's key-note."[77] They are the ongoing reminders that perhaps the pluriverse is not a destination but what activates a divergent experimentation, a hesitant opening in the midst of closure. They are the zones of indeterminacy through which the sense of activity keeps on keeping on, preventing our present from closing down upon itself, luring it toward one and many possibilities that are itching to be intensified, toward a plurality of alternative modes of cohabitation that remain to be composed and may never quite materialize. We might, then, say of this insistence, of this "perhaps" we've been calling "pluriverse," something of the order of what James once suggested of emotions. That is, that the pluriverse is not a world we dream might come about—it is what *makes us dream*. It is a nickname for the insistence of a possible that remains impossible for us to envisage but poses a problem and demands a response.[78] Which is why, if the pluriverse must be made, it must be made *endlessly*, through the very dynamic of hindrance and experiment that resonates all the way through. And if it must be made endlessly, at stake therefore is not so much the battle for the best composition of the good common world, but the ongoing and unfinished struggle to respond to the insistence that makes us strive for its recomposition in the first place, that keeps us and others keeping on, together, keeping differences proliferating, pouring over, flooding in, experimenting with ways our difficult being together could still be otherwise composed.

In relay and return, it may be that pluralism is best conceptualized in the hold of such a perhaps. It may be that, rather than describing a theory of a diverse polis, of the successful negotiation between different ontologies, or as a principle of maximal cosmological inclusion, pluralism designates a *pragmatics of the pluriverse*: the always ongoing and unfinished task of remaining attentive to fugitive shatter zones, of intensifying what still happens and can still happen in divergent spaces of refuge where differences keep on proliferating, interrupting the onslaught and persisting in spite of all, where they intimate the possibility of other worlds in this world. What differences might they make? The task is precisely to stay sensitive to the sensible tangle, alive to this buzzing, strung-along, and flowing sort of reality which we finite beings swim in. The task is to keep swimming in it so as to give to realities lost, suppressed, or derided, to stories fantastical, incomprehensible, and implausible, the power to transform our concepts, to enable us to tell our own stories otherwise, to enable them to tell theirs, to enter into generous and generative ensembles of relays with the trust of a held-out hand. All the way through, this insistence that the "pluriverse" names draws pluralism into the hold of a perhaps, groping experimentally in the dark while one still can, exploring what differences pluralism might be liable to make. After everything that our experiments can do, "there still remains the opacity of the final facts as merely given, with most of their peculiarities mutually unmediated and unexplained."[79] What is this world going to be? What is life to make of itself? The pluriverse doesn't say. It keeps on insisting, looking for differences, gaping every sacred enclosure open to what resists, exceeds, and escapes it in the still of the night.

There is no conclusion, no advice, no ethical ideal that can tidy up the loose ends that this many-storied universe makes proliferate. What has concluded, that one might conclude in regard to it?[80] And yet, what such a pragmatics of the pluriverse might nevertheless intensify in spite of all, what it may make resonate, is the dynamic of collective invention and experimentation through which myriad divergent practices in and out of Europe cultivate forms of trust in the possibility of another world while consenting to the possibility that the worlds they trust are possible are not the same world, that their stories are not the only stories, that their experimental forms of togetherness to be composed will make our modern world

tremble and might also tangle us and others in new problems no cosmological composition could accommodate, let alone anticipate. Something
always escapes, and it is by attending to what escapes that the insistence of
the pluriverse becomes bound to our ongoing existence, incarnated in the
otherwise that the activities of those who inhabit the shatter zones make
exist. And it is in and through the new threads they weave that our unfinished existence becomes inextricably bound to the pluriverse's insistence,
where the very possibility of giving refuge to the differences that lurk in
the still of the night is given a chance at all, where the insistent possibilities
for cultivating minor collective futures might momentarily be stolen back,
perhaps. Groping for possibles we dimly envisage but do not quite understand, perhaps it is through such a pragmatics of the pluriverse that a
permanent experimentation with other worlds in this world might get underway. Perhaps it is thus that glimmers of other ways of living and dying
well with others yet to be imagined might be intensified, shaping "our vital
attitude as decisively as the vital attitude of lovers is determined by the ha-
bitual sense, by which each is haunted, of the other being in the world."[81] In
the end, in the beginning, in love as much as in political cosmology, what
is this other that haunts us if not the name for an indeterminate *perhaps*?

NOTES

CHAPTER ONE: ONGOING AND UNFINISHED

1 "What can I do? / I must begin. / Begin What? / The only thing in the world that's worth beginning: / The End of the World, no less," Aimé Césaire, *Return to My Native Land*, trans. John Berger and Anna Bostock (Brooklyn: Archipelago Books, 2013), 38–39.

2 Catherine Keller, *Apocalypse Now and Then: A Feminist Guide to the End of the World* (Boston: Beacon Press, 1996).

3 Strictly speaking, the terms James occasionally used for it were "multiverse" and, more frequently, "a pluralistic universe." Even contemporary physicists begrudgingly acknowledge a connection between their cosmological theories of the multiverse and James's early use of the term. To my knowledge, it was Benjamin Paul Blood, whom James dubbed a "pluralistic mystic," who may have coined the term. The frequent attribution of the notion of "pluriverse" to James is, however, not unwarranted, because it highlights the crucial fact that, unlike the physicists' "multiverse," which connotes the hypothetical existence of multiple, parallel universes, James rejected the invitation to consent to a multiverse made of disconnected parts that are indifferent to each other. What the notion of "pluriverse" evokes, in other words, is the need to stay with both the one and the many, to attend to the fact that "[o]ur 'multiverse' still makes a 'universe'" without thereby positing "a universal co-implication, or integration of all things *durcheinander.*" See William James, *A Pluralistic Universe* (Lincoln: University of Nebraska Press, 1996), 325; Benjamin Paul Blood, *Pluriverse: An Essay in the Philosophy of Pluralism* (Boston: Marshal Jones, 1920).

4 Umberto Eco, *The Infinity of Lists*, trans. Alastair McEwen (New York: Rizzoli/Universal, 2009).

5 William James, *Pragmatism and the Meaning of Truth* (Cambridge, MA: Harvard University Press, 1975), 64.

6 James, *Pragmatism and the Meaning of Truth*, 66.

7 To speak of a process of modern monification is not to say that there haven't

been surreptitious processes of pluralization or indeed "hybridization," as Bruno Latour has classically remarked. In his argument, the modern efforts at metaphysical compartmentalization and border-policing—between nature and culture, facts and fetishes, humans and nonhumans, objects and signs, epistemology and ontology, reality and appearance—are often inconsistently produced, applying differently from case to case, and have always been fraught with all manner of side effects that engender a proliferation of multiple "hybrids," which in fact turn out to be constitutive of the "modern constitution" as such. Hence his famous phrase that "we have never been modern." And yet, this need not lead us to affirm that "modernity" is therefore nothing but a bluff, another illusion that simply ought to be unmasked and denounced as such. As a set of stories and operations that have ploughed much of the world, modernity "is a force added to others that for a long time it had the power to represent, to accelerate, or to summarize—a power that it no longer entirely holds." See Bruno Latour, *We Have Never Been Modern*, trans. Catherine Porter (Cambridge, MA: Harvard University Press, 1993), 40.

8   There is no Planet B, as activists rightly say. Yet to be in the same storm does not in any way mean that we're all in it in the same way. Many of us, moderns and other-than-moderns, humans and other-than-humans, living and dead, are already, as others have been and may end up soon, drowned at the bottom of the sea, piled up in the belly of the ship. Our togetherness is made of divergence through and through.

9   James Campbell, *Experiencing William James: Belief in a Pluralistic Universe* (Charlottesville: University of Virginia Press, 2017), 215.

10 The dominant reception of James has been adamant in casting his thought as fundamentally apolitical and has read his pragmatism as a hallmark of the American protest against philosophical questions—whatever works. A minor group of readers, scattered across the twentieth century and growing in recent years, on the other hand, have provided perceptive and lucid accounts of James as a deeply philosophical and profoundly political thinker. It is those that I pay tribute to. See among others, Henri Bergson, *The Creative Mind: An Introduction to Metaphysics*, trans. Mabelle L. Andison (Mineola, NY: Dover, 2007); Deborah J. Coon, "One Moment in the World's Salvation: Anarchism and the Radicalisation of William James," *Journal of American History* 83, no. 1 (1996): 70–99; William Connolly, *Pluralism* (Durham, NC: Duke University Press, 2005); Kennan Ferguson, *William James: Politics in the Pluriverse* (Lanham, MD: Rowman & Littlefield, 2007); Alexander Livingston, *Damn Great Empires! William James and the Politics of Pragmatism* (New York: Oxford University Press, 2016).

11 William James, *The Letters of William James*, ed. Henry James (London: Longmans, Green, 1920), 355.

12 On the experimental practice of relaying, see Isabelle Stengers, "Relaying

a War Machine?," in *The Guattari Effect*, ed. Eric Alliez and Andrew Goffey (London: Continuum, 2011), 134–57.

13 James, *The Letters of William James*, 355.

14 Walter Mignolo, *The Darker Side of Western Modernity: Global Futures, Deco-lonial Options* (Durham, NC: Duke University Press, 2011). Throughout this book, I use the term *postcolonial studies* broadly and liberally to refer to what is nevertheless a manifold of projects that go under different names. When approached as specific traditions, however, one can of course discern significant historical, geographical, and disciplinary differences. For an exploration of some of those, see Gurminder K. Bhambra, "Postcolonial and Decolonial Dialogues," *Postcolonial Studies* 17, no. 2 (2014): 115–21.

15 By now the literature on this is too vast to cite comprehensively, but for a range of thoughtful perspectives and debates, see the excellent collective volume edited by Pierre Charbonnier, Gildas Salmon, and Peter Skafish, *Comparative Metaphysics: Ontology after Anthropology* (London: Rowman & Littlefield, 2016).

16 Eduardo Viveiros de Castro, *Cannibal Metaphysics*, trans. Peter Skafish (Minneapolis: Univocal, 2014).

17 Eduardo Viveiros de Castro, *The Relative Native: Essays on Indigenous Conceptual Worlds* (Chicago: HAU Books, 2015), 46.

18 William James, *The Principles of Psychology, Volume One* (New York: Dover, 1950), 256.

19 James, *A Pluralistic Universe*, 321.

20 James, *Pragmatism and the Meaning of Truth*, 76.

21 William James, *The Principles of Psychology, Volume Two* (New York: Dover, 1950), 280.

22 William James, *Essays in Radical Empiricism* (Mineola, NY: Dover, 2003), 83.

23 James, *Essays in Radical Empiricism*, 3, 14.

24 Martin Savransky, "The Wager of an Unfinished Present: Notes on Speculative Pragmatism," in *Speculative Research: The Lure of Possible Futures*, ed. Alex Wilkie, Martin Savransky, and Marsha Rosengarten (New York: Routledge, 2017), 25–38.

25 Martin Savransky, "A Decolonial Imagination: Sociology, Anthropology, and the Politics of Reality," *Sociology* 51, no. 1 (2017): 11–26.

26 Arundhati Roy, "Confronting Empire" (paper presented at Life After Capitalism, World Social Forum, Porto Alegre, Brazil, January 27, 2003). See also Arundhati Roy, *An Ordinary Person's Guide to Empire* (New Delhi: Penguin, 2006).

27 Gilles Deleuze and Félix Guattari, *What Is Philosophy?*, trans. Graham Burchell and Hugh Thomlinson (New York: Verso, 1994), 74–75.

28 See Stefano Harney and Fred Moten, *The Undercommons: Fugitive Planning and Black Study* (New York: Minor Compositions, 2013), 118.

29 Deleuze and Guattari, *What Is Philosophy?*, 74–75.

30 Livingston, *Damn Great Empires!*

31 Max Weber, *From Max Weber: Essays in Sociology*, ed. H. H. Gerth and C. Wright Mills (Abingdon, UK: Routledge, 2009).

32 I am thankful to Sanjay Seth (personal communication) for this felicitous phrase.

33 Gabriel García Márquez, "The Solitude of Latin America," Nobel lecture delivered at the ceremony of the Nobel Prize in Literature, Stockholm, Sweden, December 8, 1982. Accessed November 28, 2019, http://www.nobelprize.org/nobel_prizes/literature/laureates/1982/marquez-lecture.html.

34 Lorraine Daston and Katherine Park, *Wonders and the Order of Nature, 1150–1750* (Brooklyn, NY: Zone Books, 2003).

35 In fact, another story of around-the-world travel prior to the first circumnavigation was a cautionary tale against imperialistic hubris from polytheistic Ancient Greece. In this story, which seems only too timely today, Phaeton (son of Helios, the Greek sun god, and a mortal woman) asks to guide Helios's solar chariot around the world for a day, only to find that he cannot control the horses and ends up wreaking havoc along its path. Gaia pleads with Zeus to stop him, and the latter strikes him with a thunderbolt, turning Phaeton's hair on fire. In a desperate attempt to put the fire out, Phaeton runs into the Eridanus River, where he finally drowns. See Ovid, *Metamorphoses*, trans. David Raeburn (London: Penguin Classics, 2004). For an interesting, historically sensitive, and theologically minded account of the logic of the One and its possible pluralistic indetermination through a theology of multiplicity, see Laurel C. Schneider, *Beyond Monotheism: A Theology of Multiplicity* (New York: Routledge, 2008).

36 Enrique Dussel, *1492: El Encubrimiento del Otro. Hacia el Origen del "Mito de la Modernidad"* (La Paz: Plural Editores, 1994).

37 See Joyce E. Chaplin, *Round About the Earth: Circumnavigation from Magellan to Orbit* (New York: Simon & Schuster, 2012), 10.

38 See García Márquez, "The Solitude of Latin America," where he recites the account of Antonio Pigafetta, a Florentine navigator who traveled with Magellan.

39 Antonio Pigafetta, *The First Voyage Around the World*, trans. Lord Stanley of Alderley (London: Hakluyt Society, 1874), 49–50.

40 Édouard Glissant, *Poetics of Relation*, trans. Betsy Wing (Ann Arbor: University of Michigan Press, 1997), 17.

41 Chaplin, *Round About the Earth*, 18.

42 Chaplin, *Round About the Earth*, 37.

43 See Jason W. Moore, "The End of Cheap Nature. Or How I Learned to Stop Worrying about 'The' Environment and Love the Crisis of Capitalism," in *Structures of the World Political Economy and the Future of Global Conflict and Cooperation*, ed. Christian Suter and Christopher Chase-Dunn (Berlin: LIT Verlag, 2014), 285–314.

44 A review of the myriad individual voices and versions in these not quite articulated debates would require a book in and of itself. Indeed, it is likely to require more than one book, as these various articulations make themselves manifest and follow a cornucopia of disparate threads in fields like philosophy, postcolonial studies, cultural anthropology, sociology, development studies, political theory, and the history of science. For a very succinct yet illuminating discussion on the merits and perils of some influential, critical stories of modernity, see Sanjay Seth, "Is Thinking with 'Modernity' Eurocentric?" *Cultural Sociology* 10, no. 3 (2016): 385–98.

45 James, *A Pluralistic Universe*, 45.

46 Gilles Deleuze, *The Logic of Sense*, trans. Mark Lester (London: Continuum, 2004), 200.

47 Stephen Jay Gould, *Dinosaur in a Haystack: Essays on Natural History* (Cambridge, MA: Harvard University Press, 1995), 42.

48 Gould, *Dinosaur in a Haystack*, 42–43.

49 Daston and Park, *Wonders and the Order of Nature*, 331.

50 Gould, *Dinosaur in a Haystack*, 47.

51 Daston and Park, *Wonders and the Order of Nature*, 350.

52 Alfred North Whitehead, *The Concept of Nature* (Mineola, NY: Dover, 1920).

53 See Lorraine Daston and Michael Stolleis, eds., *Natural Laws and Laws of Nature in Early Modern Europe: Jurisprudence, Theology, Moral and Natural Philosophy* (Farnham: Ashgate, 2008).

54 See Michel Foucault, *The Order of Things: An Archeology of the Human Sciences* (London: Routledge, 2002). For an account of the persistence of the extraordinary and the occult in the human sciences, see Jason Josephson-Storm, *The Myth of Disenchantment: Magic, Modernity and the Birth of the Human Sciences* (Chicago: University of Chicago Press, 2017).

55 Stephen Toulmin, *Cosmopolis: The Hidden Agenda of Modernity* (Chicago: University of Chicago Press, 1990).

56 Indeed, it is not a matter of conflating these, which would lead us to reject all realisms, all rationalisms, all theisms. Rather, it is always a matter of attending, in each case, to how *certain* forms of theism, rationalism, representationalism, naturalism, and imperialism become woven together in the constitution of a specific operation of disqualification.

57 Isabelle Stengers, *Cosmopolitics I* (Minneapolis: University of Minnesota Press, 2010), 29.

58 This, I'm afraid, is as much the case for many "analytical" philosophers, who have traditionally rallied around "realism" as a flag, as it is for many contemporary "continental" philosophers, who after deriding realism as a weakness of thought have recently rediscovered an appetite for realisms of various kinds. For a contemporary discussion, see, for instance, Manuel Delanda and Graham Harman, *The Rise of Realism* (Cambridge: Polity Press, 2017). For an excellent history of anti-realism in continental philosophy, see

Lee Braver, *A Thing of This World: A History of Continental Anti-Realism* (Evanston, IL: Northwestern University Press, 2007).

59 Hilary Putnam, *Representation and Reality* (Cambridge, MA: MIT Press, 1988), 107.

60 Daston and Park, *Wonders and the Order of Nature*, 350.

61 Julio Cortázar, *Clases de Literatura. Berkeley, 1980* (Madrid: Alfaguara, 2013), 50. See also Julio Cortázar, *La Vuelta al Día en Ochenta Mundos* (Madrid: Siglo XXI, 2007).

62 James, *A Pluralistic Universe*, 317.

63 Glissant, *Poetics of Relation*, 17.

64 James, *A Pluralistic Universe*, 213.

65 I borrow the term "intranslation" from Barbara Cassin, *Sophistical Practice: Toward a Consistent Relativism* (New York: Fordham University Press, 2014).

66 James, *Pragmatism and the Meaning of Truth*, 122–23.

CHAPTER TWO: RUNAWAY METAPHYSICS

1 I am thankful to Chilean filmmaker, visual sociologist, cartographer of the fantastic, and above all dear friend and comrade Felipe Palma for this suggestion.

2 Anna Tsing, *The Mushroom at the End of the World: On the Possibility of Life in Capitalist Ruins* (Princeton, NJ: Princeton University Press, 2015), 38.

3 Tsing, *The Mushroom at the End of the World*, 39.

4 Tsing, *The Mushroom at the End of the World*, 40.

5 Tsing, *The Mushroom at the End of the World*, 255.

6 James, *A Pluralistic Universe*, 213.

7 James, *A Pluralistic Universe*, 32.

8 James, *A Pluralistic Universe*, 328.

9 James, *A Pluralistic Universe*, 324.

10 James, *A Pluralistic Universe*, 324.

11 James, *A Pluralistic Universe*, 324.

12 James, *A Pluralistic Universe*, 324.

13 James, *A Pluralistic Universe*, 322.

14 Cortázar, *Clases de Literatura*, 50.

15 Harry West, *Ethnographic Sorcery* (Chicago: University of Chicago Press, 2007).

16 West, *Ethnographic Sorcery*, 1.

17 West, *Ethnographic Sorcery*, 1–2.

18 West, *Ethnographic Sorcery*, 3.

19 West, *Ethnographic Sorcery*, 3.

20 West, *Ethnographic Sorcery*, 4.

21 Latour, *We Have Never Been Modern*.

22 Valentin Y. Mudimbe, *The Invention of Africa: Gnosis, Philosophy, and the Order of Knowledge* (Bloomington and Indianapolis: Indiana University Press, 1988), 28.

23 West, *Ethnographic Sorcery*, 5.

24 Talal Asad, *Anthropology and the Colonial Encounter* (London: Ithaca Press, 1973).

25 See Peter Geschiere, *The Modernity of Witchcraft: Politics and the Occult in Postcolonial Africa* (Charlottesville: University of Virginia Press, 1997); see also Jean Comaroff and John Comaroff, "Occult Economies and the Violence of Abstraction: Notes from the South African Postcolony," *American Ethnologist* 26, no. 3 (1999): 279–301; and David Meyers and Peter Pels, eds., *Magic and Modernity: Interfaces of Revelation and Concealment* (Stanford, CA: Stanford University Press, 2001).

26 West, *Ethnographic Sorcery*, 11.

27 Mudimbe, *The Invention of Africa*, 82.

28 Edward Said, *Orientalism* (London: Penguin, 2003), 51.

29 Said, *Orientalism*, 92.

30 Said, *Orientalism*, 92.

31 Daston and Park, *Wonders and the Order of Nature*.

32 As Anouar Abdel-Malek aptly phrases it in a seminal essay: "According to the traditional orientalists, an essence should exist—sometimes even clearly described in metaphysical terms—which constitutes the inalienable and common basis of all the beings considered; this essence is both 'historical,' since it goes back to the dawn of history, and fundamentally a-historical, since it transfixes the being, 'the object' of study, within its inalienable and non-evolutive specificity, instead of defining it as all other beings, states, nations, peoples and cultures—as a product, a resultant of the vection of the forces operating in the field of historical evolution." See Anouar Abdel-Malek, "Orientalism in Crisis," *Diogenes* 11, no. 44 (1963): 108.

33 Georg Wilhelm Friedrich Hegel, *Lectures on the Philosophy of World History*, trans. H. B. Nisbet (Cambridge: Cambridge University Press, 1975), 69.

34 For an in-depth, postcolonial critique of Hegel's lectures on the Philosophy of World History, see Ranajit Guha, *History at the Limits of World-History* (New York: Columbia University Press, 2002).

35 William James, *The Will to Believe and Other Essays in Popular Philosophy* (Mineola, NY: Dover, 1956), 263.

36 James, *Pragmatism and the Meaning of Truth*, 290.

37 For some classical exemplars, see Said, *Orientalism*; Homi Bhabha, *The Location of Culture* (London: Routledge, 1994); Gayatri Chakravorty Spivak, *A Critique of Postcolonial Reason: Toward a History of the Vanishing Present* (Cambridge, MA: Harvard University Press, 1999).

38 Dipesh Chakrabarty, *Provincializing Europe: Postcolonial Thought and Historical Difference* (Princeton, NJ: Princeton University Press, 2000), 98.

39 See Walter Mignolo, *The Darker Side of Western Modernity*, 82. See also Anibal Quijano, "Coloniality and Modernity/Rationality," *Cultural Studies* 21, no. 2–3 (2007): 168–78; Boaventura de Sousa Santos, *Epistemologies of the South* (Boulder, CO: Paradigm, 2014); and Immanuel Wallerstein, *European Universalism: The Rhetoric of Power* (New York: New Press, 2006).

40 West, *Ethnographic Sorcery*, 38.

41 West, *Ethnographic Sorcery*, 70.

42 Sanjay Seth, "Reason or Reasoning? Clio or Shiva," *Social Text* 22, no. 1 (2004): 85.

43 See, for instance, Boaventura de Sousa Santos, ed., *Another Knowledge Is Possible* (London: Verso, 2008); Linda Tuhiwai Smith, *Decolonizing Methodologies: Research and Indigenous Peoples* (London: Zed Books, 2012); Warwick Anderson, "From Subjugated Knowledge to Conjugated Subjects: Science and Globalisation, or Postcolonial Studies of Science?" *Postcolonial Studies* 12, no. 4 (2009): 389–400; Wiebke Keim, Ercüment Çelik, Christian Ersche, and Veronika Wöhrer, eds., *Global Knowledge Production in the Social Sciences: Made in Circulation* (London: Routledge, 2016).

44 Martin Savransky, *The Adventure of Relevance: An Ethics of Social Inquiry* (Basingstoke: Palgrave Macmillan, 2016).

45 Said, *Orientalism*, 72.

46 Quijano, "Coloniality and Modernity/Rationality," 169.

47 See Savransky, "A Decolonial Imagination."

48 As science historians Lorraine Daston and Peter Galison put it in their monumental *Objectivity*, "Immanuel Kant's philosophical reformulation of the scholastic categories of the objective and the subjective reverberated with seismic intensity in every domain of nineteenth-century intellectual life, from science to literature." Indeed, by "the mid-nineteenth century, dictionaries and handbooks in English French, and German credited Kantian critical philosophy with the resuscitation and redefinition of the scholastic terminology of the objectivity and the subjective. Words that were once enmeshed in the realism versus nominalism debate of the fourteenth century and that had by the eighteenth century fallen into disuse except in a few treatises in logic were given a new lease on life by Kantian epistemology, ethics, and aesthetics." See Lorraine Daston and Peter Galison, *Objectivity* (Brooklyn, NY: Zone Books, 2010), 205–6.

49 Immanuel Kant, *Perpetual Peace and Other Essays on Politics, History and Morals*, trans. Ted Humphrey (Indianapolis: Hackett, 1983). For a critique of Kant's geographical imagination, see David Harvey, *Cosmopolitanism and the Geographies of Freedom* (New York: Columbia University Press, 2009).

50 West, *Ethnographic Sorcery*, 56.

51 West, *Ethnographic Sorcery*, 81.

52 Indeed, as scholars in science and technology studies have been at pains to show, such disavowals extend to the very knowledge-practices one would

be tempted to call modern, from experimental physics to modern medicine. Relevant examples are too many to cite, but see, for instance, the essays collected in John Law and Annemarie Mol, *Complexities: Social Studies of Knowledge Practices* (Durham, NC: Duke University Press, 2002).

53 See John Law, "What's Wrong with a One-world World?," *Distinktion: Scandinavian Journal of Social Theory* 16, no. 1 (2015): 126–39.

54 Ernesto de Martino, *Primitive Magic: The Psychic Powers of Shamans and Sorcerers* (Dorset: Prism Press, 1988), 3.

55 James, *The Will to Believe and Other Essays*, 3.

56 A danger I have elsewhere called "metaphysical Eurocentrism." See Martin Savransky, "In Praise of Hesitation: 'Global' Knowledge as a Cosmopolitical Adventure," in Keim et al., *Global Knowledge Production in the Social Sciences*, 237–50.

57 William James, *Essays in Philosophy* (Cambridge, MA: Harvard University Press, 1978), 139.

58 See Annemarie Mol, *The Body Multiple: Ontology in Medical Practice* (Durham, NC: Duke University Press, 2002); Marianne Elizabeth Lien, *Becoming Salmon: Aquaculture and the Domestication of Fish* (Los Angeles: University of California Press, 2015); and Helen Verran, *Science and an African Logic* (Chicago: University of Chicago Press, 2001).

59 Indeed, while the language of "ontology" has of late acquired much prominence across the humanities and the social sciences, I am in full agreement with Casper Bruun Jensen when he argues that it is a mistake to conceive this emergence of the ontological as amounting to a single "turn." More than that, I tend to think that whenever a "turn" is proclaimed, one should remain very vigilant and tread carefully: an eager contribution to the knowledge economy is likely to be in the works. The fact is that, just like the beings and modes of existence it seeks to address, there are probably as many working-notions of "ontology" as there are scholars using them in more or less explicit ways. As Jensen rightly points out, the emergence of debates around ontology in science and technology studies, in anthropology, and in philosophy each have their own divergent and complicated histories and receptions, hardly amounting to one turn. I have no intention of building up a taxonomy or of adjudicating between these. Suffice it to say that, seeking to affirm the agency and vitality of matter, exploring the multiple ways in which the very being of the human body is addressed across modern medical practices and seeking to take seriously the existence of ghosts in postwar Vietnam constitute divergent responses to three different problematics, responses that are likely to involve disparate and perhaps even less-than-compatible philosophical, political, and existential commitments, even when each of these responses may involve some notion of "ontology." For an excellent and succinct mapping of some of these multidisciplinary debates, see Casper Bruun Jensen et al., "New Ontologies?

Reflections on Some Recent 'Turns' in STS, Anthropology, and Philosophy," *Social Anthropology/Anthropologie Sociale* 25, no. 4 (2017): 525 – 45.

60 Viveiros de Castro, *Cannibal Metaphysics*, 47 – 48.

61 Eduardo Kohn, "Anthropology of Ontologies," *Annual Review of Anthropology* 44 (2015): 320.

62 Martin Holbraad and Axel Morten Pedersen, *The Ontological Turn: An Anthropological Exposition* (Cambridge: Cambridge University Press, 2017), 68.

63 Martin Holbraad, Morten Axel Pedersen, and Eduardo Viveiros de Castro, "The Politics of Ontology: Anthropological Positions," Theorizing the Contemporary, *Fieldsights*, January 13, 2014. https://culanth.org/fieldsights/the -politics-of-ontology-anthropological-positions.

64 Someone like Philippe Descola, for instance, has been pursuing this comparative project, and Bruno Latour has recently sought to redescribe what the ontology of the moderns might look like. See Philippe Descola, *Beyond Nature and Culture*, trans. Janet Lloyd (Chicago: University of Chicago Press, 2013); and Bruno Latour, *An Inquiry into Modes of Existence: An Anthropology of the Moderns*, trans. Catherine Porter (Cambridge, MA: Harvard University Press, 2013). See also the very interesting discussions in Pierre Charbonnier, Gildas Salmon, and Peter Skafish, eds., *Comparative Metaphysics* (London: Rowman & Littlefield, 2016).

65 Viveiros de Castro, *The Relative Native*, 42. See also the lively debate on the uses and abuses of ontology in anthropology by Michael Carrithers et al., "Ontology Is Just Another Word for Culture," *Critique of Anthropology* 30, no. 2 (2010): 152 – 200.

66 See Holbraad and Pedersen, *The Ontological Turn*.

67 See Mario Blaser, "Ontology and Indigeneity: On the Political Ontology of Heterogeneous Assemblages," *Cultural Geographies* 21, no. 1 (2014): 49 – 58; Mario Blaser, "Ontological Conflicts and the Stories of Peoples in Spite of Europe: Toward a Conversation on Political Ontology," *Current Anthropology* 54, no. 5 (2013): 547 – 68; Mario Blaser, *Storytelling Globalization from the Chaco and Beyond* (Durham, NC: Duke University Press, 2010); Marisol de la Cadena, *Earth-Beings: Ecologies of Practice across Andean Worlds* (Durham, NC: Duke University Press, 2015); Marisol de la Cadena, "Indigenous Cosmopolitics in the Andes: Conceptual Reflections beyond 'Politics,'" *Cultural Anthropology* 25, no. 2 (2010): 334 – 70; and Marisol de la Cadena and Mario Blaser, eds., *A World of Many Worlds* (Durham, NC: Duke University Press, 2018).

68 De la Cadena, *Earth Beings*, 275.

69 James, *A Pluralistic Universe*, 324.

70 Pierre Clastres, *Society Against the State*, trans. Robert Hurley and Abe Stein (Brooklyn, NY: Zone Books, 1989), 19.

71 On the value and function of "outrageous" propositions, see Monica Greco, "Thinking with Outrageous Propositions," in *Speculative Research: The Lure of*

Possible Futures, ed. Alex Wilkie, Martin Savransky, and Marsha Rosengarten (New York: Routledge, 2017), 218–27.

72 Isabelle Stengers, *Cosmopolitics II* (Minneapolis: University of Minnesota Press, 2011), 310.

73 I intranslate the term "intranslation" (*intraduire*) from the French philosopher Barbara Cassin (who in turn intranslates it from the term "intradução" by the Brazilian poet Augusto de Campos). In the context of Cassin's meditations on the philosophy of translation and the intranslation of philosophy, she associates it with the attempt, at once theoretical, poetical, and political, of rebuilding something new inside another language. See Barbara Cassin, *Sophistical Practice: Toward a Consistent Relativism* (New York: Fordham University Press, 2013).

74 James, *Pragmatism and the Meaning of Truth*, 30.

75 On the concept of event, see Deleuze, *The Logic of Sense*; Savransky, *The Adventure of Relevance*; and Isabelle Stengers, *The Invention of Modern Science*, trans. Daniel W. Smith (Minneapolis: University of Minnesota Press, 2000).

76 James, *The Will to Believe and Other Essays*, 150.

77 James, *Pragmatism and the Meaning of Truth*, 71.

78 James, *The Will to Believe and Other Essays*, 150.

79 William James, *Some Problems of Philosophy* (Lincoln: University of Nebraska Press, 1996), 229.

80 Marilyn Strathern, *Reproducing the Future: Anthropology, Kinship, and the New Reproductive Technologies* (London: Routledge, 1992); and Donna Haraway, *Staying with the Trouble: Making Kin in the Chthulucene* (Durham, NC: Duke University Press, 2016).

81 Roy, "Confronting Empire."

82 Gilles Deleuze, *Nietzsche and Philosophy*, trans. Hugh Tomlinson (London: Continuum, 2006), 4.

83 James, *Some Problems of Philosophy*, 230.

CHAPTER THREE: TRUST OF A HELD-OUT HAND

1 James, *The Principles of Psychology, vol. 2*, 280.

2 James, *The Principles of Psychology, vol. 2*, 295.

3 James, *The Principles of Psychology, vol. 2*, 295.

4 Vine Deloria Jr., *The Metaphysics of Modern Existence* (Golden, CO: Fulcrum, 2012), 5.

5 Vine Deloria Jr., *Spirit and Reason: The Vine Deloria Jr. Reader*, ed. Barbara Deloria, Kristen Foehner, and Samuel Scinta (Golden, CO: Fulcrum, 1999), 5.

6 As James writes in *The Varieties of Religious Experience*, the discovery of the subconscious, or the subliminal region of the self, may have been "the most

important step forward in psychology," but "if you, being Orthodox Christians, ask me as a psychologist whether the references of a phenomenon to a subliminal self does not exclude the notion of the direct presence of the Deity altogether, I have to say frankly that as a psychologist I do not see why it necessarily should." See William James, *The Varieties of Religious Experience* (London: Harper Collins, 1960), 242.

7 James, *The Principles of Psychology, vol. 2*, 297.

8 James, *The Principles of Psychology, vol. 2*, 297.

9 See Talal Asad, *Genealogies of Religion: Disciplines and Reasons of Power in Christianity and Islam* (Baltimore, MD: Johns Hopkins University Press, 1993), 43.

10 Ashis Nandy, "A Report on the Present State of Health of the Gods and Goddesses in South Asia," *Postcolonial Studies* 4, no. 2 (2001): 126.

11 Sanjay Seth, *Subject Lessons: The Western Education of Colonial India* (Durham, NC: Duke University Press, 2007), 62–63.

12 Nandy, "A Report on the Present State of Health," 126.

13 James, *The Varieties of Religious Experience*, 88.

14 William Connolly, *Capitalism and Christianity, American Style* (Durham, NC: Duke University Press, 2008).

15 See Tanya Luhrmann, *When God Talks Back: Understanding the American Evangelical Relationship with God* (New York: Vintage, 2012), 13–34.

16 See Susan Harding, "Representing Fundamentalism: The Problem of the Repugnant Cultural Other," *Social Research* 58, no. 2 (1991): 373–93.

17 See Jon Bialecki, *A Diagram for Fire: Miracles and Variation in an American Charismatic Movement* (Los Angeles: University of California Press, 2017).

18 Luhrmann, *When God Talks Back*, xv.

19 See Talal Asad, *Formations of the Secular: Christianity, Islam, Modernity* (Stanford, CA: Stanford University Press, 2003).

20 On the use of "not only" as a means of disrupting the metaphysics of identity, see Marisol de la Cadena, "Runa: Human but Not Only," *HAU: Journal of Ethnographic Theory* 4, no. 2 (2014): 253–59.

21 Gertrude Stein, *Everybody's Autobiography* (New York: Vintage, 1973).

22 James, *The Varieties of Religious Experience*, 73.

23 Luhrmann, *When God Talks Back*, 38.

24 James, *The Varieties of Religious Experience*, 78.

25 On the historical role of hearing in religious practice, see Leigh Eric Schmidt, *Hearing Things: Religion, Illusion, and the American Enlightenment* (Cambridge, MA: Harvard University Press, 2000).

26 Asad, *Formations of the Secular*, 37.

27 For a truly adventurous effort in seeking to reclaim the reality of words, see Mariam Motamedi-Fraser, *Word: Beyond Language, Beyond Image* (London: Rowman & Littlefield, 2015).

28 Asad, *Formations of the Secular*, 39.

29 Luhrmann, *When God Talks Back*, xvi.

30 Luhrmann, *When God Talks Back*, xxi.

31 Michel de Certeau, *The Practice of Everyday Life*, trans. Steven Rendall (Los Angeles: University of California Press, 1984), 137.

32 Luhrmann, *When God Talks Back*, 40–41.

33 Michel de Certeau, "What We Do When We Believe," in *On Signs*, ed. Marshall Blonsky (Baltimore, MD: Johns Hopkins University Press, 1985), 195.

34 James, *The Will to Believe and Other Essays*, 58.

35 James, *The Will to Believe and Other Essays*, 95.

36 James, *The Will to Believe and Other Essays*, 54.

37 See, for instance, Niklas Luhmann, *Trust and Power* (Toronto: Wiley, 1979); Diego Gambetta, ed., *Trust: Making and Breaking Cooperative Relations* (Oxford: Basil Blackwell, 1988); and Guido Möllering, "The Nature of Trust: From Georg Simmel to a Theory of Expectation, Interpretation and Suspension," *Sociology* 35, no. 2 (2001): 403–20. For a critique of the concept of trust as part of the new vocabulary in corporate ethics, see Alberto Corsín Jiménez, "Trust in Anthropology," *Anthropological Theory* 11, no. 2 (2011): 177–96.

38 James, *The Will to Believe and Other Essays*, 109.

39 James, *The Will to Believe and Other Essays*, 91.

40 James, *The Will to Believe and Other Essays*, 56.

41 James, *The Will to Believe and Other Essays*, 59.

42 James, *The Will to Believe and Other Essays*, 96–97.

43 Luhrmann, *When God Talks Back*, 42.

44 Luhrmann, *When God Talks Back*, 44.

45 Luhrmann, *When God Talks Back*, 42.

46 Luhrmann, *When God Talks Back*, 48.

47 Luhrmann, *When God Talks Back*, 48, 55.

48 Luhrmann, *When God Talks Back*, 53.

49 Luhrmann, *When God Talks Back*, 49.

50 Luhrmann, *When God Talks Back*, 54.

51 James, *The Will to Believe and Other Essays*, 61.

52 James, *The Will to Believe and Other Essays*, 59.

53 James, *The Will to Believe and Other Essays*, 59.

54 Luhrmann, *When God Talks Back*, 70.

55 On the notion of "doing" or "making" God, or what she calls theopoetics, see Catherine Keller, *The Cloud of the Impossible: Negative Theology and Planetary Entanglement* (New York: Columbia University Press, 2015).

56 Luhrmann, *When God Talks Back*, 84.

57 Perhaps because of the often polemical reception that the precursive dimension of trust has acquired among James's readers, the recursivity of trust has received comparatively little attention, even among some of his most creative and speculative commentators. However, a faint but nevertheless provocative intimation of its importance may be found in David Lapoujade's brilliant *William James: Empirisme et Pragmatisme* (Paris: Les Empêcheurs de

Penser en Rond, 2007), 110. There, he beautifully argues that, making itself paradoxically manifest in the indeterminate zone where the past and the future meet, trust is (precursively) the vital germ of all belief and of everything that binds us to the world. But as he indicates, it is this zone of indetermination, the very fact that the world is never fixed—for the possible is itself given in what is given—that creates the need to trust. And responding to this need involves acting not only in but *with* the world so as to exceed it and make the new a part of it. The question of *how* this indeterminate world with which we act might hold out its own hand back to those who trust it in order to render the excessive event effective is precisely what is at stake in the relation between pluralism and trust. And, as we shall see in later chapters, it is also what is required to develop a speculative appreciation of James's pragmatic account of truth and verification. See also Savransky, "The Wager of an Unfinished Present."

58 James, *Some Problems of Philosophy*, 230.
59 Luhrmann, *When God Talks Back*, 59.
60 Luhrmann, *When God Talks Back*, 52.
61 Luhrmann, *When God Talks Back*, 52.
62 Luhrmann, *When God Talks Back*, 52–53.
63 James, *The Varieties of Religious Experience*, 491.
64 James, *The Varieties of Religious Experience*, 87.
65 Luhrmann, *When God Talks Back*, 53.
66 Luhrmann, *When God Talks Back*, 287.
67 Luhrmann, *When God Talks Back*, 288.
68 James, *The Will to Believe and Other Essays*, 24.
69 See relatedly the important work of Paul Nadasdy, who, in working with the people of Kluane First Nation in the Southwest Yukon, has allowed himself to be lured by the possibility that the hunters' own account of their relationship with reindeer may be true not just metaphorically but literally. Paul Nadasdy, "The Gift in the Animal: The Ontology of Hunting and Human-Animal Sociality," *American Ethnologist* 34, no. 1 (2007): 25–43.
70 Tim Ingold, *The Perception of the Environment: Essays on Livelihood, Dwelling and Skill* (London: Routledge, 2000), 69.
71 Ingold, *The Perception of the Environment*, 13.
72 Ingold, *The Perception of the Environment*, 13.
73 Ingold, *The Perception of the Environment*, 67.
74 James, *Some Problems of Philosophy*, 228–29.
75 James, *Some Problems of Philosophy*, 229.
76 James, *Some Problems of Philosophy*, 231.

1   James, *Some Problems of Philosophy*, 46.

2   For an interesting exploration of the vicissitudes of the notion of "togetherness" in relation to James and Whitehead, see Steven Meyer, "Of 'Experiential Togetherness': Toward a More Robust Empiricism," in *The Lure of Whitehead*, ed. Nicholas Gaskill and Adam J. Nocek (Minneapolis: University of Minnesota Press, 2014), 332–59.

3   James, *Essays in Radical Empiricism*, 45.

4   For another interesting reading of this episode, see Alexander Livingston, "Excited Subjects: William James and the Politics of Radical Empiricism," *Theory & Event* 15, no. 4 (2012). Accessed August 2, 2018, https://www.muse.jhu .edu/article/491201.

5   William James, "On Some Mental Effects of the Earthquake," in *William James: Writings 1902–1910*, ed. Bruce Kurlkick (New York: Library of America, 1987), 1215.

6   James, "On Some Mental Effects of the Earthquake," 1215–16.

7   James, *A Pluralistic Universe*, 264.

8   James, "On Some Mental Effects of the Earthquake," 1216.

9   James, "On Some Mental Effects of the Earthquake," 1216.

10 James, "On Some Mental Effects of the Earthquake," 1216.

11 James, "On Some Mental Effects of the Earthquake," 1216.

12 James, "On Some Mental Effects of the Earthquake," 1217.

13 James, "On Some Mental Effects of the Earthquake," 1216–17.

14 Cortázar, *Clases de Literatura*, 50.

15 On the pluralistic problematic, see Martin Savransky, "The Pluralistic Problematic: William James and the Pragmatics of the Pluriverse," *Theory, Culture & Society* (2019): 1–19. doi.org/10.1177/0263276419848030.

16 James, *The Principles of Psychology, vol. 1*, 488.

17 Lorraine Daston, "Preternatural Philosophy," in *Biographies of Scientific Objects*, ed. Lorraine Daston (Chicago: University of Chicago Press, 2001), 15–41. See also Daston and Park, *Wonders and the Order of Nature*.

18 See Monica Greco, "Pragmatics of Explanation: Creative Accountability in the Care of 'Medically Unexplained Symptoms,'" *Sociological Review* 65, no. 2 (2017): 110–29; and Isabelle Stengers, "The Doctor and the Charlatan," *Cultural Studies Review* 9, no. 2 (2003): 12–36.

19 For a fabulous rejoinder, see Vinciane Despret, *Au Bonheur des Morts: Récits de ceux qui restent* (Paris: La Découverte, 2015).

20 It is precisely these modern-realist operations that rendered reality ordinary and regular that, today, in the face of climate catastrophe, constitute what Indian writer Amitav Ghosh has dubbed the time of the Great Derangement, when modern culture, which never ceases to praise its own self-awareness, turns out to have rendered utterly unthinkable and un

imaginable the extraordinary and metamorphic realities that now constitute the Earth. See Amitav Ghosh, *The Great Derangement: Climate Change and
the Unthinkable* (Chicago: University of Chicago Press, 2016). For a study of
the rise of literary realism, see Peter Brooks, *Realist Vision* (New Haven, CT:
Yale University Press, 2005).

21 Leela Gandhi, *Affective Communities: Anticolonial Thought, Fin-de-siècle Radicalism, and the Politics of Friendship* (Durham, NC: Duke University Press,
2006), 9.

22 William James, "Address on the Philippine Question," in *William James:
Writings 1902–1910*, ed. Bruce Kurlkick (New York: Library of America, 1987),
1130–35.

23 Gandhi, *Affective Communities*, 118.

24 Gandhi, *Affective Communities*, 133.

25 James, *Pragmatism and the Meaning of Truth*, 35.

26 This, in other words, is what Alfred North Whitehead famously called "The
Fallacy of Misplaced Concreteness," that is, the error of mistaking the ab-
stract for the concrete. See Alfred North Whitehead, *Science and the Modern
World* (New York: Free Press, 1967), 51.

27 Chakrabarty, *Provincializing Europe*, 102.

28 Chakrabarty, *Provincializing Europe*, 102. See also Ranajit Guha, "The Prose
of Counter-Insurgency," in *Selected Subaltern*, ed. Ranajit Guha and Gayatri
Chakravorty Spivak (New York and Oxford: Oxford University Press, 1988),
45–84.

29 Chakrabarty, *Provincializing Europe*, 102.

30 Chakrabarty, *Provincializing Europe*, 103.

31 As the conceptual historian Reinhardt Koselleck notes, the modern invention of the "collective singular" of "Man" as the sole subject of history ex-
pelled from it not only gods but nature as well. See Reinhardt Koselleck,
Futures Past: On the Semantics of Historical Time (New York: Columbia University Press, 2004).

32 Chakrabarty, *Provincializing Europe*, 103.

33 Chakrabarty, *Provincializing Europe*, 104.

34 Chakrabarty, *Provincializing Europe*, 101.

35 Chakrabarty, *Provincializing Europe*, 106.

36 Chakrabarty, *Provincializing Europe*, 107.

37 Chakrabarty, *Provincializing Europe*, 109.

38 Chakrabarty, *Provincializing Europe*, 110.

39 Chakrabarty, *Provincializing Europe*, 112.

40 Chakrabarty, *Provincializing Europe*, 112.

41 Chakrabarty, *Provincializing Europe*, 110.

42 Chakrabarty, *Provincializing Europe*, 110.

43 I am thankful to Sanjay Seth (personal communication) for this articula-

tion. See also Sanjay Seth, *Beyond Reason? Postcolonial Theory and the Social Sciences* (New York: Oxford University Press, 2020).

44 More recently, Chakrabarty has been exploring the imperative of crafting history otherwise in the wake of ecological devastation. See Dipesh Chakrabarty, "The Climate of History: Four Theses," *Critical Inquiry* 35, no. 2 (2009): 197–222; and Dipesh Chakrabarty, "Postcolonial Studies and the Challenge of Climate Change," *New Literary History* 43, no. 1 (2012): 1–18.

45 James, *A Pluralistic Universe*, 272.

46 James, *A Pluralistic Universe*, 272.

47 The charge of relativism is often made against even some of the most modest attempts at making the pluriverse felt. But relativism has always been a clandestine ally of a monistic rationalism. Indeed, I think there's perhaps no better way of describing a relativist than as a *defeated monist*: someone who, confronted by a worldquake, hangs on with all his/her strength to one final general principle, applicable everywhere and always: "anything goes."

48 De la Cadena, "Indigenous Cosmopolitics in the Andes," 335.

49 James, *A Pluralistic Universe*, 273.

50 Chakrabarty, *Provincializing Europe*, 101.

51 The most staggering dramatization of this experience I have come across has in fact been in the literary work of Brazilian writer Clarice Lispector, specifically in her magisterial *The Passion According to G. H.* (New York: Penguin, 2014), where the world and subjectivity of a middle-class woman is shaken to its core by the eerie encounter with a cockroach.

52 Gillian Goslinga, "Spirited Encounters: Notes on the Politics and Poetics of Representing the Uncanny in Anthropology," *Anthropological Theory* 12, no. 4 (2012): 394.

53 As Tanya Luhrmann has provocatively put it in a recent commentary, "these ontological anthropologists have not brought back observations from these local worlds in order to reimagine their own. One strongly doubts Viveiros de Castro himself believes that women can become jaguars (to borrow the famous example)." Tanya Luhrmann, "The Real Ontological Challenge," HAU: *Journal of Ethnographic Theory* 1/2 (2018): 80.

54 See Matei Candea, "We Have Never Been Pluralist: On Lateral and Frontal Comparisons in the Ontological Turn," in *Comparative Metaphysics: Ontology after Anthropology*, ed. Pierre Charbonnier, Gildas Salmon, and Peter Skafish (London: Rowman & Littlefield, 2017), 85–106.

55 See Eduardo Viveiros de Castro, "Perspectival Anthropology and the Method of Controlled Equivocation," *Tipití: Journal of the Society for the Anthropology of Lowland South America* 2, no. 1 (2004): 5. The notion and "method" of "controlled equivocation," proposed by Viveiros de Castro in relation to his own study of Amerindian perspectivism, has become one of the operational means by which the "turn to ontology" in anthropology has

developed around the day in eighty worlds. At its heart is an attempt to deal with the impossibility of translation that has preoccupied anthropologists and other allies in the humanities for decades, and to deal with it by assuming "the referential alterity between homonymic concepts." In other words, it assumes that similar concepts in different worlds may refer to radically different things. This is no doubt especially relevant to, and is an elegantly succinct way of expressing, the situated problem posed by Amerindian perspectivism itself, as the indigenous theory posits difference not in terms of a plurality of ways of looking at things but in terms of a plurality of things looked at *in the same way* by different beings. But once again, turning this into a more general methodology of translation, as it sometimes appears to have become, poses serious dangers: must all feelings of difference in the concrete come in the form of such an "equivocation"? Isn't equivocation itself relative to the particular encounter of differences?

56 Edith Turner, *Experiencing Ritual: A New Interpretation of African Healing* (Philadelphia: University of Pennsylvania Press, 1992).

57 Turner, *Experiencing Ritual*, 2.

58 Turner, *Experiencing Ritual*, 8.

59 Turner, *Experiencing Ritual*, 29.

60 Turner, *Experiencing Ritual*, 5, 12, xi.

61 Turner, *Experiencing Ritual*, 20.

62 Turner, *Experiencing Ritual*, 20.

63 Turner, *Experiencing Ritual*, 20.

64 Turner, *Experiencing Ritual*, 21.

65 Turner, *Experiencing Ritual*, 25.

66 See Martin Savransky and Marsha Rosengarten, "What Is Nature Capable Of? Evidence, Ontology, and Speculative Medical Humanities," *Medical Humanities* 42 (2016): 166–72.

67 Edith Turner, "A Visible Spirit from Zambia," in *Being Changed by Cross-Cultural Encounters: The Anthropology of Extraordinary Experience*, ed. David E. Young and Jean Guy Goulet (Ontario: Broadview Press, 1994), 73.

68 Turner, *Experiencing Ritual*, 113.

69 Turner, *Experiencing Ritual*, 27.

70 Turner, *Experiencing Ritual*, 23.

71 Turner, *Experiencing Ritual*, 96.

72 Turner, *Experiencing Ritual*, 97.

73 Turner, *Experiencing Ritual*, 96

74 Turner, *Experiencing Ritual*, 93.

75 Turner, *Experiencing Ritual*, 165.

76 Turner, "A Visible Spirit from Zambia," 73.

77 Turner, *Experiencing Ritual*, 33. *Mufungu* means "the gathering together of a herd of animals."

78 Turner, *Experiencing Ritual*, 33.

79 Turner, *Experiencing Ritual*, 34.

80 Turner, *Experiencing Ritual*, 134.

81 Turner, *Experiencing Ritual*, 148.

82 Turner, *Experiencing Ritual*, 149.

83 Turner, "A Visible Spirit from Zambia," 85.

84 Turner, *Experiencing Ritual*, 220.

85 William James, "The Confidences of a 'Psychical Researcher,'" in *William James: Writings 1902–1910*, ed. Bruce Kurlkick (New York: Library of America, 1987), 1250.

86 Turner, "A Visible Spirit from Zambia," 93.

87 Turner, "A Visible Spirit from Zambia," 93.

88 Turner, "A Visible Spirit from Zambia," 86.

89 Turner, "A Visible Spirit from Zambia," 149.

90 James, *The Will to Believe and Other Essays*, viii.

91 Turner, "A Visible Spirit from Zambia," 92.

92 Turner, "A Visible Spirit from Zambia," 87.

93 Turner, "A Visible Spirit from Zambia," 87.

94 James, *The Will to Believe and Other Essays*, 158.

95 Gilles Deleuze, *Essays Critical and Clinical*, trans. Daniel W. Smith and Michael A. Greco (Minneapolis: University of Minnesota Press, 1997), 107.

96 Turner, "A Visible Spirit from Zambia," 86. Turner would indeed go on to produce a radically understated dance of words, full of silences, that I would characterize as a kind of "practical mysticism" whose task is, above all, never to explain, nor to transpose, the way in which others inhabit the world, but to learn how to feel one's way through it.

97 On some of the problems associated with a general politics of symmetry, see Martin Savransky, "What's the Relevance of Isabelle Stengers' Philosophy to ANT?" in *The Routledge Companion to Actor-Network Theory*, ed. Anders Blok, Ignacio Farías, and Celia Roberts (London: Routledge, 2019).

98 Helen Verran, "Engagements between Disparate Knowledge Traditions: Toward Doing Difference Generatively and in Good Faith," in *Contested Ecologies: Dialogues in the South on Nature and Knowledge*, ed. Lesley Green (Cape Town: Human Sciences Research Council Press, 2013), 144.

99 Edith Turner, *Communitas: The Anthropology of Collective Joy* (New York: Palgrave Macmillan, 2012), 218.

100 James, *Some Problems of Philosophy*, 98.

101 James, *Some Problems of Philosophy*, 64.

102 James, *Some Problems of Philosophy*, 71.

103 James, *The Will to Believe and Other Essays*, 207.

104 James, *Some Problems of Philosophy*, 142.

105 James, *Pragmatism*, 122–23.

1 James, *Pragmatism and the Meaning of Truth*, 70.

2 James, *Pragmatism and the Meaning of Truth*, 139.

3 James, *Pragmatism and the Meaning of Truth*, 139.

4 Déborah Danowski and Eduardo Viveiros de Castro, "L'arret de Monde," in *De l'univers clos au monde infini*, ed. Émile Hache (Paris: Éditions Dehors, 2014), 229. See also Déborah Danowski and Eduardo Viveiros de Castro, *The Ends of the World*, trans. Rodrigo Nunes (Cambridge: Polity Press, 2016).

5 On the importance of reclaiming a tragic sensibility in postcolonial thought, the work of David Scott is exemplary. See David Scott, *Conscripts of Modernity: The Tragedy of Colonial Enlightenment* (Durham, NC: Duke University Press, 2004); David Scott, *Omens of Adversity: Tragedy, Time, Memory, Justice* (Durham, NC: Duke University Press, 2014); and David Scott, "The Tragic Vision in Postcolonial Time," PMLA 129, no. 4 (2014): 799–808.

6 James, *A Pluralistic Universe*, 321.

7 In this sense, it has to be said that while John Dewey has in some ways become the main representative of pragmatism, for all the other merits of his *The Public and Its Problems* (Carbondale: Southern Illinois University Press, 2009) Dewey remains at best a reluctant pluralist. Like many of his liberal heirs, Dewey concedes the existence of a plurality of publics but deems that fact regrettable, devoting his energies to the construction of a Great Community where the divergent problems that call for them could be brought into some form of successful reunification. On Dewey's reluctant pluralism, see Avigail Eisenberg, "Pluralism and Method at the Turn of the Century," in *Modern Pluralism: Anglo-American Debates since 1880*, ed. Mark Bevir (Cambridge: Cambridge University Press, 2017), 60–80. On the "descent" of pluralism since James, see Kennan Ferguson, *Politics in the Pluriverse* (Lanham, MD: Rowman & Littlefield, 2007).

8 James, *The Will to Believe and Other Essays*, 58.

9 Recalling that "wake" evokes a plurality of associations —the keeping watch with the dead, the path of a ship, the consequence of things, the lines of flight, the movements of bodies in water— literary scholar Christina Sharpe has generatively experimented with what it means to think (Black) existence in the wake of the ongoing and shifting present of "slavery's as yet unresolved unfolding." There are of course as many divergent wakes as there are lines of flight. We follow disparate histories and divergent paths. But just as she hopes "that the praxis of the wake and wake work might have enough capaciousness to travel and do work that I have not here been able to imagine or anticipate," I hope that perhaps some interweaving ripples from very different waves are possible when one comes to think about the manifold dead and our multiple relations to them. See Christina Sharpe, *In*

the Wake: On Blackness and Being (Durham, NC: Duke University Press, 2016), 14, 22.

10 James, *Pragmatism and the Meaning of Truth*, 23.

11 James, *Pragmatism and the Meaning of Truth*, 62.

12 James, *Pragmatism and the Meaning of Truth*, 32.

13 Failure to understand this has led many an heir of James into philosophical and political disasters of their own. To name but one example, during James's own time, and shortly after, the Italian pragmatist Giovanni Papini—who, it must be said, was otherwise an inspired writer—mesmerized by the more activist passages of James's *Pragmatism* lectures, turned pragmatism itself into a veritably Promethean program for cultivating a figure of the human endowed with unbounded powers to bend reality according to its self-deifying will. In so doing, Papini's violently optimistic figure of *Uomo-dio* created, alas, a direct connection between pragmatism and Italian fascism. See Giovanni Papini, *Sul Pragmatismo* (Milan: Libreria Editrice Milanese, 1913). For a discussion of the pragmatist-fascist connection via the work of Papini, see Livingston, *Damn Great Empires!*, 40–42. For a study of Papini as a crucial intellectual precursor laying out the foundations of Italian fascism, see the very interesting book by Andrea Righi, *Italian Reactionary Thought and Critical Theory: An Inquiry into Savage Modernities* (Basingstoke: Palgrave Macmillan, 2015).

14 James, *Pragmatism and the Meaning of Truth*, 9–10.

15 James, *Pragmatism and the Meaning of Truth*, 206.

16 See especially Coon, "One Moment in the World's Salvation," and Livingston, *Damn Great Empires!*

17 James, *The Will to Believe and Other Essays*, 37.

18 I owe this perspicacious observation to William J. Gavin's work on pragmatism and death. See William J. Gavin, "*Pragmatism* and Death: Method vs. Metaphor, Tragedy vs. the Will to Believe," in *100 Years of Pragmatism: William James's Revolutionary Philosophy*, ed. John Stuhr (Bloomington: Indiana University Press, 2010), 81–95.

19 James, *Pragmatism and the Meaning of Truth*, 122.

20 James, *Pragmatism and the Meaning of Truth*, 82.

21 James, *Pragmatism and the Meaning of Truth*, 63.

22 James, *Pragmatism and the Meaning of Truth*, 32.

23 See Wataru Suzuki et al., "Source Rupture Process of the 2011 Tohoku-Oki Earthquake Derived from the Strong-motion Records," *Proceedings of the Fifteenth World Conference on Earthquake Engineering* (2012): 1–9, accessed March 29, 2019, http://www.iitk.ac.in/nicee/wcee/article/WCEE2012_1650 .pdf; and Michael Reilly, "Japan's Quake Updated to Magnitude 9.0," *New Scientist*, March 11, 2011, accessed March 29, 2019, http://www.newscientist .com/blogs/shortsharpscience/2011/03/powerful-japan-quake-sparks-ts .html.

24 See Tania Branigan, "Tsunami, Earthquake, Nuclear Crisis—Now Japan Faces Power Cuts," *Guardian*, March 13, 2011, accessed March 29, 2019, https://www.theguardian.com/world/2011/mar/13/japan-tsunami-earthquake-power-cuts.

25 CNN wire staff, "Tsunami Warnings and Advisories Remain across Pacific Region," CNN, March 11, 2011, accessed March 29, 2019, http://edition.cnn.com/2011/WORLD/asiapcf/03/11/tsunami.warning/index.html.

26 Richard Lloyd Parry, *Ghosts of the Tsunami* (London: Vintage, 2017), 93.

27 Lloyd Parry, *Ghosts of the Tsunami*, 94.

28 Lloyd Parry, *Ghosts of the Tsunami*, 94.

29 Sabu Kohso et al., *Fukushima & Ses Invisibles: Cahiers d'enquetes politiques* (Vaulx-en-Velin, France: Les Éditions des Mondes à Faire, 2018), 19.

30 Lloyd Parry, *Ghosts of the Tsunami*, 99.

31 Lloyd Parry, *Ghosts of the Tsunami*, 95.

32 Lloyd Parry, *Ghosts of the Tsunami*, 99–100.

33 This is the case in two of the most significant global religion polls, conducted respectively by the Pew Research Center and Gallup. This is of course contrasted with but inextricably linked to the commonplace view that, as anthropologist Alan McFarlane puts it, in Japan "everything is imbued with 'spirit' or kami—pots, computers, goldfish, space, time, tea, stones, sumo, peaches, echoes." See Alan McFarlane, *Japan Through the Looking Glass* (London: Profile Books, 2007), 202. See also Michiko Iwasaka and Barre Toelken, *Ghosts and the Japanese: Cultural Experience in Japanese Death Legends* (Logan: Utah State University Press, 1994).

34 Marilyn Ivy, *Discourses of the Vanishing: Modernity, Phantasm, Japan* (Chicago: University of Chicago Press, 1995), 70.

35 On this see Gerald Figal, *Civilization and Monsters: Spirits of Modernity in Meiji Japan* (Durham, NC: Duke University Press, 1999).

36 Asad, *Genealogies of Religion*.

37 For its part, Buddhism's own relationship with ghosts rendered it the object of increasing suspicion in the late nineteenth century. As Jason Ānanda Josephson shows, the invention of religion in Japan led to accusations that Buddha's original teachings had become perverted by priests who claimed to be capable of expelling ghosts and devils, rendering popular belief in ghosts and monsters "a direct result of Buddhist fraud." Jason Ānanda Josephson, *The Invention of Religion in Japan* (Chicago: University of Chicago Press, 2012), 209.

38 Indeed, as Gerald Figal has argued, throughout the history of Japan the "control of spirits has meant the control of Spirit. Japanese spirituality was reorganised into the Japanese spirit, where spirits were relegated to the realm of folklore and superstition." Figal, *Civilization and Monsters*, 197.

39 For an in-depth, historical examination of these entangled inventions, see Josephson, *The Invention of Religion in Japan*.

40 Of course, ghosts persisted in Buddhist cosmology, as one of the realms of rebirth and existence. And the spirits of the dead also enjoy a form of survival in contemporary popular culture, not least through the annual Buddhist event known as *Obon*, dedicated to the commemoration of ancestors' spirits, who return to this world to visit their living relatives. But it is telling that, though a few reports of the presence of the dead after the tsunami were published and broadcasted in the media, these attempted "to avoid upsetting contemporary 'modern' sensibilities regarding such experiences," and thus refrained from making explicit references to ghosts, spirits, or the afterlife. See Hara Takahashi, "The Ghosts of Tsunami Dead and *Kokoro no kea* in Japan's Religious Landscape," *Journal of Religion in Japan* 5 (2016): 176–98.

41 Figal, *Civilization and Monsters*, 29.

42 Figal, *Civilization and Monsters*, 93.

43 The counterpart to this process was the buoyant generation of a field of Japanese Folklore and of a Monsterology, both of which took great interest in ghosts and spirits of all sorts, but only as objects of academic study, figments of the Japanese anthropological imagination devoid of any worldly existence. See Figal, *Civilizations and Monsters*; for a contemporary counterattempt to reclaim the reality of spirits in Japan, see Casper Bruun Jensen, Miho Ishi, and Philip Swift, "Attuning to the Webs of *en*: Ontography, Japanese Spirit Worlds, and the 'Tact' of Minakata Kumagusu," HAU: *Journal of Ethnographic Theory* 6, no. 2 (2016): 149–72.

44 Lloyd Parry, *Ghosts of the Tsunami*, 113.

45 See Takahashi, "The Ghosts of Tsunami Dead," 179.

46 James, *Pragmatism and the Meaning of Truth*, 18.

47 James, *The Varieties of Religious Experience*, 169.

48 Lloyd Parry, *Ghosts of the Tsunami*, 49.

49 Takahashi, "The Ghosts of the Tsunami Dead," 181.

50 Lloyd Parry, *Ghosts of the Tsunami*, 100.

51 James, *A Pluralistic Universe*, 353.

52 Lloyd Parry, *Ghosts of the Tsunami*, 100.

53 James, *A Pluralistic Universe*, 372.

54 Lloyd Parry, *Ghosts of the Tsunami*, 224.

55 Lloyd Parry, *Ghosts of the Tsunami*, 224.

56 Lloyd Parry, *Ghosts of the Tsunami*, 224–25.

57 Lloyd Parry, *Ghosts of the Tsunami*, 225.

58 Lloyd Parry, *Ghosts of the Tsunami*, 225.

59 Lloyd Parry, *Ghosts of the Tsunami*, 225.

60 See Martin Savransky, "Pragmatics of a World To-Be-Made," in *Thinking the Problematic: Genealogies, Tracings, and Currents of a Persistent Force*, ed. Erich Hörl and Oliver Leistert (Berlin: Transcript Verlag, 2020).

61 James, *Pragmatism and the Meaning of Truth*, 99.

62 James, *Pragmatism and the Meaning of Truth*, 32.

63 Taio Kaneta, "Listening to the Heart: Among the People in the Great East Japan Earthquake Disaster Area" (paper presented at the 3rd United Nations World Conference on Disaster Risk Reduction, Sendai, Japan, March 14–18, 2015), accessed April 4, 2019, http://drr.tohoku.ac.jp/system/wp-content /uploads/2015/01/aaf2cd443b060aaaf3090227d870528a.pdf.

64 Lloyd Parry, *Ghosts of the Tsunami*, 225.

65 Lloyd Parry, *Ghosts of the Tsunami*, 226.

66 James, *Pragmatism and the Meaning of Truth*, 44.

67 Kaneta, "Listening to the Heart."

68 Lloyd Parry, *Ghosts of the Tsunami*, 232.

69 For this and other forms of spiritual care-work set up in the wake of the tsunami, see Taniyama Yōzō, "Chaplaincy Work in Disaster Areas," in *Religion and Psychotherapy in Japan*, ed. Christopher Harding, Iwata Fumiaki, and Yoshinaga Shin'ichi (London: Routledge, 2015), 250–66.

70 Lloyd Parry, *Ghosts of the Tsunami*, 222.

71 Lloyd Parry, *Ghosts of the Tsunami*, 103. *Gaki*, of course, are familiar to Japanese Buddhism, as are *Muenbotoke*, homeless spirits. But it is one thing to know about them, and another to develop a concrete relationship with them.

72 Lloyd Parry, *Ghosts of the Tsunami*, 247.

73 Lloyd Parry, *Ghosts of the Tsunami*, 248.

74 Lloyd Parry, *Ghosts of the Tsunami*, 248.

75 Lloyd Parry, *Ghosts of the Tsunami*, 248.

76 James, *Pragmatism and the Meaning of Truth*, 97.

77 James, *Pragmatism and the Meaning of Truth*, 104.

78 Cognition is above all a matter of the production of certain existential relations between moments of experience, relations of continuity and corroboration. And "knowledge," the word by which we name such relations, is therefore an integral part (though not a necessary part) of the tissue of reality. But truth is assigned to it only retrospectively. "The 'state of mind,'" wrote James, "first treated explicitly as such in retrospection, will stand corrected or confirmed, and the retrospective experience in its turn will get a similar treatment; but the immediate experience in its passing is always 'truth,' practical truth, *something to act on*, at its own movement." See James, *Essays in Radical Empiricism*, 13.

79 James, *Pragmatism and the Meaning of Truth*, 98.

80 James, *Pragmatism and the Meaning of Truth*, 102.

81 Savransky, "The Wager of an Unfinished Present."

82 James, *Pragmatism and the Meaning of Truth*, 42.

83 Savransky, "Pragmatics of a World To-Be-Made."

84 James, *Pragmatism and the Meaning of Truth*, 28.

85 Lloyd Parry, *Ghosts of the Tsunami*, 242.

86 James, *Pragmatism and the Meaning of Truth*, 124.

87 James, *Pragmatism and the Meaning of Truth*, 124.

88 James, *Pragmatism and the Meaning of Truth*, 137.

89 James, *Pragmatism and the Meaning of Truth*, 222.

90 James, *The Letters of William James*, 89.

CHAPTER SIX: THE INSISTENCE OF THE PLURIVERSE

1 Jules Verne, *Around the World in 80 Days* (London: Penguin, 2008).

2 *Sati*, or widow sacrifice, is a Hindu practice whereby the widow is meant to ascend the pyre of the dead husband and immolate herself upon it in order to enable herself and her deceased husband to enjoy heavenly pleasures and, in some cases, to escape the cycle of life and death. Its prohibition by the British in 1829, and the debate surrounding it, became a critical episode in the history of colonialism and emancipation in India, in both colonialist and nationalist texts. It is precisely this case that Gayatri Chakravorty Spivak discusses in the crafting of the famous expression of "white men saving brown women from white men." See Gayatri Chakravorty Spivak, "Can the Subaltern Speak?," in *Marxism and The Interpretation of Culture*, ed. Cary Nelson and Lawrence Grossberg (Basingstoke: Macmillan Education, 1988), 297. For a detailed examination of the complex debates around *sati* in colonial India, see Lata Mani, *Contentious Traditions: The Debate on Sati in Colonial India* (Berkeley: University of California Press, 1998).

3 James, *A Pluralistic Universe*, 45.

4 William James, *Manuscript, Essays, and Notes* (Cambridge, MA: Harvard University Press, 1988), 5.

5 James, *Pragmatism and the Meaning of Truth*, 65.

6 James, *Pragmatism and the Meaning of Truth*, 65.

7 James, *Pragmatism and the Meaning of Truth*, 66–67.

8 James, *Manuscript, Essays, and Notes*, 13.

9 As James put it: "The whole question revolves in very truth about the word 'some.' Radical empiricism and pluralism stand out for the legitimacy of the notion of *some*: each part of the world is in some ways connected, in some other ways not connected with its other parts, and the ways can be discriminated, for many of them are obvious, and their differences are obvious to view." James, *A Pluralistic Universe*, 79.

10 James, *Essays in Radical Empiricism*, 98.

11 "Each time a story helps me remember what I thought I knew, or introduces me to new knowledge," Donna Haraway writes, "a muscle critical for caring about flourishing gets some aerobic exercise. Such exercise enhances collective thinking and movement in complexity. Each time I trace a tangle and add a few threads that at first seemed whimsical but turned out to be

essential to the fabric, I get a bit straighter that staying with the trouble of complex worlding is the name of the game of living and dying well together on terra, in Terrapolis." Donna Haraway, *Staying with the Trouble*, 29.

12 William James, *Psychology: The Briefer Course* (Mineola, NY: Dover, 2001), 321.

13 James, *Pragmatism and the Meaning of Truth*, 137.

14 James, *Some Problems of Philosophy*, 141.

15 William James, "A Pluralistic Mystic," in *William James: Writings 1902–1910*, ed. Bruce Kurlkick (New York: Library of America, 1987), 1313.

16 For a deep meditation on the depths of beginnings, on beginnings as the gaping open of the deep, see Catherine Keller, *The Face of the Deep: A Theology of Becoming* (New York: Routledge, 2003).

17 James, *Manuscript, Essays, and Notes*, 5.

18 James, *Talks to Teachers on Psychology, and to Students on Some of Life's Ideals* (London: Longmans, Green, 1907), 270.

19 James, *Talks to Teachers*, 268–69.

20 James, *Talks to Teachers*, 270.

21 James, *Talks to Teachers*, 269–70.

22 James, *The Letters of William James*, 43.

23 James, *The Letters of William James*, 271.

24 James, *Talks to Teachers*, 270.

25 See Martin Savransky, "The Pluralistic Problematic."

26 James, *Talks to Teachers*, 271.

27 James, *The Letters of William James*, 43.

28 James, *Talks to Teachers*, 272.

29 James, *Talks to Teachers*, 270.

30 James, *Talks to Teachers*, 271.

31 William James, *Essays in Religion and Morality* (Cambridge, MA: Harvard University Press, 1982), 171.

32 James, *A Pluralistic Universe*, 45.

33 James, *A Pluralistic Universe*, 45.

34 James, *The Varieties of Religious Experience*, 356.

35 James, *Talks to Teachers*, 274, 276.

36 James, *Talks to Teachers*, 283.

37 James, *Talks to Teachers*, 292.

38 James, *Talks to Teachers*, 288.

39 James, *Talks to Teachers*, 293.

40 James, *Talks to Teachers*, 292.

41 James, *Talks to Teachers*, 295–96.

42 There are many resonances between the notion of the otherwise as I use it here and the way it is mobilized by anthropologist Elizabeth Povinelli, not least in our respective debts to pragmatism. See Elizabeth Povinelli, *Economies of Abandonment: Social Belonging and Endurance in Late Liberalism* (Durham, NC: Duke University Press, 2011), 10. See also Elizabeth Povinelli,

"The Will to Be Otherwise/The Effort of Endurance," *South Atlantic Quarterly* 111, no. 3 (2012): 453–57.

43 This is indeed the way in which Jacques Derrida famously inherited Nietzsche's call for a new species of philosophers, the philosophers of the "dangerous" perhaps, and mobilized it as a way of exploring the question of friendship. See Jacques Derrida, *The Politics of Friendship*, trans. George Collins (New York: Verso, 2005). For a rich exploration of Derrida's notion of "perhaps," see Elizabeth Weber, "Suspended from the Other's Heartbeat," *South Atlantic Quarterly* 106, no. 2 (2007): 325–44.

44 James, *Essays in Radical Empiricism*, 84.

45 As James put it in a letter to his friend Josephine Lowell in December 1903, in the wake of the American annexation of the Philippines: "It seems to me that the great disease of our country now is the unwillingness of people to do anything that has no chance of succeeding. The organization of great machines for 'slick' success is the discovery of our age; and, with us, the individual, as soon as he realizes that the machine will be irresistible, *acquiesces* silently, instead of making an impotent row. The impotent row-maker becomes, in the eye of public opinion, an ass and a nuisance. . . . We want people who are willing to espouse failure as their vocation. I wish *that* could be organized—it would soon 'pass into its opposite.'" William James to Josephine Lowell, December 6, 1903, James Papers, Harvard Library Archive, cited in Coon, "One Moment in the World's Salvation," 92.

46 See de la Cadena, *Earth-Beings*.

47 Mario Blaser and Marisol de la Cadena, "Pluriverse: Proposals for a World of Many Worlds," in *A World of Many Worlds*, ed. Marisol de la Cadena and Mario Blaser (Durham, NC: Duke University Press, 2018), 4.

48 Ejército Zapatista de Liberación Nacional, "Cuarta Declaración de la Selva Lacandona," January 1, 1996. Accessed July 3, 2019, https://radiozapatista.org/?p=20287.

49 See, for instance, Paul Kingsnorth, *One No, Many Yeses: A Journey to the Heart of the Global Resistance Movement* (New York: Free Press, 2003); Alex Kasnabish, *Zapatismo beyond Borders: New Imaginations of Political Possibility* (Toronto: University of Toronto Press, 2008); and Thomas Nail, "Zapatismo and the Global Origins of Occupy," *Journal of Cultural and Religious Theory* 12, no. 3 (2013): 20–35.

50 For some of the divergent, partially connecting efforts by these allies, see, for instance, de la Cadena and Blaser, *A World of Many Worlds*; Arturo Escobar, *Designs for the Pluriverse: Radical Interdependence, Autonomy, and the Making of Worlds* (Durham, NC: Duke University Press, 2018); Ashish Kothari et al., eds., *Pluriverse: A Postdevelopment Dictionary* (New Delhi: Tulika Books, 2019); Bernd Reiter, ed., *Constructing the Pluriverse* (Durham, NC: Duke University Press, 2018); Cristina Rojas, "Contesting the Colonial Logics of the International: Towards a Relational Politics for the Pluriverse," *International*

Political Sociology 18 (2016): 369–82; and Janet Conway and Jakeet Singh, "Radical Democracy in Global Perspective: Notes from the Pluriverse," *Third World Quarterly* 32, no. 4 (2011): 689–706.

51 Mignolo, *The Darker Side of Western Modernity*, 258.

52 Mignolo, *The Darker Side of Western Modernity*, 23, 223.

53 Kothari et al., *Pluriverse: A Postdevelopment Dictionary*.

54 Blaser and de la Cadena, "Pluriverse: Proposals for a World of Many Worlds," 4.

55 Escobar, *Designs for the Pluriverse*.

56 Kothari et al., *Pluriverse: A Postdevelopment Dictionary*.

57 James, *The Varieties of Religious Experience*, 350.

58 For an excellent depiction of this emerging relational cosmology among contemporary pluralistic anthropologies, see the excellent paper by Michael W. Scott, "The Anthropology of Ontology (Religious Science?)," *Journal of the Royal Anthropological Institute* 19 (2013): 859–72.

59 Escobar, *Designs for the Pluriverse*, 95.

60 Escobar, *Designs for the Pluriverse*, 101.

61 Scott, "The Anthropology of Ontology (Religious Science?)," 864.

62 Indeed, there is an interesting etymological connection between paying attention and giving refuge. See Martin Savransky and Isabelle Stengers, "Relearning the Art of Paying Attention: A Conversation," *SubStance* 47, no. 1 (2018): 29–46.

63 Others appear less trusting of this possibility, however, arguing that relational ontologies are intrinsically depoliticizing. Of course, it all depends what one means by "politics"! See Erik Swyngedouw and Henrik Ernstson, "Interrupting the Anthropo-obScene: Immuno-biopolitics and Depoliticizing Ontologies in the Anthropocene," *Theory, Culture and Society*, 35, no. 6 (2018): 3–30. See also David Chandler and Julian Reid, *Becoming Indigenous: Governing Imaginaries in the Anthropocene* (London: Rowman & Littlefield, 2019). For an excellent pluralistic rejoinder, see Mario Blaser, "On the Properly Political (Disposition for the) Anthropocene," *Anthropological Theory* 19, no. 1 (2019): 74–94.

64 To relay James once again, whether the universe turns out to be dualistic, monistic, relational, or irrepressibly pluralistic, these are all but hypotheses that only the future can answer. What I do object to, however, is the very different gesture of positing relationalism as a foundation that, once disclosed by quantum physics or metaphysics, everyone is exhorted to adopt. On this, see Martin Savransky, "Modes of Mattering: Barad, Whitehead, and Societies," *Rhizomes: Cultural Studies of Emergent Knowledge* 30 (2016). https://doi.org/10.20415/rhiz/030.e08.

65 Escobar does recognize the risk of relying on a certain ontological dualism of his own, one that precisely draws a stark line between "modern dualists"

and "non-modern non-dualists," but makes a wager, quoting Ashis Nandy, that "the pathology of relatedness has already become less dangerous than the pathology of unrelatedness." Escobar, *Designs for the Pluriverse*, 104.

66 It is worth quoting Nietzsche's call in full: "Perhaps!—But who is willing to concern himself with such dangerous perhapses! For that we have to await the arrival of a new species of philosopher, one which possesses tastes and inclinations opposite to and different from those of its predecessors—philosophers of the dangerous 'perhaps' in every sense.—And to speak in all seriousness: I see such philosophers arising." Friedrich Nietzsche, *Beyond Good and Evil* (London: Penguin, 1990), 8.

67 Falk Xué Parra Witte, "Living the Law of Origin: The Cosmological, Ontological, Epistemological, and Ecological Framework of Kogi Environmental Politics" (PhD diss., University of Cambridge, 2017).

68 Philippe Descola, "No Politics Please," in *Making Things Public: Atmospheres of Democracy*, ed. Bruno Latour and Peter Weibel (Cambridge, MA: MIT Press, 2005), 57.

69 As Eva Giraud puts it, it is vital "to find ways of taking responsibility for the exclusions that are fostered by specific entanglements" so as to create "space for future transformation, by making exclusions visible and open to contestation by those who are most affected." Taking responsibility, of course, does not mean atoning for the actions or decisions that have led to the exclusion as if the latter was always a sin, a missed opportunity, the failure of ideal inclusion. As I read it, taking responsibility means actively and openly consenting to the fact that every decision involves a risk, a casting of one's lot with some ways of living and dying rather than others. Eva Haifa Giraud, *What Comes after Entanglement? Activism, Anthropocentrism, and an Ethics of Exclusion* (Durham, NC: Duke University Press, 2019), 172.

70 James, *The Varieties of Religious Experience*, 421.

71 This may incidentally give us another, entirely resonant way of approaching the historical and political adventures of what John Tresch has called "cosmograms," the concrete, situated renderings of one and many cosmoi in artefacts which then enjoy a life of their own, the objects of ongoing contestations, additions, deletions, and replacements. Vivid examples of these include Tibetan Mandalas, the architectural layout of certain mosques, pictorial narratives in cathedrals, and Dogon rites, as well as James Joyce's *Ulysses*, Borges's story of the Aleph, Charles Fourier's *phalanstère*, and—why not—Alfred North Whitehead's *Process and Reality*, among others. See John Tresch, "Technological World-Pictures: Cosmic Things and Cosmograms," *Isis* 98 (2007): 84–99. See also John Tresch, *The Romantic Machine: Utopian Science and Technology after Napoleon* (Chicago: University of Chicago Press, 2012).

72 James, *The Will to Believe and Other Essays*, 207.

73   James, "A Pluralistic Mystic," 1313.

74   Benjamin Paul Blood, quoted in James, *The Will to Believe and Other Essays*, ix.

75   James C. Scott, *The Art of Not Being Governed: An Anarchist History of Upland Southeast Asia* (New Haven, CT: Yale University Press, 2009).

76   Scott, *The Art of Not Being Governed*, 8.

77   James, *Pragmatism and the Meaning of Truth*, 93.

78   Relatedly, see Isabelle Stengers, "L'Insistance du Possible," in *Gestes spéculatifs*, ed. Didier Debaise and Isabelle Stengers (Paris: Les Presses du Réel, 2015), 5–22.

79   James, *The Will to Believe and Other Essays*, viii.

80   I am here paraphrasing, once again, the alluring words of Benjamin Paul Blood: "There is no conclusion. What has concluded, that we might conclude in regard to it? There are no fortunes to be told, and there is no advice to be given.—Farewell!" Quoted in William James, "A Pluralistic Mystic," 1313.

81   James, *The Varieties of Religious Experience*, 86–87.

BIBLIOGRAPHY

Abdel-Malek, Anouar. "Orientlalism in Crisis." *Diogenes* 11, no. 44 (1963): 103–40.

Anderson, Warwick. "From Subjugated Knowledge to Conjugated Subjects: Science and Globalisation, or Postcolonial Studies of Science?" *Postcolonial Studies* 12, no. 4 (2009): 389–400.

Asad, Talal. *Anthropology and the Colonial Encounter.* London: Ithaca Press, 1973.

Asad, Talal. *Genealogies of Religion: Disciplines and Reasons of Power in Christianity and Islam.* Baltimore, MD: Johns Hopkins University Press, 1993.

Asad, Talal. *Formations of the Secular: Christianity, Islam, Modernity.* Stanford, CA: Stanford University Press, 2003.

Bergson, Henri. *The Creative Mind: An Introduction to Metaphysics.* Translated by Mabelle L. Andison. Mineola, NY: Dover, 2007.

Bhabha, Homi. *The Location of Culture.* London: Routledge, 1994.

Bhambra, Gurminder K. "Postcolonial and Decolonial Dialogues." *Postcolonial Studies* 17, no. 2 (2014): 115–21.

Bialecki, Jon. *A Diagram for Fire: Miracles and Variation in an American Charismatic Movement.* Los Angeles: University of California Press, 2017.

Blaser, Mario. *Storytelling Globalization from the Chaco and Beyond.* Durham, NC: Duke University Press, 2010.

Blaser, Mario. "Ontological Conflicts and the Stories of Peoples in Spite of Europe: Toward a Conversation on Political Ontology." *Current Anthropology* 54, no. 5 (2013): 547–68.

Blaser, Mario. "Ontology and Indigeneity: On the Political Ontology of Heterogeneous Assemblages." *Cultural Geographies* 21, no. 1 (2014): 49–58.

Blaser, Mario. "On the Properly Political (Disposition for the) Anthropocene." *Anthropological Theory* 19, no. 1 (2019): 74–94.

Blaser, Mario, and Marisol de la Cadena. "Pluriverse: Proposals for a World of Many Worlds." In *A World of Many Worlds*, edited by Marisol de la Cadena and Mario Blaser, 1–22. Durham, NC: Duke University Press, 2018.

Blood, Benjamin Paul. *Pluriverse: An Essay on the Philosophy of Pluralism.* Boston: Marshal Jones, 1920.

Branigan, Tania. "Tsunami, Earthquake, Nuclear Crisis—Now Japan Faces Power Cuts." *Guardian*, March 13, 2011. Accessed March 29, 2019.

https://www.theguardian.com/world/2011/mar/13/japan-tsunami
-earthquake-power-cuts.

Braver, Lee. *A Thing of This World: A History of Continental Anti-Realism*. Evanston, IL: Northwestern University Press, 2007.

Brooks, Peter. *Realist Vision*. New Haven, CT: Yale University Press, 2005.

Campbell, James. *Experiencing William James: Belief in a Pluralistic Universe*. Charlottesville: University of Virginia Press, 2017.

Candea, Matei. "We Have Never Been Pluralist: On Lateral and Frontal Comparisons in the Ontological Turn." In *Comparative Metaphysics: Ontology After Anthropology*, edited by Pierre Charbonnier, Gildas Salmon, and Peter Skafish, 85–106. London: Rowman & Littlefield, 2017.

Carrithers, Michael, Matei Candea, Karen Skyes, Martin Holbraad, and Soumbya Venkatesan. "Ontology Is Just Another Word for Culture." *Critique of Anthropology* 30, no. 2 (2010): 152–200.

Cassin, Barbara. *Sophistical Practice: Toward a Consistent Relativism*. New York: Fordham University Press, 2013.

Césaire, Aimé. *Return to My Native Land*. Translated by John Berger and Anna Bostock. Brooklyn, NY: Archipelago Books, 2013.

Chakrabarty, Dipesh. *Provincializing Europe: Postcolonial Thought and Historical Difference*. Princeton, NJ: Princeton University Press, 2000.

Chakrabarty, Dipesh. "The Climate of History: Four Theses." *Critical Inquiry* 35, no. 2 (2009): 197–222.

Chakrabarty, Dipesh. "Postcolonial Studies and the Challenge of Climate Change." *New Literary History* 43, no. 1 (2012): 1–18.

Chandler, David, and Julian Reid. *Becoming Indigenous: Governing Imaginaries in the Anthropocene*. London: Rowman & Littlefield, 2019.

Chaplin, Joyce E. *Round About the Earth: Circumnavigation from Magellan to Orbit*. New York: Simon & Schuster, 2012.

Charbonnier, Pierre, Gildas Salmon, and Peter Skafish, eds. *Comparative Metaphysics: Ontology after Anthropology*. London: Rowman & Littlefield, 2016.

Clastres, Pierre. *Society against the State*. Translated by Robert Hurley and Abe Stein. Brooklyn, NY: Zone Books, 1989.

CNN wire staff. "Tsunami Warnings and Advisories Remain across Pacific Region." *CNN*, March 11, 2011. Accessed March 29, 2019. http://edition.cnn.com/2011/WORLD/asiapcf/03/11/tsunami.warning/index.html.

Comaroff, Jean, and John Comaroff. "Occult Economies and the Violence of Abstraction: Notes from the South African Postcolony." *American Ethnologist* 26, no. 3 (1999): 279–301.

Connolly, William. *Pluralism*. Durham, NC: Duke University Press, 2005.

Connolly, William. *Capitalism and Christianity, American Style*. Durham, NC: Duke University Press, 2008.

Coon, Deborah J. "'One Moment in the World's Salvation': Anarchism and the Radicalisation of William James." *Journal of American History*, 83, no. 1 (1996): 70–99.

Conway, Janet, and Jakeet Singh, "Radical Democracy in Global Perspective: Notes from the Pluriverse." *Third World Quarterly* 32, no. 4 (2011): 689–706.

Corsín Jiménez, Alberto. "Trust in Anthropology." *Anthropological Theory* 11, no. 2 (2011): 177–96.

Cortázar, Julio. *La Vuelta al Día en Ochenta Mundos*. Madrid: Siglo XXI, 2007.

Cortázar, Julio. *Clases de Literatura. Berkeley, 1980*. Madrid: Alfaguara, 2013.

Danowski, Déborah, and Eduardo Viveiros de Castro. "L'arret de Monde." In *De l'univers clos au monde infini*, edited by W Émile Hache, 221–39. Paris: Éditions Dehors, 2014.

Danowski, Déborah, and Eduardo Viveiros de Castro. *The Ends of the World*. Translated by Rodrigo Nunes. Cambridge: Polity Press, 2016.

Daston, Lorraine. "Preternatural Philosophy." In *Biographies of Scientific Objects*, edited by Lorraine Daston, 14–41. Chicago: University of Chicago Press, 2001.

Daston, Lorraine, and Katherine Park. *Wonders and the Order of Nature, 1150–1750*. Brooklyn, NY: Zone Books, 2003.

Daston, Lorraine, and Michael Stolleis, eds. *Natural Laws and Laws of Nature in Early Modern Europe: Jurisprudence, Theology, Moral and Natural Philosophy*. Farnham, UK: Ashgate, 2008.

Daston, Lorraine, and Peter Galison. *Objectivity*. Brooklyn, NY: Zone Books, 2010.

de Certeau, Michel. *The Practice of Everyday Life*. Translated by Steven Rendall. Los Angeles: University of California Press, 1984.

de Certeau, Michel. "What We Do When We Believe." In *On Signs*, edited by Marshall Blonsky, 192–202. Baltimore, MD: Johns Hopkins University Press, 1985.

de la Cadena, Marisol. "Indigenous Cosmopolitics in the Andes: Conceptual Reflections beyond 'Politics.'" *Cultural Anthropology* 25, no. 2 (2010): 334–70.

de la Cadena, Marisol. "Runa: Human but Not Only." HAU: *Journal of Ethnographic Theory* 4, no. 2 (2014): 253–59.

de la Cadena, Marisol. *Earth-Beings: Ecologies of Practice across Andean Worlds*. Durham, NC: Duke University Press, 2015.

de la Cadena, Marisol, and Mario Blaser, eds. *A World of Many Worlds*. Durham, NC: Duke University Press, 2018.

De Martino, Ernesto. *Primitive Magic: The Psychic Powers of Shamans and Sorcerers*. Dorset, UK: Prism Press, 1988.

Delanda, Manuel, and Graham Harman. *The Rise of Realism*. Cambridge: Polity Press, 2017.

Deleuze, Gilles. *Essays Critical and Clinical*. Translated by Daniel W. Smith and Michael A. Greco. Minneapolis: University of Minnesota Press, 1997.

Deleuze, Gilles. *The Logic of Sense*. Translated by Mark Lester. London: Continuum, 2004.

Deleuze, Gilles. *Nietzsche and Philosophy*. Translated by Hugh Thomlinson. London: Continuum, 2006.

Deleuze, Gilles, and Félix Guattari. *What Is Philosophy?* Translated by Graham Burchell and Hugh Thomlinson. New York: Verso, 1994.

Deloria Jr., Vine. *Spirit and Reason: The Vine Deloria Jr. Read*, edited by Barbara Deloria, Kristen Foehner, and Samuel Scinta. Golden, CO: Fulcrum, 1999.

Deloria Jr., Vine. *The Metaphysics of Modern Existence*. Golden, CO: Fulcrum, 2012.

Derrida, Jacques. *The Politics of Friendship*. Translated by George Collins. New York: Verso, 2005.

Descola, Philippe. "No Politics Please." In *Making Things Public: Atmospheres of Democracy*, ed. Bruno Latour and Peter Weibel, 54–57. Cambridge, MA: MIT Press, 2005.

Descola, Philippe. *Beyond Nature and Culture*. Translated by Janet Lloyd. Chicago: University of Chicago Press, 2013.

Despret, Vinciane. *Au Bonheur des Morts: Récits de ceux qui restent*. Paris: La Découverte, 2015.

Dewey, John. *The Collected Works of John Dewey. Volume 2: 1925–1927. Essays and Reviews, Miscellany, and The Public and Its Problems*. Carbondale: Southern Illinois University Press, 2009.

Dussel, Enrique. *1942: El Encubrimiento del Otro. Hacia el Origen del "Mito de la Modernidad."* La Paz: Plural Editores, 1994.

Eco, Umberto. *The Infinity of Lists*. Translated by Alastair McEwen. New York: Rizzoli/Universal, 2009.

Escobar, Arturo. *Designs for the Pluriverse: Radical Interdependence, Autonomy, and the Making of Worlds*. Durham, NC: Duke University Press, 2018.

Eisenberg, Avigail. "Pluralism and Method at the Turn of the Century." In *Modern Pluralism: Anglo-American Debates Since 1880*, edited by Mark Bevir, 60–80. Cambridge: Cambridge University Press, 2017.

Ejército Zapatista de Liberación Nacional. "Cuarta Declaración de la Selva Lacandona." January 1, 1996. Accessed July 3, 2019. https://radiozapatista .org/?p=20287.

Ferguson, Kennan. *Politics in the Pluriverse*. Lanham, MD: Rowman & Littlefield, 2007.

Figal, Gerald. *Civilization and Monsters: Spirits of Modernity in Meiji Japan*. Durham, NC: Duke University Press, 1999.

Foucault, Michel. *The Order of Things: An Archeology of the Human Sciences*. London: Routledge, 2002.

Gambetta, Diego, ed. *Trust: Making and Breaking Cooperative Relations*. Oxford: Basil Blackwell, 1988.

Gandhi, Leela. *Affective Communities: Anticolonial Thought, Fin-de-siècle Radicalism, and the Politics of Friendship*. Durham, NC: Duke University Press, 2006.

García Márquez, Gabriel. "The Solitude of Latin America." Nobel lecture delivered at the ceremony of the Nobel Prize in Literature, Stockholm, Sweden, December 8, 1982. http://www.nobelprize.org/nobel_prizes/literature/laureates/1982/marquez-lecture.html.

Gavin, William J. "*Pragmatism* and Death: Method vs. Metaphor, Tragedy vs. the Will to Believe." In *100 Years of Pragmatism: William James's Revolutionary Philosophy*, edited by John Stuhr, 81–95. Bloomington: Indiana University Press, 2010.

Geschiere, Peter. *The Modernity of Witchcraft: Politics and the Occult in Postcolonial Africa*. Charlottesville: University of Virginia Press, 1997.

Ghosh, Amitav. *The Great Derangement: Climate Change and the Unthinkable*. Chicago: University of Chicago Press, 2016.

Giraud, Eva Haifa. *What Comes after Entanglement? Activism, Anthropocentrism, and an Ethics of Exclusion*. Durham, NC: Duke University Press, 2019.

Glissant, Édouard. *Poetics of Relation*. Translated by Betsy Wing. Ann Arbor: University of Michigan Press, 1997.

Goslinga, Gillian. "Spirited Encounters: Notes on the Politics and Poetics of Representing the Uncanny in Anthropology." *Anthropological Theory* 12, no. 4 (2012): 386–406.

Gould, Stephen Jay. *Dinosaur in a Haystack: Essays on Natural History*. Cambridge, MA: Harvard University Press, 1995.

Greco, Monica. "Pragmatics of Explanation: Creative Accountability in the Care of 'Medically Unexplained Symptoms.'" *Sociological Review* 65, no. 2 (2017): 110–29.

Greco, Monica. "Thinking with Outrageous Propositions." In *Speculative Research: The Lure of Possible Futures*, edited by Alex Wilkie, Martin Savransky, and Marsha Rosengarten, 218–27. New York: Routledge, 2017.

Guha, Ranajit. "The Prose of Counter-Insurgency." In *Selected Subaltern Studies*, edited by Ranajit Guha and Gayatri Chakravorty Spivak, 45–84. New York: Oxford University Press, 1988.

Guha, Ranajit. *History at the Limits of World-History*. New York: Columbia University Press, 2002.

Haraway, Donna. *Staying with the Trouble: Making Kin in the Chthulucene*. Durham, NC: Duke University Press, 2016.

Harding, Susan. "Representing Fundamentalism: The Problem of the Repugnant Cultural Other." *Social Research* 58, no. 2 (1991): 373–93.

Harney, Stefano, and Fred Moten. *The Undercommons: Fugitive Planning and Black Study*. New York: Minor Compositions, 2013.

Harvey, David. *Cosmopolitanism and the Geographies of Freedom*. New York: Columbia University Press, 2009.

Hegel, Georg Wilhelm Friedrich. *Lectures on the Philosophy of World History.* Translated by H. B. Nisbet. Cambridge: Cambridge University Press, 1975.

Holbraad, Martin, and Morten Axel Pedersen. *The Ontological Turn: An Anthropological Exposition.* Cambridge: Cambridge University Press, 2017.

Holbraad, Martin, Morten Axel Pedersen, and Eduardo Viveiros de Castro. "The Politics of Ontology: Anthropological Positions." Theorizing the Contemporary, *Fieldsights,* January 13, 2014. https://culanth.org/fieldsights/the -politics-of-ontology-anthropological-positions.

Ingold, Tim. *The Perception of the Environment: Essays on Livelihood, Dwelling and Skill.* London: Routledge, 2000.

Ivy, Marilyn. *Discourses of the Vanishing: Modernity, Phantasm, Japan.* Chicago: University of Chicago Press, 1995.

Iwasaki, Michio, and Barre Toelken. *Ghosts and the Japanese: Cultural Experience in Japanese Death Legends.* Logan: Utah State University Press, 1994.

James, William. *Talks to Teachers on Psychology, and to Students on Some of Life's Ideals.* London: Longmans, Green, 1907.

James, William. *The Letters of William James,* edited by Henry James. London: Longmans, Green, 1920.

James, William. *The Principles of Psychology, Volume One.* Mineola, NY: Dover, 1950.

James, William. *The Principles of Psychology, Volume Two.* Mineola, NY: Dover, 1950.

James, William. *The Will to Believe and Other Essays in Popular Philosophy.* Mineola, NY: Dover, 1956.

James, William. *The Varieties of Religious Experience.* London: Harper Collins, 1960.

James, William. *Pragmatism and the Meaning of Truth.* Cambridge, MA: Harvard University Press, 1975.

James, William. *Essays in Philosophy.* Cambridge, MA: Harvard University Press, 1978.

James, William. *Essays in Religion and Morality.* Cambridge, MA: Harvard University Press, 1982.

James, William. "On Some Mental Effects of the Earthquake." In *William James: Writings 1902–1910,* edited by Bruce Kurlkick, 1215–22. New York: Library of America, 1987.

James, William. "Address on the Philippine Question." In *William James: Writings 1902–1910,* edited by Bruce Kurlkick, 1130–35. New York: Library of America, 1987.

James, William. "The Confidences of a 'Psychical Researcher.'" In *William James: Writings 1902–1910,* edited by Bruce Kurlkick, 1250–65. New York: Library of America, 1987.

James, William. "A Pluralistic Mystic." In *William James: Writings 1902–1910,* edited by Bruce Kurlkick, 1294–1313. New York: Library of America, 1987.

James, William. *A Pluralistic Universe*. Lincoln: Nebraska University Press, 1996.

James, William. *Some Problems of Philosophy*. Lincoln: Nebraska University Press, 1996.

James, William. *Psychology: The Briefer Course*. Mineola, NY: Dover, 2001.

James, William. *Essays in Radical Empiricism*. Mineola, NY: Dover, 2003.

James, William. *Manuscript, Essays, and Notes*. Cambridge, MA: Harvard University Press, 2008.

Jensen, Casper Bruun, Andrea Ballestero, Marisol de la Cadena, Michael Fisch, and Miho Ishii. "New Ontologies? Reflections on Some Recent 'Turns' in STS, Anthropology, and Philosophy." *Social Anthropology/Anthropologie Sociale* 25, no. 4 (2017): 525–45.

Jensen, Casper Bruun, Miho Ishi, and Philip Swift. "Attuning to the Webs of *en*: Ontography, Japanese Spirit Worlds, and the 'Tact' of Minakata Kumagusu." *HAU: Journal of Ethnographic Theory* 6, no. 2 (2016): 149–72.

Josephson Storm, Jason A. *The Invention of Religion in Japan*. Chicago: University of Chicago Press, 2012.

Josephson Storm, Jason A. *The Myth of Disenchantment: Magic, Modernity and the Birth of the Human Sciences*. Chicago: University of Chicago Press, 2017.

Kaneta, Taio. "Listening to the Heart: Among the People in the Great East Japan Earthquake Disaster Area." Paper presented at the 3rd United Nations World Conference on Disaster Risk Reduction, Sendai, Japan, March 14–18, 2015. Accessed April 4, 2019. http://drr.tohoku.ac.jp/system/wp-content/uploads/2015/01/aaf2cd443b060aaaf3090227d870528a.pdf.

Kant, Immanuel. *Perpetual Peace and Other Essays*. Indianapolis, IN: Hackett, 1983.

Kasnabish, Alex. *Zapatismo beyond Borders: New Imaginations of Political Possibility*. Toronto: University of Toronto Press, 2008.

Keim, Wiebke, Ercüment Çelik, Christian Ersche, and Veronika Wöhrer, eds. *Global Knowledge Production in the Social Sciences: Made in Circulation*. London: Routledge, 2016.

Keller, Catherine. *Apocalypse Now and Then: A Feminist Guide to the End of the World*. Boston: Beacon Press, 1996.

Keller, Catherine. *The Face of the Deep: A Theology of Becoming*. New York: Routledge, 2013.

Keller, Catherine. *The Cloud of the Impossible: Negative Theology and Planetary Entanglement*. New York: Columbia University Press, 2015.

Kingsnorth, Paul. *One No, Many Yeses: A Journey to the Heart of the Global Resistance Movement*. New York: Free Press, 2003.

Kohn, Eduardo. "Anthropology of Ontologies." *Annual Review of Anthropology* 44 (2015): 311–27.

Kohso, Sabu, Hapax, Yoko Hayasuke, Shiro Yabu, Mari Matsumoto, and Motonao Gensai Mori. *Fukushima & Ses Invisibles: Cahiers d'enquetes politiques*. Vaulx-en-Velin: Les Éditions des Mondes à Faire, 2018.

Koselleck, Reinhardt. *Futures Past: On the Semantics of Historical Time.* New York: Columbia University Press, 2004.

Kothari, Ashish, Ariel Salleh, Arturo Escobar, Federico Demaria, and Alberto Acosta, eds. *Pluriverse: A Post-Development Dictionary.* New Delhi: Tulika Books, 2019.

Lapoujade, David. *William James: Empirisme et Pragmatisme.* Paris: Les Empêcheurs de Penser en Rond, 2007.

Latour, Bruno. *We Have Never Been Modern.* Translated by Catherine Porter. Cambridge, MA: Harvard University Press, 1993.

Latour, Bruno. *An Inquiry into Modes of Existence: An Anthropology of the Moderns.* Translated by Catherine Porter. Cambridge, MA: Harvard University Press, 2013.

Law, John. "What's Wrong with a One-World World?" *Distinktion: Scandinavian Journal of Social Theory* 16, no. 1 (2015): 126–39.

Law, John, and Annemarie Mol. *Complexities: Social Studies of Knowledge Practices.* Durham, NC: Duke University Press, 2002.

Lien, Marianne Elizabeth. *Becoming Salmon: Aquaculture and the Domestication of Fish.* Los Angeles: University of California Press, 2015.

Lispector, Clarice. *The Passion According to G.H.* Translated by Benjamin Moser. New York: Penguin, 2014.

Livingston, Alexander. "Excited Subjects: William James and the Politics of Radical Empiricism." *Theory & Event* 15, no. 4 (2012). Accessed August 2, 2018. https://www.muse.jhu.edu/article/491201.

Livingston, Alexander. *Damn Great Empires! William James and the Politics of Pragmatism.* New York: Oxford University Press, 2016.

Lloyd Parry, Richard. *Ghosts of the Tsunami.* London: Vintage, 2017.

Luhmann, Niklas. *Trust and Power.* Toronto: Wiley, 1979.

Luhrmann, Tanya. *When God Talks Back: Understanding the American Evangelical Relationship with God.* New York: Vintage, 2012.

Luhrmann, Tanya. "The Real Ontological Challenge." HAU: *Journal of Ethnographic Theory* 1/2 (2018): 79–82.

Mani, Lata. *Contentious Traditions: The Debate on Sati in Colonial India.* Berkeley: University of California Press, 1998.

McFarlane, Alan. *Japan Through the Looking Glass.* London: Profile Books, 2007.

Meyer, Steven. "Of 'Experiential Togetherness': Toward a More Robust Empiricism." In *The Lure of Whitehead,* edited by Nicholas Gaskill and Adam J. Nocek, 332–59. Minneapolis: University of Minnesota Press, 2014.

Meyers, David, and Peter Pels, eds. *Magic and Modernity: Interfaces of Revelation and Concealment.* Stanford, CA: Stanford University Press, 2001.

Mignolo, Walter. *The Darker Side of Western Modernity: Global Futures, Decolonial Options.* Durham, NC: Duke University Press, 2011.

Mol, Annemarie. *The Body Multiple: Ontology in Medical Practice.* Durham, NC: Duke University Press, 2002.

Möllering, Guido. "The Nature of Trust: From Georg Simmel to a Theory of Expectation, Interpretation and Suspension." *Sociology* 35, no. 2 (2001): 403–20.

Moore, Jason W. "The End of Cheap Nature. Or How I Learned to Stop Worrying about 'The' Environment and Love the Crisis of Capitalism." In *Structures of the World Political Economy and the Future of Global Conflict and Cooperation*, edited by Christian Suter and Christopher Chase-Dunn, 285–314. Berlin: LIT Verlag, 2014.

Motamedi-Fraser, Mariam. *Word: Beyond Language, Beyond Image.* London: Rowman & Littlefield, 2015.

Mudimbe, Valentin Y. *The Invention of Africa: Gnosis, Philosophy, and the Order of Knowledge.* Bloomington and Indianapolis: Indiana University Press, 1988.

Nadasdy, Paul. "The Gift in the Animal: The Ontology of Hunting and Human-Animal Sociality." *American Ethnologist* 34, no. 1 (2007): 25–43.

Nail, Thomas. "Zapatismo and the Global Origins of Occupy." *Journal of Cultural and Religious Theory* 12, no. 3 (2013): 20–35.

Nandy, Ashis. "A Report on the Present State of Health of the Gods and Goddesses in South Asia." *Postcolonial Studies* 4, no. 2 (2001): 125–41.

Nietzsche, Friedrich. *Beyond Good and Evil.* London: Penguin, 1990.

Ovid. *Metamorphoses.* Translated by David Raeburn. London: Penguin Classics, 2004.

Papini, Giovanni. *Sul Pragmatismo.* Milan: Libreria Editrice Milanese, 1913.

Parra Witte, Falk Xué. "Living the Law of Origin: The Cosmological, Ontological, Epistemological, and Ecological Framework of Kogi Environmental Politics." PhD diss., University of Cambridge, 2017.

Pigafetta, A. *The First Voyage around the World.* Translated by Lord Stanley of Alderley. London: Hakluyt Society, 1874.

Povinelli, Elizabeth. *Economies of Abandonment: Social Belonging and Endurance in Late Liberalism.* Durham, NC: Duke University Press, 2011.

Povinelli, Elizabeth. "The Will to Be Otherwise/The Effort of Endurance." *South Atlantic Quarterly* 111, no. 3 (2012): 453–57.

Putnam, Hilary. *Representation and Reality.* Cambridge, MA: MIT Press, 1988.

Quijano, A. "Coloniality and Modernity/Rationality." *Cultural Studies*, 21, no. 2–3 (2007): 168–78.

Reilly, Michael. "Japan's Quake Updated to Magnitude 9.0," *New Scientist*, March 11, 2011. Accessed March 29, 2019. http://www.newscientist.com/blogs /shortsharpscience/2011/03/powerful-japan-quake-sparks-ts.html.

Reiter, Bern, ed. *Constructing the Pluriverse.* Durham, NC: Duke University Press, 2018.

Righi, Andrea. *Italian Reactionary Thought and Critical Theory: An Inquiry into Savage Modernities.* Basingstoke and New York: Palgrave Macmillan, 2015.

Rojas, Cristina. "Contesting the Colonial Logics of the International: Towards a Relational Politics for the Pluriverse." *International Political Sociology* 18 (2016): 369–82.

Roy, Arundhati. "Confronting Empire." Paper presented at Life After Capitalism, World Social Forum, Porto Alegre, Brazil, January 27, 2003.

Roy, Arundhati. *An Ordinary Person's Guide to Empire*. New Delhi: Penguin, 2006.

Said, Edward. *Orientalism*. London: Penguin, 2003.

Santos, Boaventura de Sousa, ed. *Another Knowledge Is Possible*. London: Verso, 2008.

Santos, Boaventura de Sousa. *Epistemologies of the South*. Boulder, CO: Paradigm, 2014.

Savransky, Martin. *The Adventure of Relevance: An Ethics of Social Inquiry*. Basingstoke: Palgrave Macmillan, 2016.

Savransky, Martin. "In Praise of Hesitation: 'Global' Knowledge as a Cosmopolitical Adventure." In *Global Knowledge Production in the Social Sciences: Made in Circulation*, edited by Wiebke Keim, Ercüment Çelik, Christian Ersche, and Veronika Wöhrer, 237–50. London: Routledge, 2016.

Savransky, Martin. "Modes of Mattering: Barad, Whitehead, and Societies." *Rhizomes: Cultural Studies of Emergent Knowledge* 30 (2016). https://doi.org/10.20415/rhiz/030.e08.

Savransky, Martin. "The Wager of an Unfinished Present: Notes on Speculative Pragmatism." In *Speculative Research: The Lure of Possible Futures*, edited by Alex Wilkie, Martin Savransky, and Marsha Rosengarten, 25–38. New York: Routledge, 2017.

Savransky, Martin. "A Decolonial Imagination: Sociology, Anthropology, and the Politics of Reality." *Sociology* 51, no. 1 (2017): 11–26.

Savransky, Martin. "What's the Relevance of Isabelle Stengers' Philosophy to ANT?" In *The Routledge Companion to Actor-Network Theory*, edited by Anders Blok, Ignacio Farías, and Celia Roberts, 143–54. London: Routledge, 2019.

Savransky, Martin. "The Pluralistic Problematic: William James and The Pragmatics of the Pluriverse." *Theory, Culture and Society* (2019): 1–19. doi.org/10.1177/0263276419848030.

Savransky, Martin. "Pragmatics of a World To-Be-Made." In *Thinking the Problematic: Genealogies, Tracings, and Currents of a Persistent Force*, edited by Erich Hörl and Oliver Leistert. Berlin: Transcript Verlag, 2020.

Savransky, Martin, and Marsha Rosengarten. "What Is Nature Capable Of? Evidence, Ontology, and Speculative Medical Humanities." *Medical Humanities* 42 (2016): 166–72.

Savransky, Martin, and Isabelle Stengers. "Relearning the Art of Paying Attention: A Conversation." *SubStance* 47, no. 1 (2018): 29–46.

Schmidt, Leigh Eric. *Hearing Things: Religion, Illusion, and the American Enlightenment*. Cambridge, MA: Harvard University Press, 2000.

Schneider, Laurel. *Beyond Monotheism: A Theology of Multiplicity*. New York: Routledge, 2008.

Scott, David. *Conscripts of Modernity: The Tragedy of Colonial Enlightenment.* Durham, NC: Duke University Press, 2004.

Scott, David. *Omens of Adversity: Tragedy, Time, Memory, Justice.* Durham, NC: Duke University Press, 2014.

Scott, David. "The Tragic Vision in Postcolonial Times." PMLA 129, no. 4 (2014): 799–808.

Scott, James C. *The Art of Not Being Governed: An Anarchist History of Upland Southeast Asia.* New Haven, CT: Yale University Press, 2009.

Scott, Michael W. "The Anthropology of Ontology (Religious Science?)." *Journal of the Royal Anthropological Institute* 19 (2013): 859–72.

Seth, Sanjay. "Reason or Reasoning? Clio or Shiva." *Social Text* 22, no. 1 (2004): 85–101.

Seth, Sanjay. *Subject Lessons: The Western Education of Colonial India.* Durham, NC: Duke University Press, 2007.

Seth, Sanjay. "Is Thinking with 'Modernity' Eurocentric?" *Cultural Sociology* 10, no. 3 (2016): 385–98.

Seth, Sanjay. *Beyond Reason? Postcolonial Theory and the Social Sciences.* New York: Oxford University Press, 2020.

Sharpe, Christina. *In the Wake: On Blackness and Being.* Durham, NC: Duke University Press, 2016.

Smith, Linda Tuhiwai. *Decolonizing Methodologies: Research and Indigenous Peoples.* London: Zed Books, 2012.

Spivak, Gayatri Chakravorty. "Can the Subaltern Speak?" In *Marxism and The Interpretation of Culture*, edited by Cary Nelson and Lawrence Grossberg, 271–313. Basingstoke, UK: Macmillan Education, 1988.

Spivak, Gayatri Chakravorty. *A Critique of Postcolonial Reason: Toward a History of the Vanishing Present.* Cambridge, MA: Harvard University Press, 1999.

Stein, Gertrude. *Everybody's Autobiography.* New York: Vintage, 1973.

Stengers, Isabelle. *The Invention of Modern Science.* Translated by Daniel W. Smith. Minneapolis: University of Minnesota Press, 2000.

Stengers, Isabelle. "The Doctor and the Charlatan." *Cultural Studies Review* 9, no. 2 (2003): 12–36.

Stengers, Isabelle. *Cosmopolitics I.* Minneapolis: University of Minnesota Press, 2010.

Stengers, Isabelle. *Cosmopolitics II.* Minneapolis: University of Minnesota Press, 2011.

Stengers, Isabelle. "Relaying a War Machine?" In *The Guattari Effect*, edited by Eric Alliez and Andrew Goffey, 134–57. London: Continuum, 2011.

Stengers, Isabelle. "L'Insistance du Possible." In *Gestes spéculatifs*, ed. Didier Debaise and Isabelle Stengers, 5–22. Paris: Les Presses du Réel, 2015.

Strathern, Marilyn. *Reproducing the Future: Anthropology, Kinship, and the New Reproductive Technologies.* London: Routledge, 1992.

Suzuki, Wataru, Shin Aoi, Haruko Skiguchi, and Takashi Kunugi. "Source Rupture Process of the 2011 Tohoku-Oki Earthquake Derived from the Strong-motion Records." *Proceedings of the Fifteenth World Conference on Earthquake Engineering* (2012): 1–9. Accessed March 29, 2019. http://www.iitk.ac.in /nicee/wcee/article/WCEE2012_1650.pdf.

Swyngedouw, Erik, and Henrik Ernstson. "Interrupting the Anthropo-obScene: Immuno-biopolitics and Depoliticizing Ontologies in the Anthropocene." *Theory, Culture and Society* 35, no. 6 (2018): 3–30.

Takahashi, Hara. "The Ghosts of Tsunami Dead and *Kokoro no kea* in Japan's Religious Landscape." *Journal of Religion in Japan* 5 (2016): 176–98.

Toulmin, Stephen. *Cosmopolis: The Hidden Agenda of Modernity.* Chicago: University of Chicago Press, 1990.

Tresch, John. "Technological World-Pictures: Cosmic Things and Cosmograms." *Isis* 98 (2007): 84–99.

Tresch, John. *The Romantic Machine: Utopian Science and Technology after Napoleon.* Chicago: University of Chicago Press, 2012.

Tsing, Anna Lowenhaupt. *The Mushroom at the End of the World: On the Possibility of Life in Capitalist Ruins.* Princeton, NJ: Princeton University Press, 2015.

Turner, Edith. *Experiencing Ritual: A New Interpretation of African Healing.* Philadelphia: University of Pennsylvania Press, 1992.

Turner, Edith. "A Visible Spirit from Zambia." In *Being Changed by Cross-Cultural Encounters: The Anthropology of Extraordinary Experience*, edited by David E. Young and Jean Guy Goulet, 71–95. Peterborough, Ontario: Broadview Press, 1994.

Turner, Edith. *Communitas: The Anthropology of Collective Joy.* New York: Palgrave Macmillan, 2012.

Verne, Jules. *Around the World in 80 Days.* London: Penguin, 2008.

Verran, Helen. *Science and an African Logic.* Chicago: University of Chicago Press, 2001.

Verran, Helen. "Engagements between Disparate Knowledge Traditions: Toward Doing Difference Generatively and in Good Faith." In *Contested Ecologies: Dialogues in the South on Nature and Knowledge*, edited Lesley Green, 141–61. Cape Town: Human Sciences Research Council Press, 2013.

Viveiros de Castro, Eduardo. "Perspectival Anthropology and the Method of Controlled Equivocation." *Tipití: Journal of the Society for the Anthropology of Lowland South America* 2, no. 1 (2004): 3–22.

Viveiros de Castro, Eduardo. *Cannibal Metaphysics.* Translated by Peter Skafish. Minneapolis, MN: Univocal, 2014.

Viveiros de Castro, Eduardo. *The Relative Native: Essays on Indigenous Conceptual Worlds.* Chicago: HAU Books, 2015.

Yōzō, Taniyama. "Chaplaincy Work in Disaster Areas." In *Religion and Psychotherapy in Japan*, edited by Christopher Harding, Iwata Fumiaki, and Yoshinaga Shin'ichi, 250–66. London: Routledge, 2015.

Wallerstein, Immanuel. *European Universalism: The Rhetoric of Power.* New York: New Press, 2006.

Weber, Elizabeth. "Suspended from the Other's Heartbeat." *South Atlantic Quarterly* 111, no. 3 (2012): 453–57.

Weber, Max. *From Max Weber: Essays in Sociology,* edited by H. H. Gerth and C. Wright Mills. Abingdon, UK: Routledge, 2009.

West, Harry. *Ethnographic Sorcery.* Chicago: University of Chicago Press, 2007.

Whitehead, Alfred North. *The Concept of Nature.* Mineola, NY: Dover, 1920.

Whitehead, Alfred North. *Science and the Modern World.* New York: Free Press, 1967.

Whitehead, Alfred North. *Process and Reality: An Essay in Cosmology.* New York: Free Press, 1978.

INDEX

Abdel-Malek, Anouar, 139n32

absolute, the, 103; absolution and, 35; beginnings and, 70; empire and, 35, 93; ends and, 34, 102; ideals and, 121; oneness/manyness and, 116; reason and, 16; relativism and, 35; separation, 4

activity, 23, 27, 72; composing other worlds and, 124; deconstructive theory and, 35; experience of, 123; metaphysics and, 46; "perhaps" and, 123; pluriverse and, 118; political cosmology and, 129; sense of, 123, 130

adventure, 9, 89, 92, 114, 115, 117, 161n71; anthropology and, 7; *Around the World in Eighty Days* and, 114; comparison and, 43; day-traveling and, 41; in divergence, 2, 21, 48, 50, 92, 116; ideas and, 96; Ferdinand de Magellan and, 12; metaphysics and, 97; pluriverse and, 92; radical empiricism and, 28; voyaging and, 17; William James and, 2, 118

alliance, 7, 19, 20, 23, 53, 55, 65, 69, 75, 89; divergence and, 43, 127

alternative, 14, 93, 121, 126, 130; genuine option and, 41; ontology and, 43

America, 11, 12, 13, 26

America (US), 10, 95, 97, 134n10; annexation of Philippines and, 95, 159n45

analysis, 30, 71, 73, 81

"and," 78, 109; feeling of, 7, 18, 110; *see also* experience; feeling; relations

anthropology 5, 7, 42, 81; belief and, 100; colonialism and, 29–32; economy of

inquiry and, 44; Edith Turner and 82, 88; knowledge and, 43; order and, 93; sorcery and, 39; theory and, 45, 29, 74; *see also* ontology; political ontology

anti-essentialism, 35; *see also* essentialism

anti-imperialism, 9, 53; pluralism and, 10, 38, 73; postcolonial thought and, 35

anti-realism, 9, 18, 37, 38; *see also* modern realism; pluralistic realism; realism

apocalypse, 1, 10, 19; *see also* endings; eschatology; eschaton

appositions, 92, 124

Around the World in Eighty Days (Jules Verne), 113–14

Arquivos do Patrimônio Cultural (ARPAC), 29, 36

art of living, 101, 103, 105, 107, 110–11, 130; ontology and, 43; pragmatism and, 97

arts of noticing, 19–20, 25–27, 42, 54, 81, 97; pluralism and, 28, 53; runaway metaphysics and, 49

Asad, Talal, 52, 55, 100

Asia, 11, 12, 14; belief and, 53; orientalism and, 33

"as if": believe in, 55; doubt and, 58; God and, 55–56, 60, 63, 65; as mode of experience, 55, 60

attention, 51, 54, 56, 57, 68, 97, 106, 126, 160n62

backwardness: disqualification and, 33; exoticism and, 34; ghosts and, 100; modern historiography and, 16; Muedans and, 32; Tōhoku and, 102 beginnings, vii, x, 70, 130; circumnavigations and, 13; the end of the world and, 1, 72; life and, 127; lists and, 2; openings and, 117, 158n16; pluralistic realism and, 20, 28; political cosmology and, 129; stories and, 14–15, 32, 47; throwing the dice and, 14, 36; totality and, 25; worlds and, 2, 115, 129; *see also* openings

belief, 52–54, 76, 87, 98, 101, 146n57; disqualification and, 44; etymology of, 57; evangelicals and, 54–56, 60; God and, 57, 61; modern experience and, 50; reality and, 4, 51, 59; tolerance and, 74; trust and, 57, 60; as weapon of de-realization, 21, 52, 53, 58, 100; William James and, 51–52, 55, 59

Blaser, Mario, 44, 124

Blood, Benjamin Paul, 117, 129, 133n3, 162n80

borders, 4, 9, 18, 27, 78–79, 134n7

breakdown, 86; pragmatism and, 95, 97

Bruun Jensen, Casper, 141n59

Buddhism, 23, 102, 103, 106, 107; ghosts and, 154n37, 155n40, 156n71

Café de Monku, 105–6

California, 54, 62

capitalism, 4, 32, 54, 128; cheap nature and, 13; industrialization and, 26; modern world and, 123; supply chains and, 1, 5, 82; trust and, 58; the West and, 6

Capitalist-Evangelical Resonance Machine, 54, 64

Cassin, Barbara, 138n65, 143n73

Césaire, Aimé, 1

Chakrabarty, Dipesh, 35, 76–79, 149n44

Chaplin, Joyce E., 13

Chautauqua, 23, 118–22, 124, 127

Christianity, 54, 55, 87, 100

Christians, 53, 56–57, 60, 63–66; belief and, 55

circumnavigation, 11, 14–16, 74

civilization, 1, 15, 70, 101, 121; anthropology

and, 31; Chautauqua and, 119; culture and, 34; ecological transition and, 126; Enlightenment and, 33; ruins and, 102; value systems and, 82

Clastres, Pierre, 45

coexistence, 73, 120; *see also* existence

cognition, 156n78; reality and, 71; truth and, 109, 110

colonialism, 4, 16, 19, 36, 52, 55, 82, 88, 92, 126–28, 157n2; anthropology and, 31–32; education and, 52; essentialism and, 38; exoticism and, 34, 38, 42; expansion and, 5; habits of thinking and feeling of, 29; metropolitan anticolonialism and, 75; monification and, 13; non-Western worlds and, 33; plantations and, 26; politics of knowledge and, 35; voyaging and, 17

coloniality, 6, 19, 32, 37; *see also* colonialism

Columbus, Christopher, 11–13, 115

composition, 23, 70, 99, 110, 126, 128, 130–32

concepts, 20–22, 42, 78, 86, 89, 105, 107; belief and, 53; equivocation and, 150n55; facts and, 80; intranslation and, 46; modern realism and, 29; ontology and, 44–45; percepts and, 22, 71, 76, 89; pluriverse and, 90, 131; pragmatism and, 57, 95–96, 110; reality and, 40, 43, 45, 58, 88; religion and, 100; worldquakes and, 76, 81

conceptualization, 76, 81, 86, 89; *see also* concepts

conclusions, vii, 53, 117, 131, 162n80; *see also* endings

confidence, 59, 68; *see also* trust

Connolly, William, 54

consciousness, 36, 77, 115

consent, 21, 24, 47, 55, 69, 73, 79, 80–81, 88, 92–93, 114, 120, 132, 133n3, 161n69; pragmatism and, 95, 105; trust and, 59

contingency, 22, 23, 87–89, 92

Cortázar, Julio, 18, 28, 75

cosmology, 15, 23, 46, 128; Buddhism and, 155n40; *see also* cosmos; political cosmology
cosmopolitan thought, 38
cosmopolitanism, 73; 125–26
cosmos, 4, 92, 114, 123; disaster and, 99; cosmopolitanism and, 38, 126; pinch of chaos in, 22, 46; pluralism and, 8, 130; pluriverse and, 92, 117; pragmatism and, 95, 97; *see also* cosmology; pluriverse; political cosmology
counter-renaissance, 16
Cree, the, 86–87
critique, 9, 19, 32, 38, 42, 43, 44, 53
culture, 29, 60, 98, 119, 122, 134n7, 147n20, 155n40; anthropology and, 42, 44; belief and, 53; Kant and, 38; modern realism and, 29, 74; orientalism and, 33, 139n32; problems and solutions and, 7; rationalization and, 10; techno-science and, 12
curse: ghosts and, 107; of tolerance, 45, 46, 53

Danowski, Déborah, 93
Dark Ages, 13, 15
Darwin, Charles, 15
day-traveling, 41, 43; allies and, 20, 28, 52, 53, 98, 124; modern realism and, 29; *see also* world-traveling
dead, the, 3, 17, 23, 75, 98–99, 102–3, 105–11, 134n8, 152n9, 155n40
de Certeau, Michel, 56
decolonial imagination, 9, 42; *see also* imagination
decolonial option, 6
decolonial studies. *See* postcolonial studies
decolonization, 19, 35, 125; of cosmopolitan ideals, 126; of epistemology, 37; of the plural, 21, 39; of reasons and languages, 36; of thought, 7, 42
deconstruction, 9, 19, 35, 47, 53
de la Cadena, Marisol, 44, 80, 124
Deleuze, Gilles, 9–10, 18, 48

Deloria, Vine, Jr., 50–51
de Martino, Ernesto, 40, 43
democracy, 32, 76, 78, 79, 80, 124, 126
Denkmittel, 96, 107; *see also* concepts; pragmatism
de-realization, 21–22; belief and, 52–53, 55–58; concept of religion and, 100; ghosts and, 101; language and, 56; modern realism and, 74; psychology and, 51; thereness, 60
Derrida, Jacques, 159n43
Descartes, René, 52–53, 58
Descola, Philippe, 128, 142n64
devastation: of differences, 4, 5, 47; ecological, 1, 93–94, 126, 149n44; intellectual, viii; of North East Japan, 98–99, 105; of reality, 34, 96, 108; of the world, 110–12
development, 2, 3, 34, 74, 100, 121, 124, 126
Dewey, John, 152n7
difference, 5, 7, 10, 25, 26, 38, 42, 44, 66–67, 69, 72–73, 76, 80, 82, 86, 92, 100, 114, 135n14: cosmopolitanism and, 38; events and, 47; exoticism and, 33–34; feeling and, 42, 74, 81, 87–89, 123; as generative, 32; God and, 56, 63, 65–66; as immanent, 4; modern realism and, 17; modern representation and, 35; perspectivism and, 150n55; pluralism and, 116, 132, 157n9; pluriverse and, 118, 129, 131; politics of, 21; pragmatism and, 22, 90, 95–97; stories and, 13
disasters, 83, 93, 97–99, 103, 110, 111, 130, 153n13; relief response and, 107
disenchantment, 10; *see also* enchantment
disqualification, 4, 44, 127, 137n56; colonialism and, 33–36, 42; ghosts and, 101; historiography and, 77; modern logic and, 65; modernity and, 9, 45; modern realism and 10, 17–18, 37, 65, 75; monification and, 5, 59; pluralism and, 28; trust and, 58
distrust/mistrust, 17–19, 31, 42, 59, 60, 65, 69, 75; *see also* doubt; trust

divergences, 2, 6–7, 23, 71, 127, 130–31, 141n59, 152n7, 152n9; alliance through, 43, 127; colonialism and, 42; intranslation and, 22, 46, 88; pluralistic adventure in, 2, 21, 48, 50, 92, 116; political cosmology and, 126; stories and, 16, 72; struggles and, 125; togetherness and, 4, 21, 68, 95, 116, 134n8; trust and, 66, 70, 73–74; universe and, 25–26, 111; worlds and, 18, 44, 60, 91, 94, 97, 129; *see also* difference
doubt, 3, 51, 56–58; *see also* distrust/mistrust; trust
Dussel, Enrique, 11

Earth, the, 38, 44, 71–72, 96–98, 112, 114, 126, 128, 148n20: divergent togetherness and, 95; flat-Earth story and, 11, 14–15, 17; impoverishment and, 45; living and, 120; spirituality and, 127
earthquake, 22; Japan and, 97–98; William James and, 71–72
ecumene, 73, 90, 93
empire, 9, 13, 18, 26, 34, 51–52, 74–75, 82, 95, 130; metaphysics and, 9, 19, 27, 34, 93; modern Age of, 11; 13; modern realism and, 28, 73; William James and, 35, 75; *see also* anti-imperialism
empiricism, 157n9
enchantment, 10, 118; *see also* disenchantment
enclosures, 10, 118, 113
endings, 49–50, 92–93, 112, 115, 117, 130; apocalypse and, 1, 19, 124; lists and, 2; stories and, 47, 91; *see also* apocalypse; beginnings; openings
Enlightenment, 18, 33, 55
Enrique (Malaysian Slave), 12, 14
epistemological exclusions, 35
epistemology, 6, 36, 39, 41, 43–44, 125, 134n7, 140n48; *see also* decolonization; Eurocentrism; ontology; pluralism; pluralization
equivocation, 81, 149n55; *see also* intranslation

eschatology, 10, 34–35
eschaton, 10, 73, 130
Escobar, Arturo, 126–27, 160n65
essentialism, 38; *see also* anti-essentialism
ethnography, 78, 81
Eurocentrism: cultural relativism and, 7; epistemology and, 37; history and, 77; metaphysics and, 141n56; reasons and, 35; story of modernity and, 13, 14; *see also* culture; epistemology; Europe
Europe, 20, 24, 35, 37, 52, 53, 75, 124, 131
events, 23, 32–34, 86, 97, 99, 113–14, 143n75; circumnavigation and, 11, 13–16; resonance of, 15, 27; pluralism and, 21, 47, 68; runaway metaphysics and, 27; togetherness and, 87; truth and, 109
"ever not quite," vii, 8, 14, 16, 28, 42, 74, 90, 93–94, 102, 115, 129
existence, 2–3, 79, 80, 126, 133n3, 152n7, 152n9, 155n40, 155n43; God and, 57; insistence and, 132; modes of, 9, 41, 60, 84, 141n59; other worlds and, 31, 127; possibility and, 28; pragmatism and, 95; reality and, 27; *see also* insistence
exotic, the, 33–36
exoticism, 34, 38, 42
experience, 6, 11, 26, 29–30, 55–57, 63, 65, 74, 77, 82, 84, 87, 98, 99, 107, 119, 122; Christianity and, 55; difference and, 123; ghosts and, 99, 101, 102; God and, 54, 59–61; metaphysics and, 9, 19, 32, 47, 48, 96; modes of, 7, 39; *multum in parvo* and, 28; pragmatism and, 105–7, 109; reality and, 50, 89; William James and, 8, 9; worldquakes and, 22, 72–73, 88, 92, 149n51
experimentation, viii, 8, 75, 124; metaphysics and, 19, 43, 81, 84, 94, 130; pragmatics of the pluriverse and, 132; pragmatism and, 97, 103, 105, 109
explanation, 46, 76, 87, 101, 103
extractivism, 3, 4, 123, 128
extraordinary, the, 41, 62; metaphysics and, 46; modernity and, 16; reality and, 15, 28, 33, 34, 43, 114, 148n20

facts, 33, 87, 102, 116, 129, 131; conceptualization and, 79; of cosmology, 15; fetishes and, 134; fiction and, 76; mind-independence and, 37; of struggle, 117, 124; pragmatism and, 95, 103; trust and, 60

faith, 23, 55, 57, 60, 103–4; healing and, 75; pragmatism and, 105; Shintō and, 101; trust and, 57, 63, 64; see also belief; trust

feeling, 29, 71, 79, 95, 103, 121; of "and," 18, 110; consent and, 21; of difference, 22, 42, 56, 73–75, 81, 87–89, 115, 123, 150n55; of God, 54, 65; of "if," 23, 110; intranslation and, 60; metaphysics and, 19, 73, 86; of "or," 42; of reality, 44, 49–52, 56, 58–59, 65, 68, 75, 87–88, 92, 96; the reality of the unseen and, 55; world and, 123; worldquakes and, 22, 72

feeling-with, 21, 59, 107; see also consent; feeling; trust

fieldwork, 29, 53, 81

Figal, Gerald, 101, 154n38

finality, 1, 117; see also endings

Fogg, Phileas, 12, 17, 113–15

folklore, 154n38, 155n43

foundations, 1, 28, 35, 57, 70, 72, 99, 101–2, 116, 153n13; metaphysics and, 43, 115; modern world and, 4; reason and, 6, 10, 58, 83; relationalism and, 160n64; worldquakes and, 74, 88; see also principles

fugitivity, 129

gaki, 107; 156n71; see also ghosts

Gandhi, Leela, 75

García Márquez, Gabriel, 10

genuine option, 40, 69, 93

Ghosh, Amitav, 147n20

ghosts, 2, 10, 17, 23, 35, 52, 54, 100–105, 107–11, 141n59, 154n37, 155n40, 155n43

Giraud, Eva, 161n69

Glissant, Édouard, 13, 19

globe, 11, 13–14

God, 3, 10, 17, 56, 74, 77, 80, 95, 104, 136n35;

belief and, 54; evangelicals and, 54–66; experience and, 55; feeling and, 5, 55–68; Hinduism and, 52–53; reality and, 21, 52, 54–57

good common world, 94, 117, 120, 122–24, 125, 130; see also cosmopolitanism

Gould, Stephen Jay, 15

Great Community, 94, 152n7

Great East Japan Earthquake and Tsunami, 97; see also earthquake; tsunami

grief, 101, 105, 107

Guha, Ranajit, 77–78

habitation, 99, 130

habits, 3, 7, 21, 26, 29, 40, 45–46, 54, 56, 72, 76, 79–81, 109–10

Haraway, Donna, 48, 157n11

healers, 3, 75

healing, 75, 81, 83

health, 3, 101–2

Hegel, G. W. F., 34–35, 37, 48

hesitation, 14, 29, 31, 45–46, 63, 74

Hinduism, 52

history, 11, 14–15, 32, 34, 39, 54, 56–57, 97, 102, 126, 148n31; nonsecular worlds and, 77–79; see also world history

humor, 25, 27, 46, 63, 106, 128

hypothesis, 45, 95, 103, 121, 127–28, 160n64; see also propositions

ideal, 79–80, 93, 119–22, 126, 131; pluriverse and, 117; reality as merely, 65

ideas, ix, 13, 30, 40, 52, 55, 57–58, 62, 64, 71, 119, 121; pluriverse and, 23, 38; pragmatism and, 94, 96, 109; spirits and, 89; truth and, 109

"if," 21, 59, 115, 117, 127; feeling of, 23; 110; the pluriverse hangs on, 47, 48, 68

Ihamba, 81–87

illusion, 10, 76, 119, 134n7

imagination, 6, 9, 33, 36, 43, 96, 155n43; modernity and, 16; modern realism and, 17; pragmatics of, 1; see also decolonial imagination immanence, 4; *see also* adventure; difference; experimentation; the living; "to believe in the world"; truth

impossible, the, 2, 18, 60, 88

indeterminacy, 87, 123, 130; *see also* metaphysical indetermination; perhaps; worldquakes

Ingold, Tim, 66–67

innocence, 13, 45, 93

insistence, 5, 27, 38–40, 46, 74, 89, 109, 122, 124, 130–31; existence and, 132; of the pluriverse, 4, 8, 22, 28, 53, 79, 86, 89, 109, 118, 124, 126, 131; pluralism and, 8; of the possible, 23, 27, 130; *see also* existence; the otherwise; pluriverse

interstices, ix, 4, 5, 8, 20, 35, 46, 70, 75, 117, 124, 129–30

"in the wake," 94–96, 102, 103, 107–9, 111–12, 127; Christina Sharpe and, 152n9

intranslation, 52, 60, 72, 74, 84, 88, 96; Barbara Cassin and, 138n65, 143n73; definition of, 22; translation and, 88

invitation, 55, 79, 133

Ivy, Marilyn, 100

James, William, vii, 2, 5, 7, 18, 20–21, 28, 38, 40, 47, 50, 76, 79, 90, 94, 121–22, 127, 129, 134n10; belief and, 51–52, 57; books and, vii; Chautauqua and, 118–21, 127; civilization and, 102; Deleuze and, 57, 93; earthquake and, 22, 71–72, 86; emotions and, 130; empire and, 35; experience and, 28; facts and, 87; fascism and, 153; God and, 63, 65; Hegel and, 35; Kant and, 41; Leela Gandhi and, 75; life and, 71; logic and, 65; meliorism and, 23, 117; perhaps and, 123; philosophy and, 18, 80, 115; pluralism and, 4, 9–10, 14, 125; pluriverse and, 68, 92, 117, 133n3, 160n64; pragmatism and, 23, 94–96, 105, 110; precipitousness and, 121–123; problem of the one and the many and, 8, 115–116; psychology and, 50–51; rationalism and, 53; reality and, 8, 18, 27, 45, 65, 112; the

reality of the unseen and, 55; relations and, 42; relay and, 6; sense of activity and, 123; "to believe in the world" and, 57, 93; trust and, 21, 57–59, 64, 66, 69; truth and, 109, 146n57; the world and, 27, 116; world's salvation and, 111

Japan, 23, 97, 99, 100–102, 105, 154n37; 154n38

jita funi: concept of, 107

Josephson, Jason Ānanda, 100, 154n37

justice, 2, 79–80, 119, 127; *see also* social justice

Kaneta, Taio, 103–111

Kant, Immanuel, 38, 41–42, 51, 140n48

killing, 66–67

Kohn, Eduardo, 42

Koselleck, Reinhardt, 148n31

knots, 78, 91

knowledge-making, 36–37

knowledges, 1, 5–6, 32, 40, 55, 76, 100–101, 156n78; appositions and, 92; belief and, 57; metaphysics and, 111; politics of reality and, 43; postcolonial politics of, 35–39; stories and, 157n11; trust and, 58

Lapoujade, David, 145n57

Latour, Bruno, 134n7, 142n64

Law, John, 39

laws, 47, 83, 114; cosmopolitanism and, 28; of the excluded middle, 65; language of, 36; modernity and, 76; of nature, 95; of nature and nations, 16; of noncontradiction, 84; science and, 75

Leibniz, Gottfried Wilhelm, 15

Lesseps, Ferdinand de, 33

life, ix, 4, 6, 28, 60–61, 64, 75, 79, 80, 95, 97–98, 106–107, 111, 129, 131; concepts and, 89; ideas and, 109; ideals and, 122; relationality and, 127; significance of, 120–23; transitions and, 71

linguistics, 55–56, 61

Lispector, Clarice, 149n51

listening: to the heart, 106–7
lists, 2
living, the, 75, 99, 103, 105, 107–11
living anachronisms, 16, 32
Lloyd Parry, Richard, 98–99, 104
logic, 19, 36, 48, 53, 65, 68–69, 77, 87, 95, 106, 140n48
love, 17, 21, 67, 121, 127, 132; God and, 55, 60–61, 63–64, 68, 74
Luhrmann, Tanya, 21, 54–57, 60–61, 63–66, 149n53

Magellan, Ferdinand / Fernâo de Magalhães, 12–15, 17, 19, 29, 115
magic, 10, 40
manifold, 20, 27, 126
many, the, 4, 95; intranslation and, 22, 46; pluralism and, 9, 47, 115; the one and, 6–8, 39–40, 45, 47, 70, 94, 103, 110, 133n3; see also the one; pluralism
maybe, 21, 59, 63, 68, 117, 127; see also "if"; perhaps
medicine, 75, 83, 97, 141; for Ihamba ritual, 84–85
Meiji period, 100–101
meliorism, 117, 120
metamorphosis, 7, 45
metaphysical indetermination, 19–21, 48, 54, 58, 60, 69, 73, 78–79, 86, 96, 117; definition of, 47; see also metaphysics; runaway metaphysics
metaphysics, 40–41, 50–51, 89, 115; comparative, 7; empire and, 9; experience and, 96; of identity, 144; of one-world world, 39; of ordinary nature, 16–18, 26, 47; pluralistic, 71; pragmatism and, 111
Middle Ages, 11
Mignolo, Walter, 6
mind, 42, 50–51, 62, 72, 74, 80; knowledge and, 156n78; transformation of, 56–57
Mmala, Lazaro, 20, 21, 31, 36, 38, 40, 42–43, 46
mode of existence, 9, 41, 60, 84, 141n59; see also existence

modernity, 6, 13, 34, 37, 39, 43, 46, 102, 134n7; Columbus and, 12; Japan and, 23, 105; reality and, 16; stories of, 13, 35, 137n44
"modernity of witchcraft, the," 32
modern rationality, 36, 97; see also rationality; reason
modern realism, 9, 16, 22, 37, 42, 45, 50, 60, 65, 73, 76, 102; asymmetry and, 88; and definition of, 17–18; distrust/ mistrust and, 75; tolerance and, 74; see also anti-realism; modernity; operations; realism
modern world, 4, 93, 123, 131; experience and, 50; reality and, 8; trust and, 58; see also modernity; modern realism
monification, 11, 13, 16, 28, 29, 31, 33, 35, 42, 45, 52, 73–74, 127, 133n7; definition of, 5; "ever not quite" and, 94; shatter zones and, 130; William James and, 59
monism, 58, 116; modern realism and, 19, 27
monists, 4, 27; relativism and, 149n47
Monk, Thelonious, 105
Monsterology, 155n43
Moten, Fred, 10
Mozambique. See Mueda Plateau
Mudimbe, V. Y., 31, 33
Muedans, the, 30–32, 36, 38–39, 42, 46, 81; see also Mueda Plateau; Mmala, Lazaro
Mueda Plateau (Mozambique), 21, 29, 36, 74; see also the Muedans
multifariousness, 16, 25, 28, 34, 47, 58, 72, 75
multiverse, 133n3; see also pluriverse; universe
multum in parvo, 47, 72, 109

Nadasdy, Paul, 146n69
Nandy, Ashis, 52, 54, 161n65
nature, 3, 13, 27, 30, 58, 84, 86, 98, 129, 148n31; bifurcation of, 16; experience and, 9; faith and, 55; laws of, 95; metaphysics and, 19, 25–26, 47, 88; of non-Western practices, 33; of the world, 17, 123

Ndembu, the, 82–83, 88
negotiations, 100, 131
Nietzsche, Friedrich, 128, 161n66

objectivity, 39; trust and, 57
objects, 13, 17, 50–51, 55–56, 82, 96,
    139n32, 155n43, 161n71
Obon, 155n40
one, the, 103; 136n35; *see also* the many;
    monism; theology
ontological experimentation, 84
ontology, 7–8, 81, 134n7; analytics of,
    7, 42–45; turn to, 44, 141n59; relational-
    ity and, 127; *see also* epistemology;
    pluralism; pluralization; political
    ontology
openings, 2, 7, 14, 21, 58, 73, 110, 115,
    130; origins and, 117; pluralism and,
    52, 93; pluriverse and, 111; pragmatism
    and, 105; stories and, 16; trust and,
    68
operations, 39, 46, 53, 65, 81, 86, 104,
    115; additive, 73; anaphoric, 8; de-
    exoticizing, 36; of disqualification, 45,
    101, 137n56; essentialist, 35; imperial-
    ist, 6; modern realism as, 18–20, 25,
    28–29, 31–32, 37–38, 43–44, 51–52, 65,
    68, 100; negative, 38, 47, 147n20; plan-
    tations and, 26; scalable, 33; tolerant,
    74–80
order, 16, 93, 119, 127; of the (im)possible,
    16; pluralism and, 9, 41; religion and, 52;
    theology and, 103
orientalism, 33–34, 37
origins, 22, 50, 72, 88, 124; openings and,
    117; stories of, 11, 14–15
otherwise, the, 43, 118, 123, 126–127,
    129–130, 132, 158n42
outrageous propositions, 45; *see also*
    propositions

Pacific Ocean, 12, 98
Papini, Giovanni, 153n13
paradox, 92; reality and, 65

Parra Witte, Falk Xué, 128
partial connections, 6, 17, 22, 46, 71, 87,
    92, 116
peace, 76, 92; perpetual, 38, 46, 73, 117
perception, 72, 86; of reality, 50, 55; visu-
    ality and, 56
percepts, 22, 76
perhaps, 2, 14, 20, 23, 69, 80, 105, 112; defi-
    nition of, 123; pluralism and, 123–26,
    128–31; pluriverse and, 117–18; the
    other and, 132
persistence, 32, 52, 137; *see also* insistence
perspectivism, 149n55
Phaeton, 136
philosophy, 5, 9, 16, 37–38, 41, 51, 53,
    74–75, 95–96, 119, 138n58, 140n48,
    141n59, 143n73; Hegel and, 35; modern
    realism and, 17; the one and the many
    and, 4; of sorcery, 6
Pigafetta, Antonio, 12, 136n38
plantations, 3, 26, 34
Plato, 17
plural, the, 5; decolonization of, 21, 35–40,
    42; the feeling of reality in, 9, 17, 20–21,
    45, 49, 58–59, 68, 73–75, 87, 89, 92, 96,
    109, 115, 130; truth and, 109
pluralism, 2, 4, 14, 51, 68, 73, 93, 152n7;
    epistemology and, 21, 39; metaphysics
    and, 9, 19, 27, 47; ontology and, 21, 42;
    perhaps and, 128–31; as pragmatics of
    the pluriverse, 23, 131; reality and, 8, 28,
    49; trust and, 9, 146n57; William James
    and, 6, 10, 120, 125, 157
pluralistic event, 21, 68; *see also* events
pluralistic realism, 19–20, 44, 46–48, 50,
    53, 73, 93; *see also* anti-realism; modern
    realism; realism
pluralistic universe, 2, 17, 133n3; *see also*
    pluriverse; universe
plurality, 8, 37, 46, 123; of divergent sto-
    ries, 72; of divergent practices, 111; of
    modes of cohabitation, 130; of partial
    connections, 92; perspectivism and,
    150n55; of publics, 152n9; of scientific

hypotheses, 95; of times, 78; of ways of becoming salmon, 41; of worlds, 97

pluralization, 8, 16, 28, 42–43

pluriversality, 126

pluriverse, 4–5, 7–10, 22–23, 27–28, 40–42, 47, 53–54, 59, 68, 70, 74–76, 79–80, 86, 88, 92, 95–97, 118; cosmopolitanism and, 38, 125; definition of, 2; ontological turn and, 44; perhaps and, 117, 130; pluralism and, 19, 20, 124; politics of, 22, 46, 115, 132; pragmatism and, 23, 90, 111, 131; propositions and, 48, 92; relationality and, 126–28; relativism and, 149n47; verification and, 21, 69, 109; William James and, 133n3; worldquakes and, 71, 73, 89; Zapatistas and, 125

political cosmology, 23, 125, 129, 132; see also cosmology; cosmos

political ontology, 44–45; see also ontology

possibility, 2, 5, 7, 9, 14, 19–21, 23, 26–28, 41–43, 45, 48, 59, 60, 73, 78–79, 84, 88, 90, 92, 94, 96–97, 103, 108, 110–11, 113, 117, 121, 127, 130, 132, 146n69; conditions of, 38, 123; of God's existence, 57; of justice, 80; of other worlds in this world, 1, 4, 18, 24, 63, 117, 125, 128, 131; of a pluralistic realism, 28; of a pluriverse, 10, 44, 71, 73, 88, 115; of a runaway metaphysics, 27, 37; truth and, 110

possible, the, 4, 16, 18, 105, 111, 146n57; see also the impossible; possibility

postcolonial impulse, 89

postcolonial studies, 5, 137n44; and decolonial studies, 135n14

postcolonial thought, 6, 37; tragic sensibility and, 152n5

Povinelli, Elizabeth, 158n42

practices, 8, 19, 24, 32, 41, 43–46, 75, 78, 97, 100–101, 111, 131; 157n2; collective of priests and, 23, 108; evangelicals and, 21, 55–56, 62–63; healing and, 81, 83–85, 102; listening to the heart and, 106; non-Western, 33; political ecology and, 124, 126; pragmatism and, 105, 110;

psychology and, 50–51; spiritual care and, 106–107; stories and, 13

pragmatics: of collective imagination, 1; of the pluriverse, 24, 131, 132

pragmatism, 23, 94–95, 103, 134n10, 158n42; as art of living and dying, 97; Italian fascism and, 153n13; metaphysics and, 9, 47, 110–11; truth and, 109; William James and, 95–97, 110

prayer, 56, 61–64, 68

precipitousness, 120–23

principles, 15, 22, 27–28, 34–35, 43, 45–48, 51, 58, 60, 65, 76–79, 105, 111, 115, 122, 128, 131; cosmopolitanism and, 125; empire and, 26; pragmatism and, 95, 97, 104; reality and, 49, 53; relativism and, 149n47; runaway metaphysics and, 19–20, 27; uncertainty, 84; see also foundations

problematic, 41, 122, 141n59; book as, vii; cosmos and, 95; pluralistic, 7, 41, 45, 47, 147n15; pluralism and, 8, 49; pluriverse as, 40, 92; see also problems

problems: Chautauqua and, 120–23; of difference, 73; faith and, 57; of the one and the many, 4, 6, 8, 39, 110; ontology and, 7, 43–46, 81, 128, 150n55; pluralistic realism and, 20, 40, 48, 115; pluriverse and, 111, 130, 132; pragmatism and, 65, 88; subaltern pasts and, 77–80; words and, 56; worldquakes and, 86–87, 89; worlds and, 5, 93; see also problematic

profusion, 6, 23, 52, 95, 99–100, 103

progress, 1, 11, 15, 31, 34, 76, 92, 94, 126, 127

propositions, 5, 6, 18, 20, 21, 27, 39–40, 42, 44–46, 50–51, 58, 64, 78, 93, 96, 103, 106, 121–22; pluriverse and, 48, 68, 92, 129; spirits and, 89; see also outrageous propositions

psychology, 50–51, 53, 55, 56–57, 61, 75; ritual and, 82; William James and, 8, 50

Quijano, Aníbal, 37

rationalism, 16, 53, 102, 137n56, 149n47
rationality, 35–36, 58, 75, 87, 100
realism, 20, 45, 140n48; colonization and,
    18, 37–38; contemporary philosophy
    and, 17, 137n58; epistemology and, 41;
    literature and, 75, 148n20; modernity
    and, 9, 10, 50–51, 100; monism and, 19;
    Plato and, 17; see also modern realism;
    pluralistic realism
realities, 4–5, 7–8, 10, 15, 17, 19, 21,
    26–28, 34, 39, 41–43, 45, 47–48, 52–53,
    55, 58, 60, 65, 69, 94, 96–97, 114, 131,
    148n20; see also reality
reality, 4–6, 9, 25, 27, 31, 33–34, 39–40,
    46–47, 69, 71, 75–76, 80, 87–89, 92–93,
    99, 101, 112, 125, 129, 131, 134n7, 147n20,
    155n43; belief and, 50–54, 59; concept
    of, 43, 58; decolonization and, 19, 38–41;
    essentialism and, 37; experience and, 19;
    feeling and, 8, 20–21, 29, 38, 44–45, 49,
    52, 55–57, 59–60, 63, 65–66, 68, 73–75,
    87, 88–89, 103, 115, 123; ghosts and, 105,
    109–10; God and, 54–61, 63–64, 68;
    metaphysics and, 16; modern realism
    and, 18; paradox and, 65; pluralistic pol-
    itics of, 41, 43, 48; pragmatism and, 96,
    103, 110, 153n13; profusion and, 130; psy-
    chology and, 50–51; rationalism and,
    53; realist philosophers and, 17; runaway
    metaphysics and, 20, 27; William James
    and, 8, 65; the word "or" and, 28, 45, 48,
    115; see also realities
reason, 40, 43, 94, 95, 128; contingency
    and, 87; faith and, 55; history and, 79,
    modernity and, 10–11, 16, 29, 31, 36, 51,
    76; postcolonial thought and, 6, 19, 35,
    37; reality and, 53; runaway metaphysics
    and, 22, 90; theology and, 104; see also
    rationalism; rationality
reciprocity, 66, 68, 128; see also recursivity;
    trust
recursivity, 66–67, 145n57
redemption, 1, 93, 126
reindeer, 66–68, 146

relationality, 127–29
relations, 26, 47, 57, 66, 76, 89, 100, 107,
    114, 152n9; conjunctive and disjunctive,
    28; knowledge and, 37, 156n78; realism
    and, 17; reality and, 42; trust and, 21, 59;
    universe and, 25; see also relationality;
    relationships
relationships, 18, 21–22, 54, 59, 61–68, 80,
    83, 99, 107, 113, 128, 154n37, 156n71; see
    also relations
relativism, 7, 149n47; the absolute and, 35
relay, 46; as experimental practice, 5–8,
    21, 24, 93, 125, 134n12; the pluriverse
    and, 27; trust and, 68–69, 83, 85, 131
religion, 15, 21, 60, 104, 154n33; concept of,
    52, 100–101; Hinduism as, 52
Renaissance, 15
representation, 35, 74, 81
resistance, 75, 92, 129
rituals, 61, 82–87, 103–4, 106
Roy, Arundhati, 9
ruins, 45, 93, 98–99, 102–4, 110
runaway metaphysics, 19, 21, 27–29, 32,
    37, 40, 45–49, 51, 58, 65, 68, 73, 90,
    110; see also metaphysics; pluralistic
    realism

Said, Edward, 33, 37
salvation, 92, 111, 117, 128
Santal, the, 77–80
sati, 114, 157n2
scalability, 26–27; see also scale
scale, 15, 26, 93, 119
science, 15–16, 37–38, 53, 72, 75, 101–2,
    140n48
science and technology studies, 41,
    140n52, 141n59
Scott, James C., 130
Scott, Michael W., 128
secularism, 100–101
secularization, 52, 54
Seth, Sanjay, 52
Sharpe, Christina, 152n9
shatter zones, 130–132

Shintō, 23, 101, 103
social justice, 79, 127; *see also* justice
social sciences, 35
sorcerers, 30, 39
sorcery, 30, 32, 38 – 39, 46
sorcery-lions, 3, 21, 31, 35 – 36, 38 – 39, 46, 74, 81
spirits, 3, 21 – 22, 52, 54, 63, 65, 80 – 89, 99, 101 – 2, 104, 106, 108 – 9, 155n40, 155n43, 156n71
spiritual care, 23, 105 – 6, 156n69
spirituality, 102, 127, 154n38
Spivak, Gayatri Chakravorty, 157n2
Stein, Gertrude, 55
Stengers, Isabelle, 45
stories, 1 – 4, 10 – 11, 14, 20, 29, 32, 80, 89, 96, 116 – 17, 123, 131; caring for, 23; endings and, 91, 119; ghosts and, 99 – 102, 110; modernity and, 13 – 14, 16, 35, 134n7, 137n44; of origins, 11 – 14; pragmatism and, 105 – 6, 111; within stories, 14 – 15, 52, 92, 130; universe of, 17, 79; world and, 47, 111 – 12, 115; world-quakes, 22, 72
Strathern, Marilyn, 48
struggles, 37, 117, 120, 124 – 25, 127, 130
stutter, 20, 22, 48, 49, 74, 88 – 90, 116
subaltern pasts, 77 – 78
subject: field, 82; of history, 77, 79; phe-nomenological, 8
subjectivity, 75, 77, 149n51
Suez Canal, 33
symbolic analysis, 30, 87
symbolic anthropology, 29, 30, 31, 81; *see also* anthropology
symbols, 21, 29 – 31, 36 – 38, 74,
symmetry, 88, 151n97

Thakur, 77 – 80
theology, 5, 41, 136n35
theory, 17 – 18, 97, 111, 131, 150n55
thereness, 60, 69
threads, 14, 91 – 92, 94, 102, 109, 112, 114, 116, 132, 137n44, 157n11

time, 1 – 2, 40 – 41, 47, 78, 80, 113 – 14, 117, 124, 129
"to believe in the world," 9, 10, 16, 57, 69, 91, 93 – 95, 103, 105, 109, 112, 130
togetherness, 23, 70, 75, 120 – 21, 127, 131; divergence and, 4, 116, 134n8; the Earth and, 95; pluralistic event and, 68; pluri-verse and, 117; worldquakes, 22, 72 – 73, 76, 78 – 82; 86 – 89
tolerance, 11, 76, 88, 100
Tolstoy, Leo, 121
totality, 1, 17, 25, 117; *see also* whole
Toulmin, Stephen, 16
transcendence, 23, 58, 94
transformations, 4, 15 – 16, 21, 32, 58, 60, 69, 71, 83, 99, 110, 161n69
translation. *See* intranslation
tremors, 22, 70, 72, 74, 75 – 76, 80 – 82, 86, 88, 95, 98
Tresch, John, 161n71
trust, 2 – 3, 9 – 10, 19, 24, 44, 48, 53, 70, 73 – 75, 88, 94, 123; adventure and, 117; concept of, 21, 57 – 60; confidence and, 59; as ensemble of relays, 68, 83, 85, 125, 131; faith and, 57 – 58; God and, 54 – 69; immanence and, 58; as metaphysical ultimate, 21, 51, 58, 69; as precursive, 58 – 63, 117; pluriverse and, 7, 20; prac-tice of relaying and, 6; as recursive, 66 – 69, 145; truth and, 110
truth, 80, 123, 156n78; anthropology and, 82; historiography and, 77; indu-bitable, 3; pragmatism and, 95, 97, 103, 105, 109 – 110, 146n57; rational principle of, 51
Tsing, Anna L., 26
tsunami, 23, 98 – 104, 106 – 8, 111, 155n40
Turner, Edith, 22, 81 – 88
Turner, Victor, 29 – 30, 36, 81

uncertainty principle, 84; *see also* Ihamba; principles
unexceptional, the, 17 – 18
unification, 4, 152; *see also* monification

universe, 3, 8, 18, 25–27, 35, 44, 54, 93, 96, 107, 109, 117, 123; "ever not quite" and, 94; as many-storied, 20, 34, 69, 70, 91, 117, 129, 131, 133n3, 160n64; oneness and, 115; pluriverse and, 47; pragmatism and, 111; runaway metaphysics and, 110; trust and, 59

utopia, 23, 119

values, ix, 6, 23, 80, 82, 89–90, 105, 116, 126, 128

verification, 4, 21, 63, 69, 111, 146n57; *see also* truth

Verne, Jules, 18, 114

Verran, Helen, 89

Vineyard, the, 54–57, 59–62, 66, 68, 74

Viveiros de Castro, Eduardo, 7, 42, 44, 93, 149n53, 149n55

Weber, Max, 10

West, Harry, 20, 29–33, 36, 38–39, 45, 81

"what is reality capable of?," 20, 27, 48–49, 79, 87–88, 93, 129

Whitehead, Alfred North, 147n2, 148n26, 161n71

whole, 8, 74, 78, 88, 90–91, 115, 128

words, 53, 57, 64, 144n27; dance of, 89, 151n96; divine, 55–56; metaphysics and, 111; practices and, 45; Reformation and, 55–56

world history, 34

worldquakes, 22, 72–74, 75, 78–79, 81–82, 86–89, 92, 94, 95, 97, 98, 103, 115, 130, 149n47

worlds. *See* apocalypse; cosmology; cosmos; modernity; the otherwise; pluriverse; political cosmology; stories; worldquakes

world-traveling, 18, 29, 32, 52, 114; *see also* colonialism; day-traveling; modern realism; monification

worldview, 4, 29, 38, 43, 46, 77–78

Zambia, 81–83, 85

Zapatista Army of National Liberation, 125–26